Social Responsibility in the Information Age: Issues and Controversies

Gurpreet S. Dhillon
University of Nevada, Las Vegas

D1365126

IRM Press
Publisher of innovative scholarly and professional
information technology titles in the cyberage

Hershey • London • Melbourne • Singapore • Beijing

Acquisitions Editor:	Mehdi Khosrow-Pour
Senior Managing Editor:	Jan Travers
Managing Editor:	Amanda Appicello
Development Editor:	Michele Rossi
Copy Editor:	Elizabeth Arneson
Typesetter:	LeAnn Whitcomb
Cover Design:	Deb Andree
Printed at:	Integrated Book Technology

Published in the United States of America by
    IRM Press (an imprint of Idea Group Inc.)
    701 E. Chocolate Avenue, Suite 200
    Hershey PA 17033-1240
    Tel: 717-533-8845
    Fax: 717-533-8661
    E-mail: cust@idea-group.com
    Web site: http://www.idea-group.com

and in the United Kingdom by
    IRM Press (an imprint of Idea Group Inc.)
    3 Henrietta Street
    Covent Garden
    London WC2E 8LU
    Tel: 44 20 7240 0856
    Fax: 44 20 7379 3313
    Web site: http://www.eurospan.co.uk

Library of Congress Cataloging-in-Publication Data

Social responsibility in the information age : issues and controversies / [edited by]
  Gurpreet Dhillon.
    p. cm.
  Originally published: Hershey, PA : Idea Group Publishing, c2002.
  Includes bibliographical references and index.
  ISBN 1-931777-85-3 (paper)
    1. Information society. 2. Information technology. 3. Information resources management.
  I. Dhillon, Gurpreet, 1963-

  HM851.S65 2003
  303.48'33--dc21

                  2003040626

eISBN 1-59140-008-2

Previously published in a hard cover version by Idea Group Publishing.

British Cataloguing in Publication Data
A Cataloguing in Publication record for this book is available from the British Library.

New Releases from IRM Press

Social Responsibility in the Information Age: Issues and Controversies

Table of Contents

Dedicated to the loving memory of my father
Baldev S. Dhillon

Preface

Understanding, appreciating and taking corrective steps to maintain and enhance social responsibility in the information age is important not only because of our increased dependence on information and communication technologies, but also because information and communication technologies pose complex challenges, which had a lesser significance in an earlier period. Although we have always acknowledged that increased awareness of social responsibility issues in the information age is essential, there has only been a sketchy review of the concerns and the inherent challenges. This edited book is a first step in bringing together various viewpoints from around the world and in presenting a coherent argument.

Given the technological advances and sensationalistic exposes of irresponsible handling of information, businesses have begun to act with caution. Today some companies have even appointed chief privacy officers and their likes to develop policies and programs to facilitate social responsibility in the information age. In companies such as IBM, AT&T and Eastman Kodak, such individuals have been involved in studying and assessing privacy risks ensuing from all operations, developing privacy codes of practice, interacting with concerned regulators and consumers, and conducting privacy reviews and audits of all products and Internet services. Although chief privacy officers are a new breed of executives which some of the socially conscious companies have appointed, they are as yet in a minority. A report in *The New York Times* estimated such individuals at about 100 in the United States, with expectations that the numbers will increase to 1,000 within a year (*The New York Times*, February 12, 2001). The trend is however positive. The new role offers a contact point for consumers and a responsible individual within a company.

Clearly the issue of social responsibility in the information age is an important one and it's my hope that the collection of papers by eminent scholars in the field will help in enhancing our understanding of a topic area that is in its infancy. In order to maintain the quality of the chapters, all contributions in this book were double-blind reviewed. Many of the authors also served as reviewers. I acknowledge their help in maintaining high standards and helping in the advancement of knowledge. I would also like to thank my colleagues at the College of Business, University of Nevada, Las Vegas, and numerous graduate students who have engaged in fruitful debates. This book would not have been possible without the support of my family. My parents played a significant role in making me socially aware and responsible and I wish my father could have seen the result. I dedicate this book to his loving memory. My wife rendered a lot of encouragement and provided support at every step in the completion of this book. I acknowledge her patience and support most sincerely.

Chapter I

Understanding Social Responsibility Issues in the Information Age

Gurpreet S. Dhillon
University of Nevada, Las Vegas, USA

So, you are taking a trip and have booked your flight, paid your bills, bought a travel insurance and made hotel bookings–all without talking to a single person. Of course, you used the Internet to accomplish your tasks. But how can you be sure that your personal information used to book flights, buy a travel insurance and make hotel bookings would not be used by the concerned companies to send you junk email or it is not sold to some direct marketers without your consent? How can you be sure that your personal information and credit card details were transmitted in a secure mode? How can you be sure that online businesses have proper high integrity business processes to handle your private information with due care? You may also have worries that if something does go wrong, i.e., your personal information is stolen, misused or abused, what recourse would you have. These are all legitimate social responsibility concerns which have surfaced more so in the information age because of technological advances and our growing reliance on information and communication technologies to carry out our daily work.

The purpose of this chapter is to understand the social responsibility issues in the information age. This is done by considering social responsibility concerns at five levels:

- Issues of privacy and confidentiality
- Accessibility to technology issues
- Property rights and ownership issues
- Freedom of speech issues
- Issues of quality and reliability of information and the related systems.

ISSUES OF PRIVACY AND CONFIDENTIALITY

In recent years privacy has indeed moved high on the agenda of corporations, largely because of a number of lawsuits. In 2000 DoubleClick came under criticism when it moved to merge its consumer Web surfing database with its consumers" mail-order-catalog purchases database. This had followed the acquisition of Abacus Direct by DoubleClick. Although DoubleClick has since abandoned plans to merge the databases, the case has raised a number of interesting privacy and ethical questions (see chapter 6 for further details). In another case RealNetworks apologized for the ability ingrained into RealJukeBox to capture data about a consumers musical selections. Since no consent was sought from the listener, it was clearly an infringement of privacy. Microsoft was also criticized for including a personal identifier in the Windows 98 operating system. Microsoft had to later modify the registration process so as not to create a personal identifier. U.S. Bancorp had to sign a $3 million settlement for having sold personal information to a direct marketer. Privacy and confidentiality are indeed critical to managing social responsibility in the information age. With respect to privacy Dhillon and Moores (2001) identify illegitimate sale of personal information and identity theft as the top two fundamental issues.

Two issues central to maintaining privacy, especially with respect to the Internet, relate to consent and process fairness. Clearly if an online business is requesting personal information, either for registering with them or for selling their products or services, consent must be sought from the consumer whether they wish to divulge this information. Clearly there are choices available to the consumer and the online business is aware that in order to gain the business, it cannot make revealing personal information mandatory. As has been argued elsewhere (Dhillon & Moores, 2001), once a consumer begins to trust an online business, there is an increased likelihood of the individual revealing personal information to the business in exchange for some benefit, such as customized service.

Process fairness is another issue which is critical to maintaining online privacy. If an individual is unsure as to the process followed by an online business in protecting personal information or the business process used, say, in order fulfillment, the consumer is not going to trust the nature of the transaction and the integrity of the operations. This means that the social contract between the consumer and the online business does not get established (cf. Culnan & Armstrong, 1999).

Clearly individual consumers are concerned about maintaining their privacy and perhaps protecting themselves from cybercrimes. Such concerns are also one of the main reasons for many individuals not using the Internet with a fair degree of confidence. At a technical level a number of developments are taking place which will result in enhancing chances of maintaining consumer privacy. iShopSecure, for example, has launched a Transact-Secure product that will eliminate online identification frauds and unwarranted chargebacks (see *Business Wire*, March 6, 2001). Such a product will go a long way in protecting consumers' interests even though the privacy was compromised.

ACCESSIBILITY TO TECHNOLOGY ISSUES

Accessibility to technology issues relate to the growing division between the "haves and have-nots" in the information age. Clearly there are certain groups that are more disadvantaged than the others–low-income persons living in rural areas, minorities in inner city and rural areas, young families, and families with a single parent. As Angell (2000; 1995) argues, the inequality of access to advanced electronic networks leads to divisions in the society and widening the gap between haves and have-nots. Such widening of the gap could be within countries or even at a global scale. Burn and Loch (2001) suggest that for the wealthiest nations, there are 31,046 Internet hosts per million inhabitants while for the poorest nations there are only 9 per million inhabitants.

Researchers have presented two opposing arguments to the issue of technology accessibility and the divide between the have and have-nots. The first argument, as maintained by Angell (1996), is that technological divide will give rise to a "new barbarian" and there is bound to be a lot of turmoil in the information age. Reich (1992) and Ohmae (1995) resonate somewhat with this view in their claim that in years to come we will see an emergence of the "symbolic-analyst," who could be construed as "information rich," and the others who would be "information poor." Ohmae (1995) makes an economic argument to propose that interlinked economies are the organizing logic of the future as opposed to the nation states. To a large extent this is abetted by the convergence of information and communication technologies. In many ways this dispiriting future is here. Dhillon, Moores, and Hackney (2001) illustrate this phenomena by presenting a review of networked firms operating in an interlinked economy and the challenges that a developing country faces.

The second argument, as contended by Burn and Loch (2001), is that the Internet will help in closing the divide between the haves and have-nots. Burn and Loch (2001) give the example of Egypt, where a model of technology diffusion was developed that includes education and training, infrastructure, and information technology. The applications developed in Egypt were both culturally and socially appropriate so as to gain widespread acceptance. Although education and training have been argued as cornerstones of realizing a technological diffusion, the benefits derived could be marginal since a majority of the populace may not have access to even basic education. Clearly, as with any technological innovation, the majority of the benefits reside in the related changes.

PROPERTY RIGHTS AND OWNERSHIP ISSUES

Intellectual property and ownership are crucial issues in the information age. Software piracy remains one of the foremost intellectual property right issues, and yet a complex one. Although monetary losses because of software piracy in the US have been significant ($13 billion for 1996) the software piracy rates when compared with rest of the world are rather modest. The Software and Information Industry Alliance (SIIA) has however reported a decline in software piracy in 1999 to $11 billion. The 1994 figures from Business Software Alliance estimate US software piracy rate at 35%. Although Europe has the highest overall piracy rate, piracy in Asia costs the software industry highest in monetary terms. The Hong Kong piracy rate is almost double that of the US (with an average of 72%). Hong Kong and China perhaps pose a very serious threat to the software industry. It has been estimated that there are some 26 "factories" in China that produce some 75 million pirated compact discs each year. The local market absorbs less than 1% of the total production. These copies are often smuggled to Latin American and European countries.

Numerous studies have been conducted to explain reasons behind software piracy. These have ranged from ease of theft and people's sense of proportional value (see Chapter 3) to cost, censure and availability as the main drivers (Moores & Dhillon, 2000). The SIIA has vehemently argued that since software piracy is an illegal act, the associated activities of buying and selling are also illegal and hence makes calls for increased legislation and enforcement. Although SIIA explains the decline in software piracy between 1994 and 1998 simply in terms of cost, cost per se does not seem to figure in SIIA's drive in managing piracy. This suggests that perhaps software developers are charging more than necessary for the software. One reason could be the near monopolistic environment in which most companies operate.

There are those who argue (e.g., Weckert, 1996) that unauthorized copying is not morally wrong, except when it's morally wrong to act illegally. Weckert (1996) poses three scenarios to make his point. First, where an individual may copy software just for evaluation, with the intent of buying it if it proves to be satisfactory. Second, where an individual copies a game but would never buy it because he thinks it's not worth doing so. Third, where an individual copies software for commercial gain and if the software was not available for copying, the individual would buy it. According to Weckert, clearly the owner of the software is harmed in the third case. Based on these assertions Weckert contends that copying is certainly not immoral and that a case against copying ought to be firmly established before restrictions are put in place.

There are various other viewpoints on software piracy and intellectual property rights. Swinyard, Rinne, and Kau (1990), for example, argue that the notion of copyright is a Western concept and that for the Asians becoming skilled means to copy the master. Therefore the authors contend that high piracy rates in Asia are a cultural issue with individuals viewing software piracy relative to potential benefits to self, family, and community. Conner and Rumelt (1991) argue that existence of pirated software is actually beneficial to software developers since it draws people into the software market and also is a means to distribute "free" copies to potential customers, who otherwise might not be aware.

FREEDOM OF SPEECH ISSUES

Aspects of freedom of speech have always been of concern to a broad cross section of the populace. Even today freedom of speech issues are hotly contested with the bans and destruction of paintings, sculptures, and writings. Only recently there were a lot of feelings expressed with the destruction of Buddha's statues in Afghanistan. Such occurrences have always been the musings of scholars and theologians alike. However with the recent advent of technology and the Internet, freedom of speech issues seem to have become of interest to the public.

In the United States the First Amendment to the Constitution (Freedom of Speech) has always acted as a shield between citizen and government. Individual states have tried to enact legislation to "criminalize" the intentional transmission of "obscene and indecent" messages but it has rather been difficult to define what constitutes "obscene" or "indecent." Some headway was made in the 1996 Communication Decency Act where "obscene" and "indecent" are defined as the transmission of information which depicts or describes "sexual or excretory activities or organs" in a manner deemed "offensive" by community standards. However understanding and regulating "community standards" in cyberspace is not only difficult, but also subjected to standards of the most restrictive communities in the nation. The act was challenged (and lost) on grounds that it violated the First Amendment insofar as that it caused "blanket restriction" of free speech. The act also failed to define "indecent" adequately. Although this was an attempt by the moral leaders to manage content on the Internet, at the same time it was a victory for those who supported free speech over the Internet.

Sex sites are not the only sites that are under fire. Hate speeches, online stalking and "recipe books" for terrorist groups are also of concern. As Warren and Hutchinson (2001) suggest, today a number of terrorist groups are using the Internet to further their cause. Prominent among these are the Zapatista Movement Web site, detailing their struggle against the Mexican authorities, and TamilNet, the voice of the Tamil Tigers. Many terrorists groups not only use the Internet to raise funds and disseminate information, they are also using information and communication technologies to engage in denial of service and even direct attacks. For instance the Portuguese hacker group, PHAIT (Portuguese Hackers Against Indonesian Tyranny) rewrote a number of Indonesian government and commercial Web sites to protest about East Trimor.

There are two viewpoints regarding such "bad speech" on the Internet. First, and the most obvious, is to strictly regulate the traffic. Such an action, however, comes under attack from the proponents of freedom of speech. Second, that the pursuit of truth is best served by allowing all kinds of views to be presented in the "market of ideas." The inherent contention is that only by free discussion of ideas and arguments will the real truth emerge (Elgesem, 1996).

QUALITY AND RELIABILITY OF INFORMATION AND RELATED SYSTEMS

Issues of quality and reliability of information and the related systems have perhaps received the most attention. Earlier work on quality of information was essentially carried out by software engineers (Boehm et al., 1978; McCall, 1979). The software engineers tried to describe quality of software by identifying series of attributes. Attributes in turn would have more attributes. Identifications and descriptions of such attributes helped in formulating a set of quality characteristics that could help in defining system specification and help in simplifying the quality assurance process. This earlier work went a long way in developing quality practices and in laying down the foundation for present-day software metrics.

Quality attributes were also pivotal in defining good and bad, ethical and unethical software engineering practices. For instance the software development practices followed in commissioning Therac-25 machines in the mid-1980s were criticized because basic software quality attributes had not been considered. Therac-25 was a computerized radiation therapy machine, where software from the earlier Therac-6 and Therac-20 had been reused. Following the death of six patients between 1985 and 1987, a number of social responsibility issues were raised. In the Therac-25 case the specialist machine operator upon whom the patients (and the public at large) were relying did not live up to their responsibilities. Patients were subjected to repeated radiation doses in spite of the operators knowing that the machines were malfunctioning. The manufacturer was clearly negligent in relation to this treatment equipment, from the original design stage through the much overdue safety renovations. The developers mistakenly believed that taking pieces from various proven machines would create a likewise successful new machine. This was a serious flaw in system design. More importantly, though, the priorities in system quality were poorly arranged, with simplicity of use threatening safety. There is a level of social responsibility (even greater in a industry such as medicine) that companies are entrusted with as we proceed into an era of all-consuming technology. The developers would have been far better off to meet those responsibilities proactively rather than reactively.

In recent years the social responsibility issues related to quality and reliability of information and the related systems have been repeatedly questioned. When the London Ambulance computer-aided dispatch system failed in 1992, who was to blame? London Ambulance, presumably the largest in the world, covering over 600 square miles and a resident population of nearly seven million, carries over 5,000 patients and receives between 2,000 and 2,500 calls per day. But numerous problems related to contractor selection, planning, project management and implementation resulted in complete failure of the computer-based system. The inquiries that ensued found that the system did not meet functionality or performance criteria and much of the design had fatal flaws that would, and did, cumulatively lead to all of the symptoms of system failure. This resulted in lengthy response times, numerous callbacks, and a large wait time to speak with a dispatcher.

When systems as critical as Therac-25 and London Ambulance fail, there are obviously social responsibility concerns. Clearly lack of quality in systems analysis, design and management results are the root causes. Ultimately, as observed by Bowen (2000), "it is unethical to develop software for safety-related systems without following the best practice available." As a matter of fact it is unethical to develop software without following the best practice for any kind of a system, may it be safety-critical or not. By following unethical information systems project management best practices, the baggage handling systems of the Chek Lap Kok airport in Hong Kong and Denver airport in the US resulted in disasters. The Nevada, California and Oregon Department of Motor Vehicle systems had a similar fate because corners were cut and basic guidelines for software development and project management were not followed.

OVERVIEW

This book, by considering a multitude of social responsibility issues in the information age, will help in developing a perspective to manage the ethical challenges afforded by the information and communication technologies. It is organized into 18 chapters.

Chapter 1 helps in understanding the issue of social responsibility in the information age. This is done by considering social responsibility concerns at five levels: issues of privacy and confidentiality; accessibility to technology issues; property rights and ownership issues; freedom of speech issues; issues of quality and reliability of information and the related systems.

In Chapter 2 Janice Burn and Karen Loch address the impact of information technology and the World Wide Web on the 21st century and the challenges that we will face as responsible members of a dynamically changing society. The chapter gives particular consideration to the policies, infrastructure, human resources and development responsibilities in developing societies.

Chapter 3 focuses on a more practical issue related with software piracy and Darryl Seale explores issues related to the question "Why do we do it if we know it's wrong?" A structural model of software piracy is developed. The study identifies social norms, expertise required, gender, and computer usage (both at home and at work) as having a direct effect on self-reported piracy. Furthermore ease of theft and an individual's sense of the proportional value of software were found to affect piracy indirectly. The findings hold promise for design and marketing of software.

In Chapter 4, Mark Lycett and Nancy Pouloudi discuss the issue of component-based development and the resulting data protection concerns. The authors argue that since component-based development has emerged as a software engineering approach that enables evolutionary and flexible systems development, there are inherent ethical concerns in developing software from prefabricated heterogeneous components. This is because no consent has been sought regarding data use, which is exchanged without the users or developers knowing which components will use what data and when. The discussion unveils a complex ethical debate with important and significant implications for data controllers and information systems developers.

Chapter 5 by Gurpreet Dhillon and Trevor Moores reviews issues related to the phenomenal growth in Internet commerce in recent years and the related privacy concerns. The authors argue that although privacy as a concept has been well understood with respect to brick-and-mortar businesses, there is limited research in identifying major issues of concern related to Internet privacy. The chapter systematically identifies the major Internet privacy concerns. Data for the study was collected through two panels and subjective evaluation.

Chapter 6 sensitizes readers with Internet privacy issues by reviewing the case of DoubleClick, Inc. The case study helps in identifying a number of substantive issues that need to be researched, discussed, debated and analyzed such that an efficient and effective method can be created to protect the privacy of the citizens. Scott Chapman and Gurpreet Dhillon suggest a combination of technological, legal and self-regulatory controls in order to protect privacy of individuals in the information age.

Chapter 7 presents a study by Sandra Henderson, Charles Snyder and Terry Byrd that examines the relationships between consumer privacy concerns, actual e-commerce activity, the importance of privacy policies, and regulatory preference. The study uses a model developed from existing literature and theory to develop a questionnaire to gauge the concerns of consumers. The results indicate that consumers are concerned about the protection of their personal information and feel that privacy policies are important. Consumers also indicate that they preferred government regulation over industry self-regulation to protect their personal information.

In Chapter 8, William Hutchinson and Matt Warren examine the attitudes of Australian IS/IT managers to the concept of cyber-vigilantism. The chapter reviews the policies and procedures put in place by various organizations. The authors conclude that, at the present time, only a small percentage of businesses are prepared to deal with any eventuality. This to a large extent is attributed to the complacency on part of the organizations to deal with threats posed by organized and offensive attackers.

Chapter 9 by Matt Warren and William Hutchinson addresses the issue of cyberspace ethics and information warfare. The authors consider various threats in the information age and identify the related ethical challenges. Some of the threats identified by the authors include manipulation of information, interception of information, disruption of information flows, "flooding" organizations with information, destruction of information storage media, disrupting the availability and confidentiality of data, subversion of people, and various other logical and physical attacks.

In Chapter 10, Ben Fairweather conducts a moral analysis of policies for the prevention of repetitive strain injury (RSI) among computer users. The analysis suggests that there is too much weight on individual responsibility, with little or no attention to the context in which the computers are being used, and unrealistic demands on individuals as a result. Clearly, as the author suggests, consideration needs to be given to the responsibilities of the computer suppliers and the employers. This could be in terms of availability of relatively inexpensive software and equipment to prevent RSI with the computers and clear policy initiatives on the part of the organizations.

Chapter 11 by Anastasia Papazafeiropoulou and Nancy Pouloudi examines how social concerns such as trust and digital democracy pertain to all levels of Internet and electronic commerce policy, posing dilemmas and influencing the construction of an effective and socially responsible strategy for electronic commerce. Apart from numerous technical (e.g., fast and reliable networks) and regulatory (e.g., legal frameworks and standardization) challenges, a number of social concerns have also come to the fore, necessitating policy makers to see Internet use and electronic commerce as a social as well as a technical phenomenon.

In Chapter 12, Mahesh Raisinghani and Dan Petty discuss e-commerce taxation issues. In particular their focus is on state and local taxation of Internet access fees and sales transactions on the Internet. The chapter describes viewpoints from various interest groups. Discussion of e-commerce taxation issues in this chapter presents an interesting backdrop, especially when proponents of Internet taxation are searching for technological and administrative ways to meet their goals.

In Chapter 13, James Douglas Orton looks at challenges afforded by the competitive intelligence age and considers aspects related to social responsibility. The author covers diverse topics such as: covert operations, competitive strategy, corporate intelligence, economic security, economic intelligence, competitive intelligence, economic warfare. Orton's inherent argument is that although competitive intelligence professionals are attempting to create social responsibility benchmarks in this information age, it is rather difficult to address the concerns at a global level.

Chapter 14 in this book is by Randall Reid and Mario Pascalev, addressing strategic and ethical issues in outsourcing information technologies. The analysis presented in the chapter identifies various ethical problems and suggests a systematic way of evaluating ethical conduct in the process of outsourcing IT in the context of a company's strategy. The authors incorporate various ethical challenges into outsourcing models. The ultimate aim of the study presented in this chapter is to enhance the manner in which companies look at their decision to outsource IT.

In Chapter 15 Joseph Gilbert considers aspects of managing information technology projects and the related social responsibility concerns. Gilbert analyzes social responsibilities of project managers in terms of duties to various stakeholders or constituencies. Differences between legal responsibility and moral or ethical responsibility are discussed. Furthermore, a rights and duties approach is applied to principles from business ethics to the problem of identifying project manager responsibilities. In conclusion the chapter considers how the duties or responsibilities of project managers can be viewed in a positive light as opportunities which most employees and many managers do not have.

Chapter 16 by Phil Carter discusses issues relevant to the self-employed and small-business computer users. The author argues that entering into self-employed and small-business people's lives who are using computers reveals that there are complex webs of interrelating factors that impact on their behavior with computers. Furthermore physical, psychological, social, and spiritual aspects of being human can all impact on a user's behavior with the computer. The author discusses such impacts and identifies the related challenges in the information age.

In Chapter 17 Mikko Siponen claims that the use of ethical theories and human morality is useful for security, particularly given that Hare's overriding thesis has validity. The author argues that descriptivism (including the doctrine of cultural relativism) leads to several problems and contradictions and causes detrimental effects to our well-being (and security); hence, an alternative approach to using ethics in minimizing security breaches is proposed.

Chapter 18 presents a description of various aspects of a viable social responsibility program in the information age. It is hoped that this will enable individuals, organizations and society at large to cope with diverse challenges afforded in the information age.

REFERENCES

Angell, I. O. (1995). Winners and losers in the information age. *LSE Magazine*, 7(1), 10-12.

Angell, I. O. (1996). Economic crime: Beyond good and evil. *Journal of Financial Regulation and Compliance*, 4(1).

Angell, I. O. (2000). *The New Barbarian Manifesto: How to Survive the Information Age*. London: Kogan Page.

Boehm, B. W., et al. (1978). *Characteristics of Software Quality*. Amsterdam: North Holland.

Bowen, J. (2000). The ethics of safety-critical systems. *Communications of the ACM*, 43(4), 91-97.

Burn, J. M. and Loch, K. D. (2001). The societal impact of the World Wide Web-Key challenges for the 21st century. *Information Resources Management Journal*, 14(4).

Conner, K. R. and Rumelt, R. P. (1991). Software piracy: An analysis of protection strategies. *Management Science*, 37(2), 125-139.

Culnan, M. J. and Armstrong, P. K. (1999). Information privacy concerns, procedural fairness, and impersonal trust: An empirical investigation. *Organization Science*, 10(1), 104-115.

Dhillon, G. and Moores, T. (2001). Internet privacy: Interpreting key issues. *Information Resources Management Journal*, 14(4).

Dhillon, G., Moores, T. and Hackney, R. (2001). The emergence of networked organizations in India: A misalignment of interests? *Journal of Global*

Information Management, 9(1), 25-30.

Elgesem, D. (1996). Freedom of expression and the regulation of Internet access in academia. Paper presented at the *3rd International Conference on Values and Social Responsibilities of Computer Science (ETHICOMP96)*, Madrid, Spain, November.

McCall, J. A. (1979). An introduction to software quality metrics. In Coper, J. B. and Fisher, M. J. (Eds.), *Software Quality Management*. New York: PBI.

Moores, T. and Dhillon, G. (2000). Software piracy: A view from Hong Kong. *Communications of the ACM*, 43(12), 88-93.

Ohmae, K. (1995). *The End of the Nation State*. New York: The Free Press.

Reich, R. B. (1992). *The Work of Nations*. New York: Vintage Books.

Seale, D. A. (2002). Why do we do it if we know it's wrong? A structural model of software piracy. In Dhillon, G. (Ed.), *Social Responsibility in the Information Age: Issues and Controversies*. Hershey, USA: Idea Group Publishing.

Swinyard, W., Rinne, H. and Kau, A. (1990). The morality of software piracy: a cross cultural analysis. *Journal of Business Ethics*, 9(655-664).

Warren, M. and Hutchinson, W. (2001). Cyber terrorism and the contemporary corporation. In Dhillon, G. (Ed.), *Information Security Management: Global Challenges in the New Millennium*, 53-64. Hershey, USA: Idea Group Publishing.

Weckert, J. (1996). Intellectual property rights and computer software. Paper presented at the *3rd International Conference on Values and Social Responsibilities of Computer Science (ETHICOMP96)*, Madrid, Spain, November.

Chapter II

The Societal Impact of the World Wide Web– Key Challenges for the 21st Century

Janice M. Burn
Edith Cowan University, Australia

Karen D. Loch
Georgia State University, USA

INTRODUCTION

Many lessons from history offer strong evidence that technology can have a definite effect on the social and political aspects of human life. At times it is difficult to grasp how supposedly neutral technology might lead to social upheavals, mass migrations of people, and shifts in wealth and power. Yet a quick retrospective look at the last few centuries finds that various technologies have done just that, challenging the notion of the neutrality of technology. Some examples include the printing press, railways, and the telephone.

The effects of these technologies usually begin in our minds by changing the way we view time and space. Railways made the world seem smaller by enabling us to send goods, people, and information to many parts of the world in a fraction of the time it took before. Telephones changed the way we think about both time and distance, enabling us to stay connected without needing to be physically displaced. While new technologies create new opportunities for certain individuals or groups to gain wealth, there are other economic implications with a wider ranging impact, political and social. Eventually, as the technology matures, social upheavals, mass

This chapter originally appeared in the Information Resources Management Journal, Vol. 14, No. 4.
Copyright © 2001, Idea Group Publishing.

migrations and shifts in economic and political power can be observed. We find concrete examples of this dynamic phenomenon during the Reformation, the industrial revolution, and more recently, as we witness the ongoing information technology revolution.

Before the Reformation, the church controlled an effective monopoly on knowledge and education. The introduction of the printing press in Western Europe in the mid-15th century made knowledge and ideas in book form widely available to a great many more people. Printing hastened the Reformation, and the Reformation spread printing further. By the early 16th century, when Martin Luther posted his 95 theses on the castle church, the political movement was well underway. The printing press changed the way in which we collected, transmitted, and preserved information prior to that time. Mass production and dissemination of new ideas, and more rapid response from others were instrumental in launching a worldwide social phenomenon.

Dramatic changes in the economic and social structures in the 18th century characterized the industrial revolution. Technological innovations were made in transportation and communication with the development of the steam engine, steam shipping, and the telegraph. These inventions and technological innovations were integral in creating the factory system and large-scale machine production. Owners of factories were the new wealthy. The laboring population, formerly employed predominantly in agriculture, moved in mass to the factory urban centers. This led to social changes as women and children were introduced into the workforce. Factory labor separated work from the home and there was a decline of skilled crafts as work became more specialized along the assembly line.

The inventions of the telegraph and telephone dramatically changed the manner in which we conduct business and live our daily lives. They allowed the collection, validation, and dissemination of information in a timely and financially efficient manner. More recently, we are experiencing the information technology revolution, led by the introduction of computers. The rate of change has accelerated from previous times–with generations of technology passing us by in matters of months rather than decades. We are witnessing significant shifts in wealth and power before our eyes. Small start-up high technology and Internet companies, and their young owners, represent a very wealthy class–and an extremely powerful one. Small countries such as Singapore and Ireland, through the strategic use of information technology and aggressive national policy, have transformed their respective economies and positioned themselves in the competitive global economy.

The Internet, a complex network of networks, is frequently spoken of as a tool for countries to do likewise. The Internet removes the geographical and time limitations of operating in a global economy. The banking industry has been revolutionized with Internet banks who can collect, validate, and disseminate information and services to any people group–internal to the organization and external to its customers-in a timely and financially efficient manner. Similar scenarios exist in the worlds of retail, healthcare, and transportation.

There is an underlying assumption in the popular belief that the Internet may be the savior to the developing countries of the world. Such thinking is dependent on a single premise: the belief that access to information gives access to the global marketplace, which in turn leads to economic growth. Information is power; knowledge is wealth. The vehicle for access is information technology and communications infrastructure (ITC). Mohammad Nasim, the minister for post and telecommunications in Bangladesh, one of the poorest countries in the world, restated the premise, saying, "We know full well how important a role telecommunications play in a country's economic development" (Zaman, 1999). The converse is also true. Lack of IT access leads to an increased inability to compete in the global marketplace, which leads to further economic poverty. What we are witnessing is therefore either an upward or downward spiral phenomenon. This raises some interesting and important questions for society, such as: What is the current information access through the Internet? Who are the "haves" and the "have-nots" of information access? How can the Internet address the societal challenges?

This paper attempts to address these questions and related issues. In the first section we document the current state of information technology diffusion and connectivity, and related factors such as GDP, population density, and cultural attitudes. The second section examines more fully the question of who comprises the "haves" and the "have-nots" so frequently mentioned. Across and within country comparisons are made, noting in particular disadvantaged groups, urban vs. rural communities, and women and children as groups that are frequently forgotten, but who are vital to true transformation to a global information society. The third section offers some concrete suggestions as to how the Internet may be used to address the growing gap between those who have and those who don't. We report some country examples which illustrate both the progress and the magnitude of the challenge as societies, governments, and other key change agents attempt to redress the problem. Finally, we make two observations. One is that for those who don't have, there is little demand to have, as well. This is in large part explained by the second observation, which is that a multilevel complex challenge must be overcome in order to leverage technology-based services, such as offered by the Internet, as a sociological tool to reduce economic disparity. We challenge the reader to look inward for each one's individual responsibility in this big picture.

INFORMATION TECHNOLOGY ACCESS

In 1995, the world IT market as measured by the revenue of primary vendors was worth an estimated US$527.9 billion. Between 1987 and 1994, its growth rate averaged nearly twice that of GDP worldwide. It was particularly high in Asia climbing from 17.5% to 20.9% of world share during that time. Nevertheless this strong growth did little to redress the geographical imbalance in the world IT market—markets outside Asia and the OECD area (ROW) accounted for only 4% of the world total.

From a world population of 5.53 billion, ROW accounts for 82.6% of the total population yet from a world GDP of US$25,223 billion, ROW accounts for only 19.2% (decreasing >2% over the last 7 years) and from a total IT market of US$ 455 billion, ROW accounts for only 8.4%. See Figure 1.

The IT market has remained concentrated within the G7 countries at around 88%, with the United States accounting for 46% of the market. In terms of installed PC base the US was by far the world leader with 86.3 million units well ahead of Japan (19.1m), Germany (13.5m) and the UK (10.9m). In the US this averages at 32.8 PCs per 100 inhabitants. The Internet now reaches into every part of the globe with the number of host computers connected to the Internet increasing from 3.2 million in July 1994 to 6.6 million in July 1995, 12.9 million in 1996, 16.1 million by January 1997 and 29.7 million by January 1998 (Network Wizards). This is more than a tenfold increase since July 1993 as shown in Figure 2.

Recent estimates indicate that some 90 countries, just under 5 million machines and some 100 million users worldwide are connected to the Internet (NUA Internets Survey, 1998). However, Internet hosts per 1 million inhabitants by country income show huge differences between the rich and the poor, with 31,046 hosts for the highest income countries and only 9 per million inhabitants in the poorest. The level of LAN implementation differs significantly across countries, with the US accounting for 55%, Western Europe 32% and ROW only 13% of the installed base of LAN servers.

This has to be examined at two levels: the rates of PC diffusion and connectivity. In terms of the number of corporate PCs per 100 white-collar workers, leading countries such as Norway, Switzerland and the US have more than 100, major Western European countries 60-80 and Japan only 24 (see Figure 3). As for PCs

Figure 1: Share of OECD member countries in world population, GDP and IT market, 1987–1994

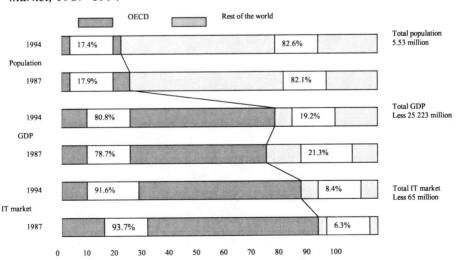

Source: *World Bank* based on IDC (1995b), *World Bank* (1995), and *OECD* (ANA Database)

connected to LANs, 64% of corporate PCs are on a network in the US but only 21% in Japan (Dataquest, 1995). Corporate cultures in Asia may be less conducive to online management.

Access to telephone service is a good indicator of the state of a country's telecommunications infrastructure as this plays a large role in accessibility to information. More than 90% of households in high-income countries have a

Figure 2: Internet host computers (millions)

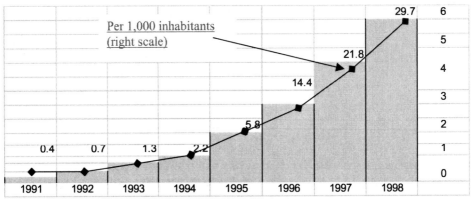

Source: Network Wizards

Figure 3: Number of PCs per 100 white collar workers

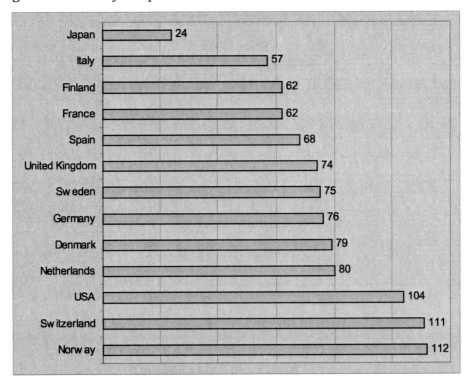

telephone line (and some have more than one), whereas only 2% of households in low-income countries are similarly served. Of 950 million households in the world, 65% of the total do not have a telephone. Figure 4 shows the distribution of telecommunications against wealth.

The technology gap is strikingly apparent in telephone usage, where consumers in the United States make an average of 2,170 calls per inhabitant annually, which converts into just under seven calls a day. Only Canada and Singapore come close to the American average; Canada because of the similarity of culture and technological deployment, and Singapore by virtue of the heavy concentration of business within the small city-state. The United States' use of the telephone remains approximately three times higher than the European, Japanese and Australian averages, which seem to be clustered at between the 600-800 call per inhabitant level.

The difference between the United States and the Latin American and some of the Asian countries is even more striking. The average American makes 10 times as many calls as the average Mexican, 20 times as many calls as the average Chinese, and 40 times as many as the average Indian (see Figure 5). As the developing countries make greater inroads into extending their networks and their inhabitants succeed in integrating the telephone more into their daily lives, it is to be expected that their telephone usage will eventually start to catch up to that of the more developed countries, but it will undoubtedly take some time to do so.

While the technology invasion has offered developing countries amazing opportunities to leapfrog over stages of growth in their programs for industrialisation and advancement, the drive for information can often occur only at the expense of other basic infrastructure needs which are regarded as norms for advanced societies. Illustrative of these trade-offs are countries who are currently making major investments into their ITC infrastructure, as shown in Table 1. China aims to enter the 21st century as an information economy yet has an average GDP which is only 1/50th of the US; Argentina has a school life expectancy of less than 4 years compared to over 16 in Australia, and India boasts a female adult illiteracy problem of 62.3%. The statistics are even more alarming when comparisons are made

Figure 4: Lines per 100 inhabitants in relation to GDP

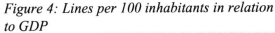

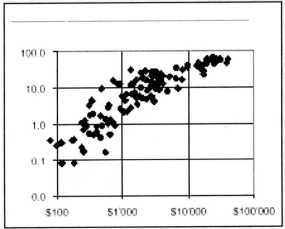

Source: International Telecommunication Union, 1998

Figure 5: Number of calls per capita by country

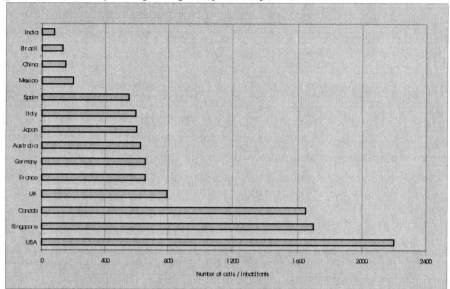

Source: International Telecommunication Union, 1998

Table 1: Worldwide indicators

	1995 US$ gdp pc	School life expectancy	Adult (F) illiteracy	Economic Rural Activity %	% access to sanitation
USA	26037	15.8	3.1	59.9	*
Japan	41718	14.8	*	50.0	*
UK	18913	16.3	*	52.8	*
Australia	20046	16.2	*	48.1	*
China	582	*	27.3	72.9	7
India	365	*	62.3	*	14
Philippines	1093	11.0	5.7	49.0	67
Argentina	8055	3.8	3.8	41.3	2
Vietnam	270	*	8.8	74.1	15

* not available

Source: UN statistics, 1997

with rural communities, where only 7% of the rural population in China and 2% in Argentina have access to sanitation.

The Haves and the Have-Nots

The haves and have-nots are generally differentiated based on a variety of factors such as income and education levels. We generally think of the haves and the have-nots from the perspective of the international arena, dividing countries into two large categories: developed and developing, with the greater proportion of countries considered developing. There is a tight coupling between the ITC infrastructure of a country and its income status. It comes as little surprise then that despite rapid growth of the Internet, some 97% of users are in high-income countries which account for just 15% of the world's population (Tarjanne, 1996). The US boasts four out of ten homes owning a personal computer and one in three of these has a modem enabling the computer and telephone to be connected (see Figure 6). By the year 2000 at least half of all US homes will have two or more telecommunications lines. At present the median age of users is 32 years and dropping, 64% have college degrees and 25% have an annual income higher than $80,000. Half of Internet users have managerial or professional jobs and 31% are women. There are now more than a million Web sites for them to visit.

It is also useful to examine the question of the haves and have-nots from a second vantage point–a within country perspective. In fact, while the majority of the population within a developed country may qualify as "have," there is a subset of the population which does not meet the criteria. For example, the United States is considered a developed country, but the poorest 20% of households receive a smaller share of income than in almost any other developed country. Over six million homes did not have phone service in 1997 (ITU, 1998). By regions, households in Oceania (predominantly Australia and New Zealand) are the most wired, with penetration rates of over 90%. This is in contrast to Asia, where about 20% of households have a telephone, and to Africa, where the figure drops to 6% (ITU, 1998). Within country comparison by urban and rural areas also shows marked differences. Over 80% of Thailand's population still lives in rural areas, yet less than 40% of telephone lines in the country are in non-urban areas. These within country variances at best retard the overall economic growth of the respective countries.

Whether developed or developing, we also observe significant segments of the population that do not have access to the ITC infrastructure. These groups are

Figure 6: Percent of US households with a telephone, computer and Internet use

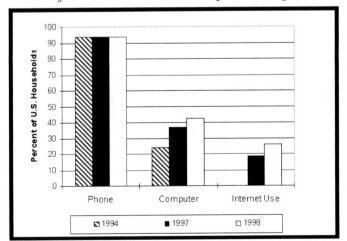

Source: Falling Through the Net, 1999

characterized by low income, young limited education, member of a minority group, elderly, handicapped, and rural. The irony is that it is these groups that, were they to have access, would be simultaneously empowered to take steps to improve their economic well-being. It is these groups that receive huge benefits from being able to engage in job search activities, take educational classes, or access government reports online for example.

Falling Through the Net : Defining the Digital Divide. A 1999 survey of the digital divide in the US (third in a series from 1995) shows that whilst there is expanded information access, there is a persisting "digital divide" which has actually increased since the first survey (see Figures 7 and 8). The least connected are typically lower income groups, and Blacks and Hispanics. Additional geographical locations (urban, central city, and rural), age, education and household type are additional factors leading to disadvantaged groups. The following are profiles of groups that are among the "least connected," according to the 1999 data:

• **Rural Poor**-Those living in rural areas at the lowest income levels are among the least connected. Rural households earning less than $5,000 per year have the lowest telephone penetration rates (74.4%), followed by central cities (75.2%) and urban areas (76.8%). In 1994, by contrast, central city poor were the least connected. Rural households earning between $5,000-$10,000 have the lowest PC-ownership rates (7.9%) and online access rates (2.3%), followed by urban areas (10.5%, 4.4%) and central cities (11%, 4.6%).

A high-income household in an urban area is more than 20 times as likely as a rural, low-income household to have Internet access.

• **Rural and Central City Minorities**-"Other non-Hispanic" households, including Native Americans, Asian Americans, and Eskimos, are least likely to have telephone service in rural areas (82.8%), particularly at low incomes (64.3%). Black and Hispanic households also have low telephone rates in rural areas (83.2% and 85%), especially at low incomes (73.6% and 72.2%). As in 1994, Blacks have the lowest PC-ownership rates in rural areas (14.9%), followed by Blacks and Hispanics in central cities (17.1% and 16.2%, respectively). Online access is also the lowest for Black households in rural areas (5.5%) and central cities (5.8%), followed by Hispanic households in central cities (7.0%) and rural areas (7.3%).

To put this in simple terms: a child in a low-income White family is three times as likely to have Internet access as a child in a comparable Black family and four times as likely as children in a comparable Hispanic household.

• **Young Households**-Young households (below age 25) also appear to be particularly burdened. Young, rural, low-income households have telephone penetration rates of only 65.4%, and only 15.5% of these households are likely to own a PC. Similarly, young households with children are also less likely to have phones or PCs: Those in central cities have the lowest rates (73.4% for phones, 13.3% for PCs), followed by urban (76% for phones, 14.5% for PCs) and rural locales (79.6% for phones, 21.2% for PCs).

Figure 7: Percent of US households with a computer by income

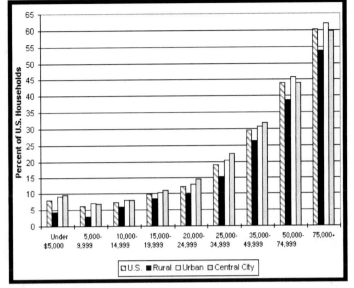

Source: Falling Through the Net, 1999

- **Female-Headed Households**-Single-parent, female households also lag significantly behind the national average. They trail the telephone rate for married
couples with children by 10 percentage points (86.3% versus 96%). They are
also significantly less likely than dual-parent households to have a PC (25%
versus 57.2%) or to have online access (9.2% versus 29.4%). Female-headed
households in central cities are particularly unlikely to own PCs or have online
access (20.2%, 6.4%), compared to dual-parent households (52%, 27.3%) or
even male-headed households (28%, 11.2%) in the same areas.

The data reveal that the digital divide–the disparities in access to telephones,
personal computers and the Internet across certain demographic groups–still exists
and in many cases has widened significantly. The gap for computers and Internet
access has generally grown larger by categories of education, income and race. This
remains the chief concern as those already with access to electronic resources make
rapid gains while leaving other households behind. We are witnessing the wholesale
disappearance of work accessible to the urban poor. Without intervention, unem-
ployment, poverty, and out-migration will likely increase, exacerbating the structural problems typical of rural areas (OTA, 1996).

In Australia, the picture is very similar. The report "Women's Access to Online
Services," produced by the Office of the Status of Women in December 1996, states:
"The Governments' focus on commerce has meant that the social consequences of
becoming an 'information society' have been largely ignored. This may have been
exacerbated by the apparent lack of women in decision-making positions in industry
and relevant departments." The most recent data from the Australian Bureau of

Figure 8: Percent of US households using the Internet by income

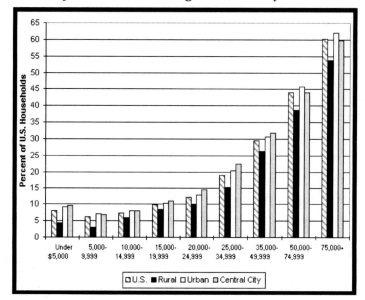

Source: Falling Through the Net, 1999

Statistics (1998) estimated 262,000 users who indicated use of the Internet at home, with about 178,000 being men and 84,000 women (68%:32%). Women's represen- tation amongst email users was even lower-at only 26%. Women over the age of 55 were extremely poorly represented. However, perhaps a more important issue is "What access opportunities are open to women who don't have a computer and modem at home?" AGB McNair estimates that in the region of only 13% of Australian women over the age of 14 have ever accessed the Internet!

Other countries' digital divides also persist; the percentages are simply higher for the have-nots. For example, Egypt's "haves/have-nots" ratio, a lower-middle income country as defined by the World Bank,[1] represents less than 8% of its 60 million plus population.

There are astonishing exceptions to the rule—one example is women farmers. The DSS CRP case studies found that women farmers "were the enthusiasts, the main drivers, while their husbands, if they had no prior computer experience, were reluctant to touch the CIN (Community Information Network)". Weather informa- tion, farming practices, health and education were all foci but, further, email was used to develop support networks, thereby reducing social and cultural isolation. Strangely it is not only those women typically identified as culturally isolated (aboriginal, non-English speaking, remote communities such as mining) but also professionally educated women whose need for professional support, continuing education and contact with like-minded peers is not adequately met.

Increasingly, education, health, legal services and social communications are moving to computer-based technology. The success of the Ipswich Global Infolinks project "SeniorNet" is another startling example. One resident said "I personally find the Internet to be a fascinating medium where any information seems available. … [IT] opens up a whole new world for elderly people and keeps the mind active. … There is no age limit to having a good time surfing the Net (des Artes, 1996).

The Internet is increasingly viewed as the window to the global economy. Is then the Internet the secret weapon for the have-nots? Is it for the masses? One may argue that what subsistence farmers in Afghanistan, or Korea, or Cambodia need is NOT high-tech science and complex systems, but immunizations, basic literacy, disease- and drought-resistant cereals and oilseeds, simple pumps, or deep-drop toilets. The fallacy of the pro-Internet argument is that it ignores the social and economic implications of the technology, as highlighted in this discussion.

A second argument in favor of the technology is that it will assist developing countries in leapfrogging stages in the development process. Many highly successful initiatives are taking place in developing countries to promote community-based Internet access for health (effective water sourcing, sanitation, bioengineering of crop production), educational (electronic network of schools), and other applications. The Mbendi AfroPaedia Web site (www.mbendi.co.za), the pan-European FRIENDS (Farming and Rural Information Expertise and News Dissemination Service) project, and the Mediterranean Institute of Teleactivity (IMeT) are representative of these types of initiatives (Stratte-McClure, 1999). Compelling examples demonstrate the pay-off: In rural southern Ghana, petrol stations are able to place orders with suppliers by phone when previously they could only be made by traveling to Accra; in Zimbabwe, one company generated $15 million of business by advertising on the Internet; in China, a little girl's life was saved when her doctor posted her symptoms to an Internet discussion group and received an immediate answer. Sam Pitroda, Indian government advisor, states, "IT is not a luxury but VITAL to basic activities, such as bringing food to market, preventing drought, a major source of new jobs and wealth." The conundrum is that sustainable development is an immensely complex process having its roots in educational and infrastructural building; what then is the role for the Internet in this process?

HOW CAN THE INTERNET ADDRESS THE CHALLENGE?

It is recognized that an educated population with skills and knowledge in information technology is an instrumental part of sustainable development. The irony is that while the volume of information and knowledge that is available is increasing, the percentage of the world population able to have access to and derive value from it seems to be becoming smaller. The gap between the haves and the have-nots is increasing significantly–both on a global and local basis (Novak & Hoffman, 1998). The magnitude of the challenge within countries is related to income distribution and country size. Central and Eastern European countries enjoy high teledensities in relation to their income levels because they have more even levels of income distribution than other regions (ITU, 1998). In terms of size, smaller countries are more able to reinvent themselves than countries such as China with massive populations and huge geographic expanse. Ireland and Singapore are good examples of small countries who, through aggressive national policy towards technology and education, repositioned themselves in the global market.

Is the Internet the secret weapon to bring equality to the masses-to close the gap? Fact one: Information represents power in both the political and economic spheres. Fact two: Almost every emerging society, has made it a priority to participate in the global information society bearing witness to the belief in its ability positively to affect their country's well-being. Fact three: The Internet is the technological innovation that can provide access to the same markets and the same information within the same time frame as is the case with more developed countries. It would seem therefore that the answer to the question is "yes"-but that access is a necessary albeit insufficient solution. What then are the implications?

The traditional approach for introducing technological innovations has been through the educational system and the workplace. The problem is that a significant portion of the have-not segment does not participate in these venues. A nontraditional approach must be taken.

If access to the have-nots is to be achieved, then technological innovations, such as the Internet, need to be brought specifically to the target group and on their level. Venues where Internet' awareness, exposure, and ultimately, familiarity need to be developed. Candidate sites include communal gatherings such as the post office, hospitals, banks, and the local merchant. Furthermore, the have-nots must perceive value, an incentive to take the steps to go beyond simple awareness to becoming an actual user of the technology. The success of this effort is necessarily linked with the extent to which applications are socially and culturally appropriate and specifically address those daily life issues that concern the intended users, such as registering to vote, access to government information, access to medical information and assistance, or bus schedules.

In the local village or community where the deployment is being made, co-opting a key individual is instrumental to success. The key individual receives the benefits of training plus the respect of his or her community as the knowledge broker. They are instrumental in introducing the technology to others. Use of the systems, at least initially, will likely need to be heavily if not totally subsidized. This certainly raises the bar for many developing countries and also illustrates how country size quickly becomes a significant factor.

Egypt is an example of a country that developed a model that includes education and training, infrastructure, and IT in general and Internet access over time, all together. Moreover, it developed applications that would be culturally and socially appropriate so as to gain widespread support for the effort. But, results do not come overnight: There is a requirement for champions and long-term commitment on the behalf of the sponsor-in this case, the Egyptian government. In the late 1980s, Egypt began to deploy computer-based systems in its 27 governorates, creating Information and Decision Support Centers (IDSC) (Nidumolu et. al., 1996; Kamel, 1995, 1997; El-Sherif & El-Sawy, 1988). The effort was part of a comprehensive plan to introduce and rationalize the use of information technology in key sectors in the economy. Over time, the IDSCs have been extended into the local villages and more rural areas. There are currently 1,102 IDSC facilities. Technology Community Centers represent the most recent efforts to introduce and rationalize the use of information technology in general, and specifically the Internet, to the general populace (Loch et al., 1999). The focus of the community centers is on children up to the age of 20. Egypt's income distribution and population demographics are typical of many developing countries. Less than 10% of the population comprises the haves subset of the population. More than 60% of its population is under the age of 30; of that segment, more than 50% is under 20 years of age. The implication is that the extent to which these segments are exposed to advanced technologies and educational and training opportunities is highly correlated with the future economic well-being of the country.

The International Telecommunication Union's (ITU) Telecommunication Development Bureau (BDT) has a program for Multipurpose Community Telecentres (MCTs) for rural and remote areas. The ITU is working in partnership with other international organizations and the private sector, installing pilot MCTs in and around a dozen countries. The operating principal of this effort is the information premise: Access to information (services) brings about improved access to the local marketplace which in turn enhances economic growth and which ultimately impacts the global competitiveness of the country. MCTs articulate the premise slightly differently, also arguing that access to information services can also help to lessen isolation and combat the problem of brain drain from rural to urban areas. Contrary to past history, where technological innovations were contributors to mass migration of people, the Internet might allow people to remain in place while making available needed information.

The project in Uganda subsidized by the BDT exemplifies the above. The MCT will be installed in Nakaseke to provide individuals with access to telephones, facsimile machines and computing facilities, including Internet access. It offers training, technical support, and professional guidance to produce electronic information reflecting local knowledge and requirements. The library is integrated into the telecentre. The MCT will provide support to teachers in the local school system through information support to the school libraries, the provision of visual resources, training for teachers in the use of computers, and distance education. The staff of the local hospital will use the facility for telemedicine applications, continuing education for health staff, and access for local health workers to medical-related resources on the Internet. Other targeted local user groups include small businesses and farmers, local councils, the women's training organization, nongovernmental organizations, and the general public (ITU, 1998, box 5.1).

SUMMARY OBSERVATIONS

True, the Internet and its associated developments, such as the World Wide Web, are a developed global phenomenon. True, the gap between the economically advantaged and disadvantaged continues to increase in both developed and developing economies. With the experiences in Egypt and Uganda as exemplars, we can make several observations that may be useful to other organizations and governmental agencies considering such initiatives or for researchers examining such initiatives.

First, existing articulated demand for technology-based services by the have-not group for such services is likely to be small to nonexistent. Hence the effort is very much characteristic of a push phenomenon (Gilbert, 1996; Gurbaxani et al., 1990). Central and local government authorities, international agencies, and leading entities from the private sector are playing, and must continue to play, key roles. Aggressive IT policy by the Singaporean government transformed Singapore within a 20-year time frame. Other countries, such as Uganda and Egypt as highlighted in this paper, are making inroads, but one must acknowledge that it is a long road to travel.

Second, there are three levels of challenges that are part of this effort. The first level is a human resource challenge. The availability of quality education and the level of literacy are both part of this challenge. The second level is the economic challenge. On an individual basis, the ability to pay for service is minimal. This places additional pressure on the providers to make the service inexpensive and widely available. On a country/governmental level, such efforts stretch the economic resources of the providing agencies. The geographic size and population distribution and size are all factors that make this level a particularly difficult challenge. The magnitude of the task for China, for example, far exceeds that of Singapore simply due to its geographic span and population demographics.

The third level is the technological innovation itself. In the case of the Internet, a base level of infrastructure must be in place to be able to deliver access to the Internet and, in turn, access to the global marketplace. All three levels are interrelated. The simple availability of the technology is insufficient; training to support its use must also be available. All levels reside in a political environment which varies from country to country. Figure 9 depicts these levels in context.

THE REAL CHALLENGE?

Information technology is generally perceived as a major facilitator for globalization, with the implication that hitherto underdeveloped regions can now gain access to worldwide resources and expertise, which will in turn lead to enhanced economic development. Globalization theorists, however, argue that it is only capital that has escaped the confines of space (Bauman, 1998; Beck, 2000). Capital has gained almost unlimited, instantaneous mobility, whereas people

Figure 9: Three challenges to technological innovation deployment

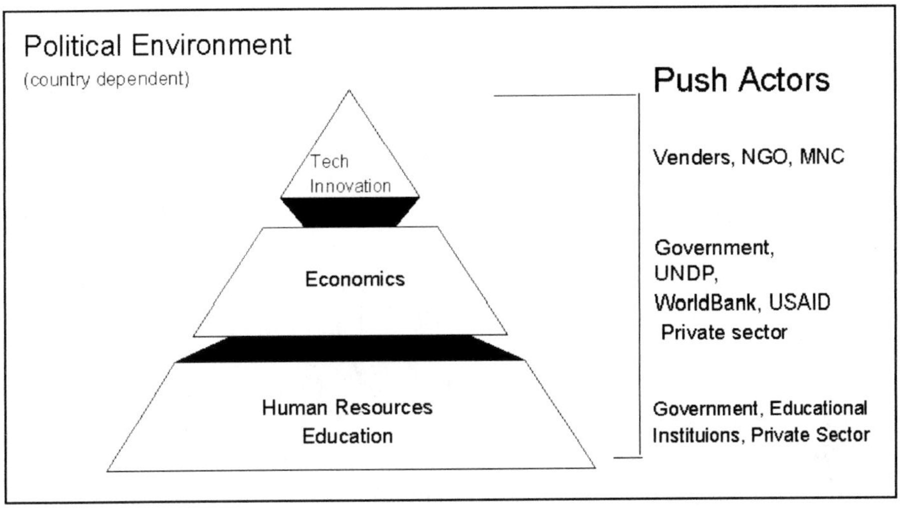

remain relatively immobile. One could argue that the development of global networks serves only to enhance the more developed nations and support the most dominant values, leading to increased exploitation of the less developed nations and the more disadvantaged sectors of society (Castells, 2000).

A powerful tool such as the Internet, used creatively, can serve to begin to reduce the growing and persistent gap between the haves and the have-nots but only if we begin to address the kind of problems identified in this paper.

Consider these words which come from the Cyberspace Declaration of Independence (Barlow, 1996):

- Cyberspace is a world that is both everywhere and nowhere
- A world that all may enter without privilege or prejudice accorded by race, economic power, military force, or station of birth
- A world where anyone, anywhere may express his or her beliefs
- A world where legal concepts of property, expression, identity, movement and context do not apply
- A world of no matter.

It is in our hands to make our new world matter and for it to be a cyber civilisation to be proud of. Otherwise the proud boast that: "We will create a civilisation of the Mind in Cyberspace. May it be more humane and fair than the world your governments have made before" (Barlow, 1996) will remain empty rhetoric.

ENDNOTE

1 The World Bank has defined economic groupings of countries based on Gross National Product (GNP) per capita. Economies are currently classified based on their 1995 GNP per capita as follows: low income–economies with a GNP per

capita of US$75 or less; lower-middle income–economies with a GNP per capita of more than US$ 766 and less than US$3,035; upper-middle income–economies with a GNP per capita of more than US$ 3,035 and less than $9,386; and high income–economies with a GNP per capita of more than US$8,956 (ITU, 1998).

REFERENCES

Australian Bureau of Statistics. (1998). *Household Use of Information Technology*, Australia. Cat no. 8146.0.

Barlow, J. P. (1996). *DBLP: John Perry Barlow*. Retrieved on the World Wide Web: http://www.cse.unsw.edu.au/dblp/db/indices/a-tree/b/Barlow:John_Perry.html

Bauman, Z. (1998). *Globalization: The Human Consequences*. Cambridge, Polity Press.

Beck, U. (2000). *What is Globalization?* Cambridge, Polity Press.

Castells, M. (2000). Information technology and global capitalism. In Hutton, W. and Giddens, A. (Eds.), *On the Edge: Living with Global Capitalism*. London: Jonathon Cape.

CommerceNet. (1998). *Knowledge-Internet Statistics*. Retrieved on the World Wide Web: http://www.commerce.net/research/stats/wwstats.html

Dixon, P. (1999). *Cyber Reality*. Retrieved on the World Wide Web: http://www.globalchange.com/cyberr_index.htm

El-Sherif, H. and El-Sawy, O. (1988). Issue-based decision support systems for the Cabinet of Egypt. *MIS Quarterly*, December.

Falling Through The Net: Defining the Digital Divide. (1999). Retrieved on the World Wide Web: http://www.ntia.doc.gov/ntiahome/digitaldivide/.

Gilbert, A.L. (1996). A framework for building national information infrastructure: The evolution of increased reach and range in Singapore. In Palvia, P., Palvia, S. and Roche, E. (Eds.), *Global Information Technology and Systems Management: Key Issues and Trends*, 55-76. Nashua, NH: Ivy League Publishing.

Gurbuxani, V., King, J. L., Kraemer, K. L., McFarlan, F. W., Raman, K. S. and Yap, C. S. (1990). Institutions in the international diffusion of information technology. In *Proceedings of 11th International Conference on Information Systems*, Copenhagen, Denmark, December, 87-98.

Gokalp, I. (1992). On the analysis of large technical systems. *Science, Technology & Human Values*, 17 (1), 57(22).

International Telecommunication Union. (1998). *World Telecommunication Development Report 1998*. ITU, Geneva, Switzerland.

Kamel, S. (1997). *DSS to Support Socio-Economic Development in Egypt*. HICSS-30.

Kamel, S. (1995). IT diffusion and socio-economic change in Egypt. *Journal of Global Information Management*, Spring, 3(2).

Loch, K. D., Straub, D. and Hill, C. (1999) Field interviews-Egypt, March-May.

Network Wizards. (2000). *Internet Domain Survey*. Retrieved on the World Wide Web: http://www.isc.org/ds/.

Nidomolu, S., Goodman, S. E., Vogle, D. R. and Danowitz, A. K. (1996). Information technology for the local administration support: The governorates project in Egypt. *MIS Quarterly*, June, 197-224.

Novak, T. P. and Hoffman, D. L. (1998). Bridging the digital divide: The impact of race on computer access and Internet use. *Science*, April, 17.

OECD. (1997). Information Technology Outlook. Retrieved on the World Wide Web: http://www.oecd.org/.

OECD. (1998). Electronic Commerce. Retrieved on the World Wide Web: http://www.oecd.org/subject/e_commerce/summary.htm.

Office of the Status of Women, Department of Prime Minister and Cabinet, Australia. (1996). *Regulating the Internet: Issues for Women*, December.

Office of the Status of Women, Department of Prime Minister and Cabinet, Australia. (1996). *Women's Access to Online Services, December.*

Pitroda, S. (1993). Development, democracy, and the village telephone. *Harvard Business Review*, November-December, 66(11).

Stratte-McClure, J. (1999). Trade and exchange on the Net. *International Herald Tribune*, October, 14.

Tarjanne, P. (1996). The Internet and thin information infrastructure: What is the difference? *SMPTE Journal*, October, 657-658.

The World Bank Group. (2000). Retrieved on the World Wide Web: http://www.worldbank.org/.

Zaman, R. (1999). The mobilization of Bangladesh. *International Herald Tribune*, October, 14.

Chapter III

Why Do We Do It If We Know It's Wrong? A Structural Model of Software Piracy

Darryl A. Seale
University of Nevada, Las Vegas, USA

This study examines predictors of software piracy, a practice estimated to cost the software industry nearly $11 billion in lost revenue annually. Correlates with software piracy were explored using responses from a university wide survey (n=589). Forty-four percent of university employees reported having copies of pirated software (mean = 5.0 programs), while 31 percent said they have made unauthorized copies (mean = 4.2 programs). A structural model, based in part on the theory of planned behavior (Ajzen, 1985) and the theory of reasoned action as applied to moral behavior (Vallerand, Pelletier, Cuerrier, Cuerrier & Mongeau, 1992), was developed which suggests that social norms, expertise required, gender, and computer usage (both home and at work) all have direct effects on self-reported piracy. In addition, ease of theft, people's sense of the proportional value of software, and various other demographic factors were found to affect piracy indirectly. Theoretical as well as practical implications for the design and marketing of software are discussed.

INTRODUCTION

If dollar estimates are correct, software piracy rivals organized crime as one of our nation's most costly offenses. Although scholars are far from agreement on the level of legal protection that should be afforded software and other forms of intellectual property (Nelson, 1995) and engage in considerable debate regarding the actual costs of software piracy (Masland, 2000), most researchers agree that piracy is widespread. Industry surveys estimate that for every legitimate copy of software, there are between two and ten illegal copies (James, 2000; Conner & Rumelt, 1991). In some studies, over half of those surveyed admitted that they had made unauthorized copies of computer software. Even in the more conservative business arena, estimates suggest that in the US 25% of all installed applications are pirated. The Business Software Alliance (1999) estimates that, worldwide, the industry is losing nearly $11 billion annually in lost revenue. In the US alone, lost sales are estimated at $2.8 billion, plus a loss of over 100,000 jobs, amounting to $4.5 billion in wages and $991 million in tax revenues.

Beyond the economic impact, studying software piracy is important for other reasons. First, it may help us better understand how social norms and moral standards develop for new technologies, especially technologies involving intellectual property issues. Second, research on software piracy may expand the important philosophical debate on intellectual property. A central controversy in this debate is that many of the owner's rights commonly associated with tangible property are not violated when intellectual property is copied or used by others. Further, many philosophers and economists contend that intellectual property rights should not be protected by law (Davidson, 1989), arguing the such protection is anticompetitive, monopolistic, and can stifle creativity and progress (Abbott, 1990; Cooper-Dreyfuss, 1989; Davidson, 1989; Samuelson, 1989; Wells-Branscomb, 1990). The many proponents of stronger copyright and patent protection argue that property rights should be strictly enforced, claiming that piracy is an insult to hardworking inventors and essential to foster innovation in one of the largest value-added industries in the world (Schuler, 1998). A final reason for studying piracy behavior, and an important theme of this book, is that understanding society's norms and values regarding piracy adds to our understanding of social responsibility in the information age, which has widespread implications for design and marketing in the software industry.

THEORY AND MODEL DEVELOPMENT

Software piracy has been investigated from varied disciplinary perspectives, including: (1) economics (Gopal & Sanders, 1998; Bologna, 1982); (2) those that attempt to deter or detect would-be offenders (Holsing & Yen, 1999; Jackson, 1999; Sacco & Zureik, 1990); (3) as a risk-taking phenomenon (Parker, 1976); (4) or simply by the failure of society's morals to keep up with the growth in technology (Johnson, 1985). Much of the empirical research on software piracy has focused on ethical and legal aspects (Im & Koen, 1990) while a few studies have dealt with the social costs (Briggins, 1998; Conner & Rumlet, 1991; Mason, 1990), or attitudes (Reid, Thompson & Logsdon, 1992; Sacco & Zureik, 1990; O'Brien & Solomon, 1991; Taylor & Shim, 1993). While these studies offer some insight into various motivations to pirate, a more encompassing and plausible model for software piracy has yet to emerge. An important aim of this chapter is to develop a model that both predicts and explains incidents of software piracy.

We begin by examining previous studies that report correlates of software piracy behavior and computer use. Recognizing that the act of piracy may hinge on moral, ethical or attitudinal concerns, we turn next to several popular theories of reasoned action for guidance. Finally, to ensure that the model generalizes to a broader class of items deemed intellectual property, we examine several important aspects that distinguish tangible from intellectual property. The model that emerges integrates previous research on correlates of piracy behavior and a rational action perspective on moral behavior with several defining characteristics of software and other forms of intellectual property.

Computer Usage and Demographic Factors

Earlier research aimed at understanding software piracy approached this behavior as a dimension of computer use or, more specifically, misuse. Sacco and Zureik (1990) found that piracy was the most frequently reported misuse of computers, with 62% of respondents reporting that they had made illegal copies of software. Respondents also reported that they believed a great deal of illegal copying was going on, and that the likelihood of detection (getting caught) was very low. Previous research that examined personal and/or demographic factors has yielded mixed results regarding the relationship between gender and software piracy. One study found a significant relationship (O'Brien & Solomon, 1991), while another study (Sacco & Zureik, 1990) did not. The effects of age and computer use have also yielded divergent levels of software piracy across studies. In addition, studies have found that software pirates are generally bright, eager, motivated, and well qualified (Parker, 1976). These are the same characteristics we value in people, and beg the question: Are we trying to predict software piracy or good citizenship? Thus, a more definitive relationship between demographic variables and software piracy remains an empirical question.

Morality, Ethics and Reasoned Action

Several studies have examined software piracy with a moral or ethical focus. Im and Van Epps (1991) see piracy as yet another sign of the moral decay in corporate America. To combat the problem, they offer three prescriptions centering on educating employees concerning what is acceptable and unacceptable behavior. Swinyard, Rinne and Kau (1990) argue that many people weigh the outcomes or benefits of illegal copying more than the legal concerns of getting caught. Their results also indicate that morality judgments likely differ by culture or national origin, adding yet another dimension to be addressed in our understanding of software piracy. Although the two studies mentioned above offer somewhat different perspectives on piracy, both point toward morality and ethics and important considerations for any theory of software piracy.

Although important, theories of morality and ethics are not sufficient for developing a predictive model of piracy behavior. Here we turn to the theory of reasoned action (Fishbein & Ajzen, 1975) and two important extensions: the theory of planned behavior (Ajzen, 1985) and the theory of reasoned action as applied to moral behavior (Vallerand et al., 1992). A central feature in the theory of reasoned action is the individual's intention to perform a given behavior. Intentions capture the sum of an individual's motivational influences; they are indications of planned effort or of how hard one is willing to work to perform a behavior. Accordingly, there are two main determinants of intention: a personal or "attitudinal" factor and a social or "normative" factor. Attitude, in this context, refers to the favorable or unfavorable evaluation of behavior. It is a function of the salient beliefs one holds regarding the perceived consequences of performing a behavior and the evaluation of these consequences. Social norms consist of a person's perception of what important referent groups think he or she should do. These subjective norms are often determined by normative belief structures and motivations to comply with the behavior. Therefore, when attitudes and subjective norms coincide there is a greater intention to perform the behavior.

The hypothetical independence of attitudinal and normative factors has been seriously challenged by research showing significant correlations between these constructs (Miniard & Cohen, 1981; Ryan, 1982; Shephard & O'Keefe, 1984). These findings are particularly interesting because they suggest that either a common antecedent exists, or one's normative beliefs causally affect one's attitudes. Causality questions take on added importance when the behavior in question has moral implications.

Vallerand et al. (1992) extended the basic rational action perspective by incorporating moral behavior. They contend that a person's normative beliefs, i.e., what important others may view as appropriate behavior, are common determinants of an individual's attitudes and subjective norms. Therefore, when confronted with a moral situation, such as software piracy, individuals decide on the basis of their attitudes toward the behavior (determined in part by the probabilities and consequences of getting caught) and their perceptions of what important others (e.g., parents, other relatives, friends, professors) think is appropriate. This view is similar to differential association, a "learning" theory of deviant/criminal behavior, that suggests we adopt attitudes favorable or unfavorable to deviance based partially upon the acceptance of the attitudes and behaviors of esteemed others with whom we interact or observe (Sutherland, 1947; Akers 1994).[1]

A somewhat different configuration of measures leading to behavioral intentions is derived from a theory of planned behavior (Ajzen, 1985), however, they retain, largely, the same meaning outlined above. Attitudes, subjective norms, and perceived behavioral control are proposed as theoretically independent determinants of intended behavior. The latter concept represents the perceived difficulty of performing the behavior based upon past experience and anticipated barriers or hurdles (e.g., time, skills, cooperation of others; see Ajzen, 1985, for a more complete discussion). The relative importance of these concepts in predicting behavioral intention is expected to vary across behaviors and populations. However, generally, as attitudes and subjective norms become more favorable and the level of perceived behavioral control increases, the intention to perform a particular act should become more likely.

Modeling Conceptual Differences in Software and Intellectual Property

The theories and extensions outlined above provide an important framework from which to examine software piracy. However, due to important conceptual differences, a theory of software piracy or a more general theory covering intellectual property may differ in certain respects to reasoned action theories. Consistent with reasoned action theories both attitudinal and social factors are expected to be important determinants of piracy. People make bootlegged copies of software, music, or VHS tapes with little regard for the legality of copyrights or patents. The awareness that others are doing it can help establish a social norm that software piracy is acceptable. Among computer users, for instance, general agreement that software is overpriced or that copying is appropriate when the original software was purchased may lead to widespread approval of software "sharing" without any remorse.

If, as past research suggests, a moral component of software piracy exists, then personal attitudes and social norms are likely to be determined by common antecedents. Thus, a model of software piracy should include certain exogenous factors, such as age, income and employment, that serve to shape one's normative beliefs. These normative beliefs, in turn, are important determinants of both attitudes and subjective norms. Yet, little guidance exists regarding how such a perspective might be empirically modeled.

Additionally, perceived behavioral control is expected to play an important role within this integrated perspective. Software piracy requires certain skills and expertise, as well as opportunity. If the required abilities are beyond an individual's perceived control, software piracy is not likely to emerge. Thus, level of expertise (perceived behavioral control) is expected to have a direct effect on piracy behavior. Similarly, logistical concerns such as likelihood of being detected, ease of piracy, and opportunity should also be related to software piracy.

Notwithstanding the considerable agreement outlined above, there are several reasons to expect differences between reasoned action theories and a general theory of software piracy. Intellectual property has unique qualities that differ substantially from tangible property (Cooper-Dreyfuss, 1989). For example, it is harder to maintain exclusive use over intellectual property than it is to control tangible property. Theft of tangible property, say, a car, deprives the owner of its use as well as the right to sell it, borrow it, or trade it in on a newer model. Intellectual property, on the other hand, is not consumed by its use and can be many places at once; therefore, the possession or use by one person does not preclude others from using it (Cooper-Dreyfuss, 1989; Hettinger, 1989). Such differences outline the *nonexclusive* nature of intellectual property, which may also increase the likelihood of piracy.

Another aspect common to intellectual property is that its retail price often does not reflect its production cost. Potential purchasers may sense an inherent unfairness in the price of software; that is, they may recognize the low marginal cost to the manufacturer of producing one more copy compared to the high retail purchase price. Perceptions of price and value are important to consumers (Zeithaml, 1988), and our sense of *proportional value* requires that the price of our purchase be reflected in its cost (Hettinger, 1989). Thus, people who report an inherent unfairness in the price or proportional value of software may be more likely to engage in piracy. Moreover, the violation of one's proportional expectations may also have consequences in shaping one's attitudes or subjective norms.

The foregoing discussion provides a partial list of the items that one might expect to affect software piracy. Computer use, demographic factors or other personal attributes, social norms, proportional value, the nonexclusive nature of software, expertise, and ease of piracy were identified as likely predictors. The temporal order of several of these items, however, remains unclear. If, as past research suggests, a moral component of software piracy exists, then judgments concerning proportional value, expertise and social norms are likely to be determined by common antecedents, like personal attributes and demographics. We would also expect attitudes, like one's sense of proportional value, might have consequences in shaping social norms. Thus, regarding temporal order, proportional value is seen as an antecedent to social norms. Similarly, the level of expertise required to pirate software might be impacted by one's impression of the difficulty of pirating software. Thus, we might expect ease of theft to come before expertise.

METHOD

Thus far we have identified likely predictors of software piracy and suggested a possible temporal order for many of the variables. To test these conjectures, a questionnaire was designed that captures computer use and demographics using several single-item measures, and proportionality, ease of theft, social norms and expertise required with four multi-item measures. After appropriate pretesting, the survey was conducted and the data analysis submitted to structural equations modeling (specifically, LISREL). This technique has been used in a variety of research domains in the behavioral and social sciences and is well suited to test relationships between single and/or multi-item measures where temporal order remains important. We begin by describing the sample, survey design, and procedure.

Sample

The study was conducted at a large southwestern university. The sampling frame was a mailing list of 9550 names purchased from the university that included everyone on the university payroll, from high level administrators to full-time gardeners and part-time graduate students. In total, 1910 surveys were distributed to a random sample of employees. Of the total distributed, 589 surveys were returned (gross response rate of 31%). The study excluded 66 respondents who did not report microcomputer use (17 respondents did not answer questions concerning their microcomputer use, and 49 respondents reported they did not have access to a microcomputer either at home or at work). Thus, the final sample included 523 returned surveys from university employees who reported some microcomputer use.

The respondents represent a wide cross section of employees. Approximately 42% were classified staff, 20% faculty, 18% professional staff, 12% graduate students, and 8% administration. Men and women were equally represented (49% versus 51%, respectively), with an average age of 39.7 years old and a median education level of a college degree.

Survey Design

The survey was divided into three sections. The first section contained questions addressing general aspects of computer use: frequency of computer use, types of computer use and software applications, access to personal computers, and purchases of software. This section also contained three questions concerning self-reported piracy behavior, as well as a question concerning perceptions about the frequency of piracy among computer owners.

The second portion of the survey addressed attitudes and perceptions regarding unauthorized copying of software. Multi-item scales were developed to measure proportionality, social norms, expertise required, and ease of piracy. Response categories were 7-point Likert scales where 1 is "strongly disagree" and 7 is "strongly agree."

Nonexclusivity (nonexclusive nature) was measured by comparing responses to two questions: 1) It's alright to take home up to $25 worth of company office supplies, and 2) It's alright to copy company software that costs as much as $25. Although the dollar amounts were chosen arbitrarily, the distinction between tangible and intangible property is clear. Further, the questions were spaced to impede deliberate comparison. If the arithmetic difference between the two responses was positive, the respondent felt it was more acceptable to take home an unauthorized copy of company software than it was to take home company office supplies that have similar value. If the arithmetic difference was zero, this is an indication that the respondent sees no difference between these actions.

The third section of the survey contained the standard demographic questions of age, education, gender, religious affiliation, employment status, and income.

Procedure

The survey was pretested among select faculty, staff and graduate students. After some modifications, the instrument was distributed through campus mail to a systematic random sample of employees. As software piracy is a controversial topic, underreporting of piracy was a concern. To address this concern, the cover letter assured complete anonymity. To enhance response rate, everyone who received the initial questionnaire was sent a follow-up postcard two weeks later which asked them to respond if they had not already done so.

RESULTS

Descriptive Statistics

Of the employees surveyed, 44% reported that they have received unauthorized copies of software from friends or relatives. When asked "how many copies," the mean response was 5.0 programs (sd = 1.30). Thirty-one percent of those surveyed said that they have made unauthorized copies. When asked "how many copies," the mean response was 4.2 programs (sd = 1.32). When asked to estimate what percent of microcomputer owners have unauthorized copies, the mean response was 66% (sd = 8.30). Several questions were asked regarding the respondent's level of computer experience. Only 49% of those surveyed said they had taken two or more formal computer courses. Yet, 88% reported that they use a PC at work. Of these, 83% reported more than two years experience. Word processing (91%), spreadsheet (46%), and email (41%) were the most frequently cited applications. Using a PC at home was reported by 58% of the respondents. Word processing (95%), games (48%), and spreadsheets (44%) were the most common home uses. When asked if they have ever purchased PC software, 62% said yes. Of those that own or have access to a PC at home, 86% reported purchasing software.

Indicators of the Measurement Model

The 18 indicators presented in Table 1 were employed to operationalize a measurement model of software piracy perceptions that ranged from computer knowledge required to social norms surrounding the unauthorized use of software. As outlined in the table, the survey questions crossed employment, social, and personal boundaries where software piracy may occur. Indicator variables were collected using seven-point Likert scales, with four variables (overpriced, profitable, permission and obtained) reverse scored. For a more detailed discussion of the indicators, including a discussion of skewness and kurtosis, see the appendix.

Empirical Assessment of the Measurement Model

In exploratory analyses not shown here, several additional factors of deterrence, or detectability, and nonexclusivity were included. However, these factors

Table 1: Means, standard deviations, skewness and kurtosisof measurement model indicators

	Indicator Variable	Mean	SD	Skewness	Kurtosis	
1.	Overpriced: (Software is)	2.78	(1.46)	0.480	-0.336	R*
2.	Profitable: (companies developing software are)	2.63	(1.37)	0.600	-0.117	R*
3.	Value: (compared to other goods software is a)	3.94	(1.46)	-0.091	-0.221	
4.	Fairly priced; (software is)	3.35	(1.44)	0.109	-0.334	
5.	Obtained: (PC owners can easily obtain unauthorized software)	5.06	(1.49)	-0.540	-0.191	
6.	Installed: (Unauth. Software is easily)	4.83	(1.48)	-0.446	-0.010	
7.	Copies Made: (It is easy to copy unauthorized software)	5.41	(1.42)	-0.872	0.594	
8	Needs: (It's alright to copy software for bus./prof.)	2.69	(1.75)	0.938	-0.088	
9.	Workcopy: (It's alright for employees to copy company software costing $25)	2.26	(1.59)	1.301	0.935	
10.	Copy: (It's alright to copy microcomputer software)	2.89	(1.73)	0.707	-0.341	
11.	Permission: (It's wrong to copy software without)	2.64	(1.77)	0.988	0.012	R*
12.	Borrow: (Copying software is more like borrowing than theft)	2.73	(1.70)	0.751	-0.383	
13.	Friends: (It's wrong to copy software obtained from a friend)	3.25	(1.92)	0.492	-0.883	
14.	Personal: (It's alright to copy software for personal use)	2.99	(1.83)	0.583	-0.710	
15.	Make: (After purchasing software it is okay to copy it for friends)	2.90	(1.75)	0.629	-0.575	
16.	School/work: (It's wrong to copy software obtained from school or work)	2.89	(1.83)	0.730	-0.502	R*
17.	Computer Knowledge: (People would purchase if they did not have knowledge to copy)	3.85	(1.96)	0.149	-1.180	
18.	Computer Skills: (People making copies possess special skill)	2.98	(1.63)	0.622	-0.355	

NOTE: Items scored 1=strongly disagree, 7=strongly agree. Items marked with an (R*) were reverse scored to coincide with the remaining items in the factor.

were found to have no empirical basis. Further, the single indicators of deterrence and nonexclusivity were found to be unrelated to software piracy and are not included in the structural model. Several indicators were also eliminated from the analyses since they did not sufficiently cohere to their assumed latent structures, social norms and expertise, or the remaining factors in the model.

Figure 1 depicts the measurement model relating to software piracy perceptions. Proportionality, for instance, represents an unobserved construct that generates the structure of relationships among its indicators--overpriced, profitable, value, and fairly priced. Each indicator is a linear combination of the latent measure proportionality, plus a random measurement error component. The initial model estimated assumes that these measurement errors are uncorrelated with the latent unobserved construct or with one another. The program computes asymptotically unbiased and efficient maximum likelihood estimates of parameters, as well as a likelihood ratio statistic that approximates a chi-square distribution in large samples.

Table 2 presents chi-square statistics and other relative fit comparisons for a model of software perceptions and piracy. As expected, the baseline model does not fit the data well (x^2=369.20; d.f.=129; ratio=2.862; GFI=.922). In relatively large samples a general rule-of-thumb is that the chi-square/d.f. ratio should be less than 2.0 and the goodness of fit index (GFI) should exceed 0.95. While the results from Model 1 approach the GFI threshold, they do not approach the appropriate ratio. However, this is largely because error correlations were not allowed between the observed indicators in the model. A review of the 18 indicators suggests that many of them tap similar beliefs, perceptions, or ideas even though they are not perfect replications of one another. Therefore, in Model 2 twelve error correlations are included, although the basic four-factor structure depicted in Figure 1 is retained.

Figure 1: Measurement model: Software piracy perceptions

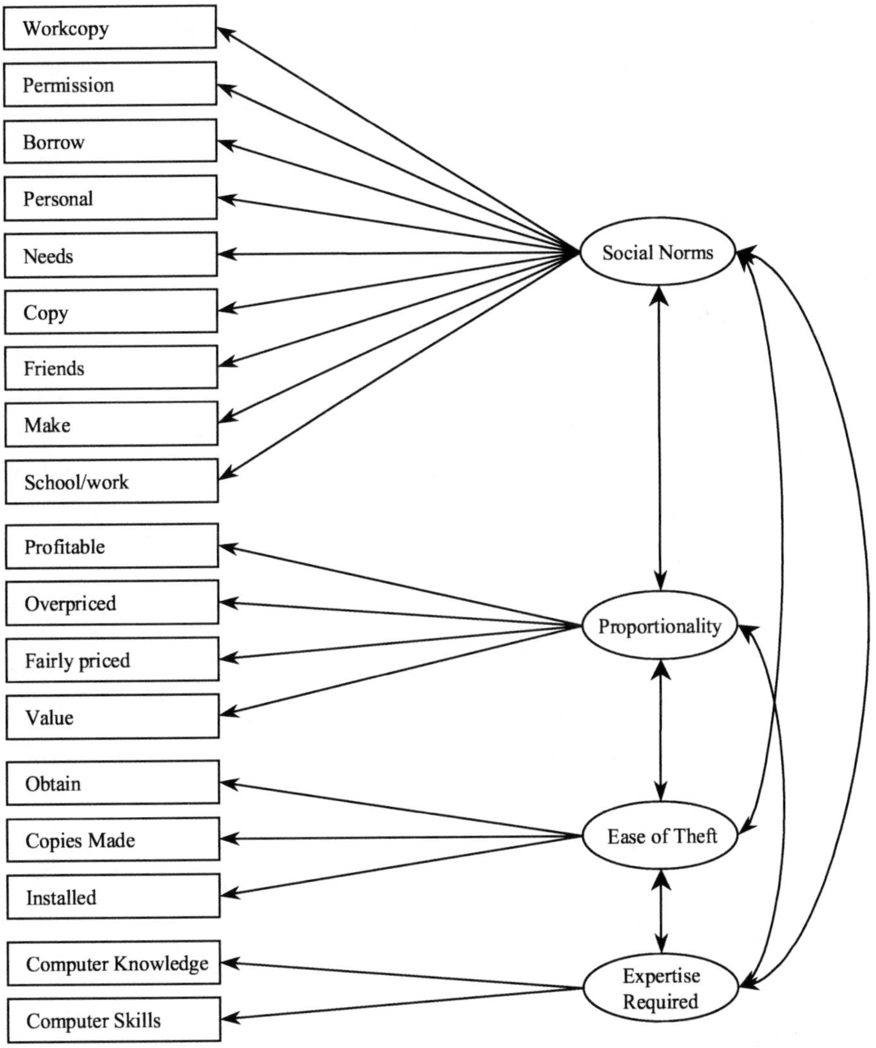

Table 2: Comparison of relative fit statistics for measurement and structural models of software piracy

Measurement Models

	Model Description	Chi-square Statistic	D.F.	In Fit	In D.F.	X2/df	GFI
				Differences			
1.	18 indicators, 4 latent factors, no error correlations.	369.20	129	----	----	2.862	.922
2.	12 error correlations allowed between indicators tapping similar perceptions.	157.11	117	212.09**	12	1.343	.968

Structural Models

	Model Description	Chi-square Statistic	D.F.	In Fit	In D.F.	X2/df	GFI	
				Differences				
3.	Simultaneous est. of meas. and struc. models. Direct effects from exogenous measures.	464.13	313	----	----	1.483	.950	.288
4.	Introduce direct effects from measurement structure.	464.13	313	no change				.411
5.	Delete direct effects from several demographic measures.	473.04	323	8.91	10	1.465	.949	.402
6.	Delete direct effects from proportionality and ease of theft factors.	474.83	325	1.79	2	1.461	.949	.413
7.	Add direct effects from proportionality to social norms and easy to knowledge.	480.24	327	5.41	2	1.468	.948	.413

Probability level: *<.05; **<.001.
Note: Models 5, 6, and 7 are significantly improved due to the additional degrees of freedom saved by altering the direct effects allowed in the model structure. GFI is the goodness of fit index provided by LISREL.

As expected, the fit of Model 2 is a dramatic improvement over Model 1 (ratio=1.343; GFI=.968). While other structural configurations were examined, none were found to fit the data as well as Model 2. For instance, the latent factors of expertise and ease of theft might appear to overlap by looking at the indicators of each; however, the correlation between these structures is only .375. In addition, analyses combining the five indicators under one factor yield a reduction in the number of degrees of freedom but a large decrement in the chi-square statistic. Therefore, the four-factor structure is retained.

Empirical Assessment of the Structural Model

Due to its highly technical nature, a more detailed discussion of the empirical assessment of the structural model can be found in the appendix. This discussion tracks systematic changes to the proposed model and the resulting measures that assess goodness of fit. A summary description of this empirical assessment is provided in Table 2. Briefly, LISREL analysis was performed on 18 indicator variables comprising four latent factors. Various causal effects from both the latent factors and error terms were then systematically added or removed, and the resulting models, seven in all, were tested for relative goodness of fit. No improvement was possible from Model 6, which is displayed in Figure 2 and discussed next.

Table 3: Measurement model of software pirating perceptions (N=523; chi-square=157.11; d. f.=117; GFI=.968)

Indicator Variable	Proportionality		Ease of Theft		Social Norms		Expertise Required	
Overpriced	1.000 [0.953]	(0.000)						
Profitable	0.393 [0.397]	(0.049)						
Value	0.575 [0.552]	(0.058)						
Fairly Priced	0.746 [0.722]	(0.064)						
Obtained			0.662 [0.542]	(0.064)				
Installed			0.874 [0.719]	(.0730)				
Copies Made			1.000 [0.860]	(0.000)				
Needs			0.794 [0.709]	(0.043)				
Workcopy					0.722 [0.712]	(0.039)		
Copy					0.805 [0.730]	(0.042)		
Permission					0.717 [0.635]	(0.048)		
Borrow					0.753 [0.696]	(0.042)		
Friends					0.684 [0.557]	(0.052)		
Personal					1.000 [0.856]	(0.000)		
Make					0.940 [0.837]	(0.040)		
School/work					0.647 [0.556]	(0.049)		
Computer Knowledge							0.595 [0.500]	(.177)
Computer Skills							1.000 [0.809]	(0.000)
Reliability	0.7672		0.7409		0.9013		0.4328	

Note: Maximum-likelihood coefficients reported first. Standard errors reported in (), standardized solution reported in brackets. GFI is a goodness of fit index provided by LISREL.

A four-factor structure was retained in Model 6. Four indicator variables (overpriced, profitable, value and fairly priced) loaded on the proportionality factor (see Table 1 for a more detailed description of the variables, and Table 3 for the maximum-likelihood coefficients and standard errors). The reliability measure was 0.7672. Four indicators (obtained, installed, copies made, needs) also loaded on ease of theft, with a reliability measure of 0.7409. The social norms factor was comprised of eight indicator variables (workcopy, copy, permission, borrow, friends, personal, make and education) and yielded the highest reliability measure at 0.9013. Finally, two variables (computer knowledge and computer skills) loaded

Figure 2: Structural model of software piracy

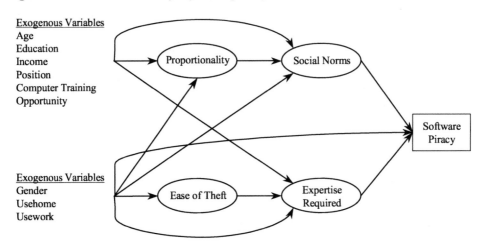

on expertise required. The reliability measure, 0.4328, is much lower than the three previous measures, but fairly typical of two-item measures.

Table 4 presents the maximum-likelihood and standardized coefficients for the model depicted in Figure 2. The final column of this table depicts the five direct effects on software piracy. Men are significantly more likely to pirate software than women as are those individuals who report using computers in their home or at work. In addition, those individuals who agree that using unauthorized software is not really theft are significantly more likely to do so than their contemporaries. Of these five direct effects, the standardized coefficients suggest that the strongest effects come from social norms and expertise. Therefore, the relatively high r-squared is largely the result of a person's perceived norms relating to computer software usage and expertise with computers.

Of the four factors in the model, only social norms (sc = 0.366, p < 0.001) and expertise required (sc = -0.301, p < 0.001) were found to have significant direct effects on reported software piracy. The positive standard coefficient (sc) on social norms indicates that the more one views piracy as acceptable, the more one is likely to engage in this behavior. Similarly, the negative standard coefficient on expertise required suggests that the greater the perceived difficulty of making illegal copies, the less likely the behavior. Proportionality affected software piracy indirectly through social norms (sc = -0.271, p < 0.001). This result suggests that the greater the perceived proportional value of software, the less likely one is to view piracy as acceptable. Ease of theft also affected software piracy indirectly. The significant direct effect on expertise required (sc = -0.426, p < 0.001) indicates, as common sense would predict, that as the perceived ease of making illegal copies increases, less expertise is required to pirate software.

Turning next to the exogenous variables specified in the model, age was positively related to proportionality (sc = 0.154, p < 0.05) and expertise required (sc

Table 4: Parameter estimates of structural model predicting software piracy (X2-480 .24, d. f.=327, GFI=.948)

Predetermined Variables	Endogenous Measures				
	Proportionality	Ease of Theft	Social Norms	Expertise Required	Software Piracy
Age	0.019 [0.154]*	-0.024 [-0.025]	-0.030 [-0.205]**	0.013 [0.179]*	
Sex	0.271 [0.100]*	0.257 [0.104]*	0.038 [0.012]	-0.082 [-0.054]	0.310 [0.143]**
Education	0.091 [0.064]	0.053 [0.041]	0.079 [0.048]	-0.132 [-0.165]*	
Employed	0.015 [0.071]	0.029 [0.149]	-0.004 [-0.017]	-.0013 [-0.111]	
Income	0.038 [0.052]	0.096 [0.143]*	-0.052 [-0.060]	-0.045 [-0.108]	
University Position					
Admin.	0.334 [0.063]	1.260 [-0.259]**	-0.154 [-0.250]	0.700 [0.232]*	
Class. Staff	0.112 [-0.040]	-0.487 [-0.192]	-0.215 [-0.067]	0.235 [0.150]	
Prof. Staff	0.138 [0.039]	-0.471 [-0.147]*	0.142 [0.035]	0.327 [0.165]	
Faculty	0.001 [0.000]	-0.413 [-0.136]	0.312 [0.080]	0.429 [0.228]*	
Computer Experience					
Training	0.162 [0.123]*	0.015 [0.012]	-0.092 [-0.060]	-0.103 [-0.138]	
Home Use	0.044 [-0.155]*	0.003 [0.013]	0.019 [0.058]	-0.059 [-0.366]**	0.035 [0.155]*
Work Use	.0002 [-0.006]	0.040 [0.106]*	-0.006 [-0.012]	-0.035 [-0.152]	0.034 [0.103]*
Opportunity	0.094 [-0.096]	0.217 [0.240]**	0.248 [0.215]**	0.034 [0.061]	
Factors					
Proportionality			-0.316 [-0.271]**		
Ease of Theft				-0.263 [-0.426]**	
Social Norms					0.252 [0.366]**
Expertise					-0.427 [-0.301]**
R-squared	0.117	0.204	0.273	0.683	0.413

Note: Standardized coefficients in [ ]. Significant effects: *p <.05; **p < .001.

= 0.179, p <0.05) and negatively related to social norms (sc = -0.205, p < 0.05). This suggests that, as we pass our twenties, we are more likely to appreciate the proportional value of software and the expertise required to make illegal copies, and less likely to condone piracy behavior. We also found significant effects for gender, with males more likely to view piracy with greater proportional value (sc = 0.100, p < 0.05) and ease of theft (sc = 0.104, p < 0.05) and more likely to engage in self-reported piracy (sc = 0.143, p < 0.001).

Interestingly, computer experience worked in opposite directions. Formal training in computers was positively related to the perceived proportional value of software (sc = 0.123, p < 0.05), but using a computer at home was negatively related (sc = -0.155, p < 0.05). Increased home use of computers also lowered impressions of the expertise required to pirate software (sc = -0.366, p < 0.001) and had a positive and direct effect on self-reported piracy (sc = 0.155, p < 0.05). The opportunity to pirate software was positively and highly significantly related to both the ease of theft factor (sc = 0.240, p < 0.001) and social norms (sc = 0.215, p < 0.001). This indicates that those with a greater opportunity to pirate software view the action as less difficult and more acceptable.

DISCUSSION

Microcomputer software is protected under US Code, Section 17, of the copyright law (Mason, 1990). Although the maximum penalties for copyright infringement have recently been increased, results from this and other studies confirm that a high proportion of people believe the behavior is permissible. Thus, empirical research or theory that begins by assuming software piracy is universally accepted as inappropriate behavior fails to recognize the attitudes and evaluations

Starting from this vantage point, our research makes several contributions to the study of software piracy, ethics, and technology. First, the results support and extend those of previous studies concerning piracy behavior. A sizeable proportion of the respondents reported incidents of piracy, which is consistent with previous research (O'Brien & Solomon, 1991; Sacco & Zureik, 1990). Our results also indicate that gender affects reported piracy behavior, with males more likely to pirate software than females. However, while age has been reported in some studies as having direct effects on piracy, our findings indicate that age is related to piracy behavior indirectly by significantly affecting three of the four endogenous factors making up the measurement model.

Second, by modifying the theories of reasoned action (and the Vallerand et al. extension applied to moral behavior) and planned behavior, the present investigation had a firm foundation on which to develop a model of software piracy. The factor representing social norms, for instance, is the strongest predictor of pirating behavior. Although survey questions addressed both attitudinal (personal) and normative (social) criteria, separate factors failed to emerge. This finding coincides with those studies (Miniard & Cohen, 1981; Ryan, 1982; Shephard & O'Keefe, 1984) that challenge the independence of the attitudinal and normative factors. Further, we also identify several antecedent variables that are likely to affect an individual's normative beliefs and, in turn, their social norms. In agreement with the theory of planned behavior, we find that perceived behavioral control (expertise required) has an important direct effect on self-reported piracy.

Third, certain conceptual distinctions characterizing software and other forms of intellectual property were investigated. One's perception of proportional value was found to be indirectly related to software piracy. Proportionality was negatively related to social norms; that is, if individuals perceived the price of software to be unfair they were more likely to report social norms in favor of software piracy. To our knowledge, this was the first attempt to investigate the concept of software as nonexclusive property. We operationalized the construct as the difference in an individual's attitude towards the theft of tangible versus intellectual property. The greater this perceived difference, the more likely the individual was to report social norms in favor of software piracy. Nonexclusivity, although found to be positively related to social norms, did not survive the model construction phase of our analysis. Thus, future investigations should develop a variety of means by which to investigate this concept since it would seem to have a common-sense relation to deviant behavior.

Understanding the attitudes and perceptions of those who pirate software may point toward those areas holding the greatest promise for solutions. For example, if people copy software because the price violates their sense of proportional value, software firms may consider two solutions: raise the perceived value of the product through marketing efforts or lower the price (Zeithaml, 1988). Similarly, if existing social norms are contributing to the growth in unauthorized software, several remedies are available to software manufacturers. Two such solutions include (1) changing the image offenders have of the industry through a public relations campaign or (2) encouraging institutional customers to develop software policies which discourage unauthorized copying. To our knowledge, software associations have not considered this first alternative. They are, however, actively engaged in the second. Software associations are hard at work, both in and out of court, to establish standards and guidelines for their institutional customers. Interestingly, our results suggest that part of this effort may be misguided. We find no relationship between awareness of employer's software policies and reported piracy. Similarly, Taylor and Shim (1993) also report no relationship. Reid et al. (1992) found no relationship between awareness of copyright law and unauthorized copying. However, before we can confidently exclude such policy considerations from the model, a more in-depth analysis across different institutions, particularly nonacademic institutions, is required.

Companies that develop commercial software applications must carefully consider the issue of copy protection. Protection methods, which range from dongles to key diskettes and access codes, complicate the product, add additional cost, and may require added support. However, when done correctly, the company may reap the rewards from increased sales of its product. Advice on copy protection methods generally touch on several points, including choosing a method that is difficult to "crack," simple to apply, requires a minimum amount of technical support, and does not involve special manufacturing techniques.

It's important to point out that this model is an individual-level one, which only tangentially addresses many of the important macro-level issues of software piracy. One of the primary issues concerning intellectual property involves whether legally protecting it encourages or stifles innovation. As one scholar argues, "The fundamental bargain made for either patent or copyright protection is disclosure to the public in return for a monopoly of either limited duration (for patents) or limited scope (for copyrights) (Davidson, 1989, p. 163)." The debate is far from resolved in favor of protection. Conner and Rumlet (1991) conclude that not protecting software may, paradoxically, increase profits while lowering the cost for the consumer. Pirates may actually create a market for a particular type of software by making it the operating standard in a particular organization or industry. While the piracy model reported here does not directly address the merits of legal protection, it certainly makes clear that consumers do not view software piracy the same as theft of tangible goods, regardless of whether such activity is illegal or against company policy.

A related debate concerns the ability of legal standards to actually protect intellectual property from unauthorized copying. For example, software piracy is much more prevalent in foreign countries with weak legal protection of intellectual property rights (Weisband & Goodman, 1992). An interesting area for future research would be a cross-cultural examination of attitudes and behavior regarding software piracy in countries with varying legal protection (Swinyard, Rinne, & Kau, 1990). Such research would be particularly illuminating if it were longitudinal. As many countries adopt stricter intellectual property laws in order to comply with international trade standards, we could measure how legislation affects social norms regarding intellectual property.

There are several concerns that must be addressed before generalizing these results to other populations or other types of intellectual property. First, piracy was self-reported. Though we promised anonymity, we still could not ensure that all respondents were truthful. Second, attitude and value scales are difficult to validate and may have limited reliability (Grosof & Sardy, 1985). Third, there may be non-respondent bias; respondents may have been less likely to copy software than non-respondents. These concerns are somewhat allayed by the fact that the frequency of reported software piracy was quite high. Furthermore, ethical and legal concerns make it unfeasible to observe participants actually copying software illegally during an experiment. Thus, in spite of their weaknesses, surveys such as this one play an important role in the study of sensitive topics such as software piracy. The model proposed here is not meant to be definitive. It needs to be refined and tested with other populations as well as other types of intellectual property. The current research is meant to be a starting point for further work in this important and developing area.

ENDNOTE

1 We raise this link with deviance research since the behaviors investigated with such perspectives are similar to software piracy in value of the item stolen (criminologists often ask whether individuals have taken anything less than $50) and seriousness of the crime (seriousness remains a vague concept but is often used to rank order level of criminal activity).

REFERENCES

Abbott, A. F. (1990). Developing a framework for intellectual property protection to advance innovation. In Rushing, F. W. and Ganz Brown, C. (Eds.), *Intellectual Property Rights in Science, Technology and Economic Performance*, 311-339. Boulder, CO: Westview Press.

Ajzen, I. (1985). From intentions to actions: A theory of planned behavior. In Kuhl, J. and Beckmann. (Eds.), *Action-Control: From Cognition to Behavior*, 11-39. Heidelberg: Springer.

Akers, R. F. (1994). *Criminological Theories: Introduction and Evaluation*. CA: Roxbury.

Bologna, J. (1982). *Computer Crime: Wave of the Future*. San Francisco: Assets Protection.

Briggins, A. (1998). Soft on software piracy? Your loss. *Management Review*, June.

Cloward, R. and Ohlin, L. (1960). *Delinquency and Opportunity*. New York: Free Press.

Conner, K. R. and Rumlet, R. P. (1991). Software piracy: an analysis of protection strategies. *Management Science*, 37, 125-139.

Cooper-Dreyfuss, R. (1989). General overview of the intellectual property system. In Weil, V. and Snapper, J. W. (Eds.), *Owning Scientific and Technical Information*, 17-40. New Brunswick: Rutgers University Press.

Davidson, D. M. (1989). Reverse engineering software under copyright law: The IBM PC BIOS. In Weil, V. and Snapper, J. W. (Eds.), *Owning Scientific and Technical Information*, 147-168. New Brunswick: Rutgers University Press.

Fishbein, M. and Ajzen, I. (1975). *Belief, Attitude, Intention and Behavior: An Introduction to Theory and Research*. Reading, MA: Addison-Wesley.

Gopal, R. D. and Sanders, F. L. (1998). International software piracy: Analysis of key issues and impacts. *Information Systems Research*, December.

Grosof, M. S. and Sardy, H. (1985). *A Research Primer for the Social and Behavioral Sciences*. New York: Academic Press, Inc.

Hayduk, L. (1987). *Structural Equation Modeling with LISREL*. Baltimore, MD: John Hopkins Press.

Hettinger, E. C. (1989). Justifying intellectual property. *Philosophy & Public Affairs*, 18, 31-52.

Holsing, N. F. and Yen, D. C. (1999). Software asset management: Analysis, development, and implementation. *Information Resources Management Journal*, July-September.

Im, J. H. and Koen, C. (1990). Software piracy and responsibilities of educational institutions. *Information & Management*, 18, 189-194.

Jackson, W. (1999). *Yo, Ho, Ho, and A CD ROM!* New Zealand Management, December.

James, G. (2000). Organized crime and the software biz. *MC Technology Marketing Intelligence*. January.

Johnson, D. G. (1985). *Computer Ethics*. Englewood Cliffs, NJ: Prentice-Hall.

Joreskog, K. G. and Sorbom, D. (1989). *LISREL VII. User's Guide*. Chicago: National Educational Resources.

Long, J. S. (1983). *Confirmatory Factor Analysis*. Beverly Hills, CA: Sage.

Masland, M. (2000). Software Piracy A Booming Net Trade. *MSNBC News*. Retrieved on the World Wide Web: http://www.msnbc.com/news/177396.asp?cp1=1.

Mason, J. (1990). Software pirates in the boardroom. *Management Review*, 40-43.

Matsueda, R.L., Gartner, R., Piliavin, I. and Polakowski, M. (1992). The prestige of criminal and conventional occupations: A subcultural model of criminal activity. *American Sociological Review*, 57, 752-771.

Matza, D. and Sykes, G. M. (1961). Juvenile delinquency and subterranean values. *American Sociological Review*. 26, 712-719.

Miniard, P. W. and Cohen, J. B. (1981). An examination of the Fishbein-Azjen behavioral-intention model's concepts and measures. *Journal of Experimental Social Psychology*, 17, 303-309.

Nelson, R. R. (1995). Why should managers be thinking about technology policy? *Strategic Management Journal*. 16, 581-588.

Nesselroade, J. R. (1983). Temporal selection and factori invariance in the study of development and change. *Life Span Development and Behavior*, 5, 60-89.

O'Brien, J. A. and Solomon, S. L. (1991). Demographic factors and attitudes toward software piracy. *Information Executive*, 12, 61-64.

Parker, D. (1976). *Crime by Computer*. New York: Charles Scriber's Sons.

Reid, R. A., Thompson, J. K. and Logsdon, J. M. (1992). Knowledge and attitudes of management students toward software piracy. *Journal of Computer Information Systems*, 33, 46-51.

Ryan, M. J. (1982). Behavioral intention formation: The interdependency of attitudinal and social influence variables. *Journal of Consumer Research*, 9, 263-278.

Sacco, V. F. and Zureik, E. (1990). Correlates of computer misuse: Data from a self-reporting sample. *Behaviour & Information Technology*, 9, 353-369.

Samuelson, P. (1989). Innovation and competition: Conflicts over intellectual property rights in new technologies. In Weil, V. and Snapper, J. W. (Eds.), *Owning Scientific and Technical Information*, 169-192. New Brunswick: Rutgers University Press.

Schuler, C. (1998). Make Software Piracy Meet its Doom. CeePrompt! *Computer Connection*. Retrieved on the World Wide Web: http://www/ceeprompt.com/articles/030998.html.

Shepard, G. J. and O'Keefe, D. J. (1984). Seperability of attitudinal and normative influences on behavioral intentions in the Fishbein-Azjen model. *The Journal of Social Psychology*, 122, 287-288.

Sutherland, E. H. (1947). *Principles of Criminology*. 4th Ed. Philadelphia: J.B. Lippincott.

Swinyard, W. R., Rinne, H. and Kau, A. K. (1990). The morality of software piracy: A cross-cultural analysis. *Journal of Business Ethics*, 9, 655-664.

Taylor, G. S. and Shim, J. P. (1993). A comparative examination of attitudes toward software piracy among business professors and executives. *Human Relations*, 46, 419-433.

Vallerand, R. J., Pelletier, L. G., Cuerrier, P. D., J. P. and Mongeau, C. (1992). Ajzen and Fishbein's theory of reasoned action as applied to moral behavior: A confirmatory analysis. *Journal of Personality and Social Psychology*, 62(1), 98-109.

Weisband, S. P. and Goodman, S. E. (1992). News from the committee on public policy: International software piracy. *IEEE Computer*, November, 87-90.

Wells-Branscomb, A. (1990). Computer software: Protecting the crown jewels of the information economy. In Rushing, F. W. and Ganz Brown, C. (Eds.), *Intellectual Property Rights in Science, Technology and Economic Performance*, 47-60. Boulder CO: Westview Press.

Zeithaml, V. (1988). Consumer perceptions of price, quality, and value: A means-end model and synthesis of evidence. *Journal of Marketing*, 52, 2-22.

APPENDIX

Indicators of the Measurement Model

The multi-context character of the survey, even though it remains a cross-sectional design, is significant since it affords the opportunity to empirically distinguish whether some of these perceptions pertain only to work/personal settings or are more general in nature. In addition, Table 1 presents information on the distributions of these 18 measures. The measures of skewness and kurtosis do not appear to evidence any dramatic departure from normality (Hayduk, 1987). Nevertheless, methods of analysis that do not require that all assumptions of multivariate normality are have been conducted and are referred to below.

Statistical Methods

LISREL was used to estimate both the measurement and substantive structural models. In analyzing the measurement (factor) model we empirically examine: (1) which observed variables are affected by which latent factors; (2) which pairs of factors are correlated; (3) which observed variables are assumed to be measured with error; and (4) which error component of the observed variables is correlated (Long, 1983). The LISREL program also affords the ability to estimate a covariance structure model that simultaneously specifies a factor and a structural equation, or causal, model. Factor models explain the covariation among a set of observed variables in terms of a smaller number of common unobserved, or latent, structures (Long, 1983; Nesselroade, 1983).

After achieving the most parsimonious factor structure, the measurement model is simultaneously estimated within a more complex recursive structural model that incorporates variables according to their perceived temporal priority. Moreover, these initial structures can be empirically tested against alternative nested models that can be compared by several statistical measures derived from the LISREL program.

As a whole, the present data are well suited to the type of analysis outlined above. However, several limitations of the data do exist. Since there is little substantive theoretical research upon which the present data were based, we examined a variety of alternative structures, using exploratory factor modeling, but present the confirmatory analysis for the most substantively plausible models. Second, since the data were collected using cross-sectional survey methods the investigators impose the temporal priority outlined in the structural model explored. Nevertheless, the included measures provide an excellent opportunity to examine the possibility of describing software piracy by using unobserved latent models of perceptions that may mitigate the effect of demographic measures. Moreover, in examining the proper structural configuration we are careful to note that this is an area of research that provides little theoretical guidance; therefore, we have investigated a variety of alternatives not presented in the tables.

Finally, the present sample is sufficiently large (N=523) to capitalize on asymptotic properties of statistical estimators, such as maximum likelihood. However, since the distribution of software piracy was found to be positively skewed, additional analyses were conducted using unweighted and generalized least squares methods that do not require that all of the assumptions of multivariate normality be met. The results were extremely robust and appeared to be unaffected by the method of estimation; therefore, the maximum-likelihood estimates are presented. Additionally, past research suggests that the presence of skewed or kurtotic variables makes the chi-square distribution larger than expected so that the results are actually more conservative than necessary (Hayduk, 1987).

Empirical Assessment of the Measurement Model

Both the standardized and maximum-likelihood coefficients are presented in Table 3. As evident in the table, each of the coefficients is several times larger than its standard error. Substantively the factors represent significant perceptions held by the respondents regarding their views of the propriety, ease, and skill needed to pirate software. For instance, expertise required is a combination of statements suggesting that people perceive that those who might be able to pirate software need to have special computer knowledge and skills, while ease of theft represents an underlying dimension implying that anyone with access to a computer can easily obtain and install software that is received in an unauthorized fashion. As outlined above, each of these factors appears to be a separate dimension surrounding software piracy. In addition, proportionality represents a dimension that taps the relative fairness of the profits and costs related to computer software. In contrast, the social norms factor appears to coalesce indicators that minimize the negative connotation, or consequence, of pirating software. For instance, the indicator "borrow" suggests that the copying of software is more like borrowing than theft, and "needs" implies that it is alright to copy software for particular business or professional needs. Thus, we appear to have a mixture of factors assessing the relative expertise of persons who might pirate software as well as the norms surrounding access to unauthorized software, whether this relates to the perceived fairness of software pricing or general norms of conduct.

Empirical Assessment of the Structural Model Predicting Piracy

The following analysis describes the outcome of the simultaneous estimation of the measurement model as part of a more complex recursive structural model predicting software piracy. Figure 2 presents a model that includes as exogenous measures (those that are determined outside the model) several demographic, employment, and computer abilities of the respondents and five endogenous measures (those that are causally dependent on other endogenous variables as well as the exogenous measures) including the measurement model. Figure 2 represents the final version of the model discovered through empirical analysis. However, the structural model began as a fully saturated recursive model; that is, each exogenous measure directly affected each endogenous measure, including piracy, and all four factors in the measurement model had a direct effect on the dependent measure of software piracy.

Model 3 represents the initial estimation of the fully saturated model. As the model becomes more complex, in comparison to the measurement model, there is a slight decrement in the ratio (1.483) and GFI (.95); however, each of these values are within acceptable ranges. Additionally, Table 2 also includes a column presenting the explained variance (r-squared, or R2) of the equation being investigated. Model 3 allows each exogenous measure to have a direct effect on software piracy, however, only five measures were found to have a significant impact. As the age of the respondent rises, the likelihood that they pirated software significantly declined. In contrast, being a male and using a computer at home or at work significantly increased the likelihood of software piracy. Moreover, software piracy appears to depend upon one's perception of opportunities to pirate.

In the next equation the factors making up the measurement model were allowed to have direct effects on software piracy.[1] While the overall fit of the model is not altered, the explained variance (R2) is significantly increased to .411. The addition of direct effects from the factor structure significantly mitigates the effects from the exogenous measures previously described. In fact, both the age and opportunity measures are found to no longer differ significantly from zero; i.e., thus, having no direct impact. Further, the effects from sex, usehome, and usework are halved but still significant at the (.05) level.

Due to these results, the direct effect of 10 of the exogenous measures to software piracy have been eliminated in Model 5 of Table 2. There is a slight decrement in the chi-square statistic of this model, however, by constraining these effects to zero we have saved 10 degrees of freedom. Therefore, overall, Model 5 is a dramatic improvement over Model 4. The only two factors that were found to have a significant and direct effect on software piracy were expertise and social norms; that is, if one perceives that a person requires expertise to pirate software they are significantly less likely to do so themselves and if one generally agrees that making copies of software is borrowing and not theft they are significantly more likely to possess unauthorized copies of software.

In Model 6 we investigate these issues further by eliminating the direct effects of proportionality and ease of theft on software piracy. As in the earlier discussion there is only a small decrement in the chi-square statistic but we gain two additional degrees of freedom. It is also important to note that even though proportionality and ease of theft do not have direct effects on software piracy it appears that they are significantly related to social norms and expertise, respectively. Therefore, the final model investigated in Table 2 restructures the measurement model slightly into one that coincides with that depicted in Figure 2. In this model proportionality has a causal impact on social norms while ease of theft has a causal relationship to expertise. The fit of Model 7 is not dramatically different from Model 6; therefore, by the rules of parsimony since Model 7 eliminates insignificant paths to software pirating it is preferred over the others investigated.

Table 4 also presents information regarding the effects of demographic, computer experiences, and university position measures on the four factors previously discussed. For instance age positively affects social norms but negatively impacts perceptions of expertise. Moreover, age is the only measure that significantly affects all four of the factors in the analysis. The only other measure that comes close to this impact is opportunity, which significantly affects three of the four factors.

The R-squared for each of the equations shows a wide variation in explanatory ability of the model. With regard to the reconfigured factor structure we can see that as proportionality, or the belief that software is fairly priced and accessible, increases, social norms corresponding to unauthorized use of software significantly decreases. Additionally, if one perceives that software theft is easy to do their belief that special computer skills are required to commit the theft is decreased. These are fairly straightforward findings that coincide with expectations, however, the particular temporal sequencing of the factor structure was unexpected.

ENDNOTE

1 This process is similar to a path model or stepwise regression that allows direct effects to be incrementally added or deleted from the model.

Chapter IV

Component-Based Development: Issues of Data Protection

Mark G. Lycett and Athanasia Pouloudi
Brunel University, UK

This chapter focuses on the issues raised by component-based development in the light of new data protection legislation recently introduced in the European Union. Component-based development has been proposed as a software engineering approach that can enable the development of flexible and evolutionary systems. The approach aims at the dynamic composition of information systems from pre-fabricated heterogeneous software components. The integration of components, however, potentially creates ethical issues as data need to be exchanged without the users or developers knowing which components will use what data and when. Our discussion unveils a complex ethical debate with important implications for data controllers and information systems developers.

INTRODUCTION

A fundamental challenge for information systems professionals is the development of information systems that are flexible and can respond to changing user needs within an unstable business environment. System flexibility is a problem that has long haunted the profession and it may be argued that traditional approaches to system development result in static systems that have to work in a dynamic world. This is witnessed in both statistics related to the cost and time devoted to software maintenance (Swanson & Beath, 1989) and the literature devoted to understanding information systems failure (Beynon-Davies, 1995; Poulymenakou & Holmes, 1996; Sauer, 1993). Building on the foundations of object-oriented approaches to development, "component-based development" has been proposed as a software engineering approach that can enable the development of flexible and evolutionary systems. This is primarily a consequence of mixing the flexibility of object-orientation with the encapsulation of earlier modular approaches to software development. From an object perspective, components may be simplistically viewed as collections of related classes that are strongly encapsulated, communicating with the outside world only via interfaces. With significant behavioral characteristics embedded, this allows them to be viewed as independent units of production, acquisition and deployment. Ideally, the component-based approach aims at the dynamic composition of information systems from prefabricated heterogeneous software components in a "plug-and-play" fashion. Organizations can thus acquire "black-box" components from different sources at different times and deploy them as they see fit.

From an organizational perspective, this ideal places an emphasis on systems integration as opposed to development. Components, potentially drawn from a number of diverse sources, will be integrated together and allowed to operate on data that may be sensitive at both the individual and corporate level. The notion of "black boxes" becomes relevant here: "No matter how controversial their history, how complex their inner workings, how large the commercial or academic networks that hold them in place, only their input and output count" (Latour, 1987, p. 3). Implicit in this notion is an assumption that a black box encapsulates a common understanding about *what* the technology does and *how* the technology works. The black-box nature of a component mandates that the user organization will understand it only in terms of what is stated in its interface specification(s) and any additional documentation that is supplied. Concomitantly, it is not necessarily possible to know which components will use what data and when. This feature of component-based development has interesting ramifications in ethical terms that relate strongly to the concept of data protection. The chapter focuses on the issues of data protection and the social considerations that arise for systems development and integration when component-based development is used. The chapter considers the above points in the context of the provisions of recently adopted data protection legislation in the European Union.

In order to present a focused discussion of this legislation, the following section explores the history of data protection in the UK and the adoption and implications of the European Union Data Directive (95/46/EC) in this country. Section 3 describes the principles and advantages of component-based development, focusing in particular on the way in which data are stored and used by applications. Section 4 then discusses why data protection can be an issue in component-based development and highlights the need for better awareness and understanding of the issues involved. Section 5 presents the increasing challenges that affect component-based development, especially in the electronic commerce era where data needs to be exchanged not only across legal entities (organizations), but also across jurisdictions (countries and regions). The chapter concludes with the need and implications of an ethical debate in this area.

DATA PROTECTION IN THE UK

This section provides some background information and a description of recent developments for data protection in the UK. The experience of this country provides a specific and well researched context to present the issues of the principles and implications of the European approach to data protection. It also sets the scene for a broader discussion of issues of data protection in a contemporary development environment in the later sections.

In Britain, the concerns over the abuse and misuse of personal data date back to the 1960s when the government passed a number of parliamentary bills, reports and white papers covering the subject of data protection and privacy (Bainbridge, 1996). The most important developments, however, took place in the last two decades. In 1980, the development of the first international treaty in the area of data protection, the Council of Europe "Convention for the Protection of Individuals with regard to Automatic Processing of Personal Data" (Treaty 108), triggered the need for the introduction of appropriate legislation in EU countries. The 1984 Data Protection Act was the first piece of legislation in the UK regarding the use of computers (Barber et al., 1998; Bott et al., 1995). This legislation protected individuals in circumstances where information about them was processed automatically.

Treaty 108, however, created problems in the interpretation and, hence, for the harmonization of data protection legislation within the EU as well. Following these problems the European Parliament and Council adopted the 95/46/EC EU Data Directive. The directive aimed to "protect the fundamental rights and freedoms of natural persons, and in particular their right to privacy with respect to the processing of personal data," but also to harmonize data protection legislation and aid free flow of personal information within the EU. In response to the directive, the UK adopted the 1998 Data Protection Act. This is a revision of the 1984 Data Protection Act, which also caters for the processing of manual data and recognizes the importance of the transfer of data outside the European Economic Area as well (France, 1998; Data Protection Act, 1998; Barber et al., 1998).

The most important changes in the new Act that are relevant to our discussion here are the enhanced provisions for *data subjects* (i.e., the individuals who are the subject of personal data). Data subjects are entitled to:

(a) a description of the data being processed,
(b) a description of the purposes for which it is being processed,
(c) a description of any potential recipients of their data and, except in limited circumstances, and
(d) any information as to the source of their data (where available). In addition, where the data is processed automatically and is likely to form the sole basis for any decision significantly affecting the data subject, then they will also be entitled to know the logic involved in that decision making.

Data subjects also have the right to stop particular kinds of processing, for example, in the case that it is likely to cause them damage or distress. There are also wider rights for an individual to ask a court for the "rectification, blocking, erasure or destruction" of inaccurate data and a right to compensation if damage or damage and distress and been caused by the breach of the act. The new act still poses problems of interpretation, regarding its impact in businesses, particularly its financial implications (Hunt, 1998; Nicolle, 1998; Warren, 1998). As a result, the information commissioner, the person responsible for the promotion of good information handling and the encouragement of related codes of practice (previously called the data protection registrar), has been publishing relevant guidance and advice (available at www.dataprotection.gov.uk) to facilitate the interpretation and adoption of the act.

Regardless of the present difficulties in adapting information systems use to the new legislation, businesses need to prepare for and adopt the Data Protection Act. In practice, this means recognizing the implications and changes that need to be made at an organizational level, but also at a technical level. This is an issue that has not been adequately studied, particularly in relation to new technologies and development approaches, like component-based development. The next sections present some challenges that the latter approach creates for data protection.

COMPONENT-BASED DEVELOPMENT

Component-based development is the latest in a line of approaches that promise to minimize development cost, compress cycle-time and improve flexibility. It is an approach that strongly espouses the "plug-and-play" perspective, as the software element of component-based information systems is viewed as a dynamic composition of reusable, pretested components that can be upgraded independently (Adler, 1995; Nierstrasz & Dami, 1995; Szyperski, 1998). Composition is enabled through a software architecture that allows components to be removed, replaced and reconfigured in a dynamic fashion, which provides the primary mechanism for flexibility in the face of change (Nierstrasz & Meijler, 1995). Components, as constituents of this architecture, represent units of independent production, acquisition and deployment that interact to form a functioning system (Szyperski, 1998).

As independent units of production, different people can develop components at different times, in complete ignorance of each other. As independent units of acquisition and deployment, organizations potentially benefit from reduced cost and risk associated with commercial off-the-shelf software. In ideal terms, an organization thus selects the functionality they require, purchases or builds the appropriate component(s) and "composes" a system from them (Weck, 1997). Component-based development thus aims to provide a software environment where reuse and interoperability are the rule, as opposed to the exception, and that is independently extensible, scaleable and thus more flexible in the face of changing business needs (see Figure 1).

Figure 1: Component-based development in a business context

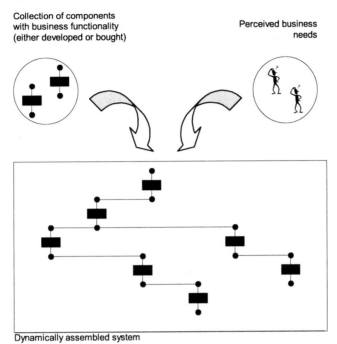

The implications of the approach are significant here for the following reasons. Firstly, the ability of components to act as independent units of development, acquisition and deployment allows for a sharp divorce between component "producers" and "consumers." The black-box nature of components mandates that the consumer organization will understand a component only in terms of what is stated in its interface specification(s) and any additional documentation that is supplied. This means that the consumer organization will have to trust:

(a)   that a component does exactly what it says that it does,
(b)   that a component does not inadvertently mishandle the data that it operates with/ upon, and
(c)   that a component does not covertly pass data to entities outside the originating organization's sphere of control.

Secondly, the emphasis on architecture indicates that significant investment in infrastructure is required to enable the widespread reuse of common assets. In this respect it is increasingly recognized that architecture has to blend different perspectives that are context dependent and often evolutionary in nature (see Kruchen, 1995, for example perspectives). In light of the above points, however, ethical concerns about data protection may well have to be included in these perspectives.

COMPONENT-BASED DEVELOPMENT AND DATA PROTECTION

As an evolution of the object/distributed object approach, components may be simplistically viewed as collections of related classes that are strongly encapsulated, communicating with the outside world only via interfaces. To allow producers a marketable degree of context independence, as well as enabling interoperation, these interfaces may be classified into those which supply information on the services "provided" by that component and those which supply information on services "required" from other components (Syzperski, 1998). These offer the means for integration, which can be supplemented with three primary and non-mutually exclusive mechanisms of integration. Firstly, via a direct "call" from a required interface to a provided interface. Secondly, via an intermediate messaging mechanism such as a queue or blackboard. Thirdly, a meta-level entity can be used to coordinate lower level ones. Lastly, via a third party such as a relational or object database. The latter mechanism is also important because it provides the predominant means of persistence or perpetuity within a system (see Sessions, 1998). For reasons of distribution efficiency, components are stateless entities, which means that they maintain state only during the execution of a service and thus require the use of data files to store and restore data.

Returning to the conversation of trust raised above, this means that a disparate and dynamic collection of components may be both operating upon and passing potentially sensitive individual and corporate data. None of the points on trust raised, however, are straightforward. Firstly, though there is active research in the area, the richness of semantic information at the component interface is currently very limited (see De Hondt et al., 1997; Helm et al., 1990; Steyaert et al., 1996, for approaches). This means that it is not easy for a consumer to understand exactly what a component does.

Secondly, it may be argued that the requirement not to mishandle data places an added stress on both the design process of the producer and the composition process of the consumer. If markets mediate between producers and consumers, a component designer is unlikely to know the sensitivity of the data utilized by the component. Supplement to this, it may not be easy for the consumer to keep audit trails of data handling in systems that are (a) dynamically configurable and (b) independently extensible. On one hand, mistakes can easily be made as witnessed in a recent case where it was discovered that users registering Microsoft's Windows 98 online were inadvertently sending a number that would identify their PCs. On the other hand, the issues of component design and assembly could intentionally be used for subterfuge. The technology-led world may be argued to be far from a perfect place as witnessed in the US Federal Trade Commission's (FTC) announcement that GeoCities had agreed to settle their charges of deceptively collecting personal information (Benassi, 1999).

DISCUSSION AND FUTURE TRENDS

Data protection is closely interlinked with the three general principles of information systems security: confidentiality, integrity, and availability. This section discusses component-based development in relation to each of these principles in order to present the general challenges for data protection in this area as well as the likely directions for dealing with these challenges in the future.

Confidentiality, Integrity and Availability in Component-Based Development

Confidentiality is generally realized by restricting data access to those who are authorized. This might be seen as difficult in component-based systems, which are independently extensible. This difficulty is best explained through a discussion of **integrity** and **availability**. In abstract terms, component **integrity** is provided via encapsulation; that is, the data "owned" by a component can only be accessed and manipulated by the services provided by that component. This cohesion (cf. Latour, 1987) is one of the virtues of the black-box approach. It is the case, however, that components are stateless in nature (Szyperski, 1998). Persistent state (i.e., data) is normally held within a database and marshalled to and from a component on an as-needed basis, where it is manipulated via one or more services in direct response to a request for those services. In the centralized world of many organizations this might mean very many components manipulating data from few databases. This, in the context of points (a) to (c) in Section 3, provides for a high level of complexity and danger where components are independently produced and integrated where-upon confidentiality and integrity may be compromised.

Meta-level coordination entities, noted in Section 4, provide a current means for handling such danger by defining the model, control flow and interaction between independently produced components. "Frameworks" represent the common instantiation of such coordination entities, and black-box variants implement a set of "policy decisions" that provides the common ground for multiple components to coexist in a single environment (Weck, 1997). To this extent frameworks represent a dedicated and focused architecture providing the protocols or contracts for interaction alongside the dimensions in which a framework may be independently extended. In general, however, frameworks are noted to be both difficult to design and to re-factor in the face of change (Bäumer et al., 1997; Fayed & Schmidt, 1997; Johnson, 1997). Either as an addition or alternative to the meta-level view, Sparling (2000) proposes that the single integrated database approach needs to be replaced by components implementing isolated data stores. This view is based on experience from the development of component-based systems, but is noted as requiring considerable work in educating data management professionals on the importance of encapsulation at all levels–in this case to provide confidentiality.

Component-based systems also raise an issue related to maintaining the **availability** of systems when they are needed. The independent production of components means that current conceptions of testing are challenged. In notional terms, current unit testing strategies may be argued to remain suitable at the level of individual components. Clearly, however, there needs to be some guarantee provided that any fault within a component would be contained within that component and/or that the assembled system could degrade gracefully (the black box is "dismantled") if faults occurred (e.g., the system architecture localizes the fault). The implication of this is that component testing would need to be backed up with certification (or suchlike) if the results are to be trusted in market-like situations. Similarly, demands are made on framework design if a responsibility for fault tolerance is dictated at this level. Given the dynamics of a component's life cycle within an organizational context, commitments also have to be made, and assurances given, that changes in the specification or behavior of a component over time will not result in dependency problems at the system level.

Each of these problems is magnified as a component-based system moves toward the (Utopian) ideal of independent extensibility. Currently some distinction is still required between design time and run time to allow the testing of solutions before live release. Based on experience it is noted that there is significant overhead involved in testing components that have multiple roles (Sparling, 2000). This is important as it indicates that significant investment is required if trust is to be obtained at the market level. Issues of trust become increasingly relevant as systems development takes place outside the organizational context (e.g., outsourcing, application service provision), but also as applications span organizational and national boundaries. Indeed lack of trust in online transactions is one of the main reasons reported for the relatively low electronic commerce adoption today. Trust is a key issue and its existence among the business community and the end-consumers will increase the willingness of trading partners to expand their electronic transactions (e.g., Hart & Saunders, 1997; Ratnasingham, 1998; Wilson, 1997). Thus, issues of data protection in component-based development go well beyond technical concerns about the behavior of the "black box." Future developments in this area need therefore to consider both technical developments in the area of security and component-based development but also more general trends in the applications of these technologies in the current interorganizational context. The next section reviews some of these developments.

Future Trends

As problems arise, so does the awareness of those problems and research into solutions. There is extensive research into technological issues relating to security and component-based development that are expected to improve the provisions for data protection. One approach of use might be that of adapting the Platform for Privacy Preferences Project's (P3P) proposal concept and using it in "the small" (see Reagle & Cranor, 1999). This would provide a harmonized vocabulary designed to describe what the services of a component do that could, for example, be parsed by the component architecture/infrastructure and compared with organizational policy on data protection and privacy. The approach could also be used to allow components to negotiate the level and purpose of data exchange. A second approach, which can be considered complimentary, is that of verification/certification. This utilizes "digital signatures" to provide confirmation that data has not been changed since it was sent and/or to verify that the components used to compose a system were really written by a genuine producer and not by a "hormone-impaired teenage hacker" (Sessions, 1998, p. 409). As information is increasingly exchanged through networks, the integrity of the transmission requires the authentication of the message, the recipient and the sender. Bertino et al., (2000) present several approaches and authorization schemes that are in use or are being explored for dealing with information protection in the context of "the peculiar characteristics of this environment."

More generally, in the electronic commerce era, there are several actions that can be taken to respond to user uncertainty (Johnston, 1999). First, users need to be educated about privacy and security issues. We would argue that this is also essential for developers. Despite the well established codes of ethics in computing (e.g., Anderson, 1993), developers may be unaware of the challenges that contemporary development environments raise for data protection. Second, the perceptions about technology, often seen as a tool than can threaten trust, need to change to acknowledge that technology can also be applied for the users' protection, for example, using encryption mechanisms. However, it is also important to recognize the limitations of technology in addressing security issues, as there are also organizational and social aspects that need to be taken into account (Dhillon, 1997). Third, the necessary legislation framework that protects trading partners must be developed. In Europe, for example, governments try to balance the desire for international competitiveness, that presumes the electronic exchange of information at a global level, with the need to safeguard the protection of personal data. The recent data protection legislation in Europe (described in this paper in the UK context) has created tensions in the commercial relations between the European Union (EU) and the United States (Swire & Litan, 1998). In practice it has been overcome as American companies that catered for data protection (as opposed to *all* American companies) were considered trustworthy partners for electronic transactions with European companies. The use of model contract clauses has also been considered as another mechanism for enabling transfers outside the European Union while still providing protection for personal data (Data Protection Registrar, 1998). This is an example where, following commercial interest, electronic commerce acted as a catalyst, motivating (or forcing) global stakeholders to think about bringing together different legislative frameworks. At the same time as data protection legislation is debated at a global level, governments in Europe and the US support the effort to enhance the awareness and confidence of citizens and companies in electronic commerce and the development of relevant skills and network literacy (EU-US, 1997).

In combination, technological, organizational and political means become important in promoting confidence in new information technologies and development strategies by at least providing guard mechanisms and audit capabilities.

Clarke (1999) argues, however, that such initiatives will ultimately have to evolve a form of intellectual property rights in personal data, which are vested in the individual whom can trade them. Whatever the result, it is our contention that the most fundamental prerequisites are those of awareness and understanding. For component producers, this mandates the integration of such awareness and understanding in component-based analysis and design techniques. For component consumers, a similar argument applies at the architectural level, as it is here that the rules, policies and ethical guidelines of an organization are made concrete.

CONCLUSIONS

The chapter presented issues of data protection and considered the challenges it may present to a component-based development environment, particularly within contemporary business environments where electronic transactions are increasing. In view of recent data protection legislation, information systems developers and users need to consider, on the one hand, the ways in which data protection legislation restricts information systems development and, on the other hand, the ways in which information systems development practices limit or enable data protection. In this respect, we have attempted to elucidate some of these issues with respect to component-based development.

We believe that our study of data protection in a component-based development environment contributes to the ethical discussion about the implications of new information technologies and development strategies. Importantly, it unveils a complex ethical debate, in which data controllers (i.e., those who determine the purposes for which and the manner in which any personal data may be processed), the supervisory authority that oversees data protection, and information systems developers need to be involved. This debate spans technical, organizational, and social issues. The ethical awareness and understanding that arises from such debate have strong implications. First, it is people that have to implement development practices and institutionalize relevant policy. This makes demands on the existing knowledge and education of component analysts, designers and architects. In particular, new and updated skills are required. Secondly, architectural and other mechanisms are required that implement ethical awareness and understanding. The aim of this chapter has been to raise the level of awareness. Given the level of interpretation that can be applied to the Data Protection Act, the ethics of new approaches to development is an area that clearly requires further research.

REFERENCES

Adler, R. M. (1995). Emerging standards for component software. *IEEE Computer*, 28(3), 68-77.

Anderson, R. E. (1993). Using the new ACM code of ethics in decision making. *Communications of the ACM*, 36(2), 98-107.

Bainbridge, D. (1996). *Introduction to Computer Law*, 3rd edition, Pitman Publishing.

Barber, B., Leslie, D., Elbra, T., Green, N. and Gilbey, J. (1998). *Data Protection–Everybody's Business*. Prepared by a Working Party of the British Computer Society's Data Protection Committee.

Bäumer, D. and Gryczan, G. et al. (1997). Framework development for large systems. *Communications of the ACM*, 40(10), 52-59.

Benassi, P. (1999). TRUSTe: An online privacy seal program, *Communications of the ACM*, 42(2), 56-59.

Bertino, E., Pagani, E., Rossi, G. P. and Samarati, P. (2000). Protecting information on the Web. *Communications of the ACM*, 43(11).

Beynon-Davies, P. (1995). Information systems 'failure': The case of the London Ambulance Service's Computer Aided Despatch project. *European Journal of Information Systems*, 4, 171-184.

Bott, F., Coleman, A., Eaton, J. and Rowland, D. (1995). *Professional Issues in Software Engineering*. 2nd edition. UCL Press Limited.

Clarke, R. (1999). Internet privacy concerns confirm the case for intervention. *Communications of the ACM*, 42(2), 60-67.

Data Protection Act. (1998). *London: The Stationery Office Limited*. Retrieved March 22, 2001 on the World Wide Web: http://www.hmso.gov.uk/acts/acts1998/19980029.htm.

Data Protection Registrar. (1998). *The Fourteenth Annual Report of the Data Protection Registrar*, London: HMSO.

De Hondt, K., Lucas, C. and Steyaert, P. (1997). Reuse contracts as component interface descriptions. *Second International Workshop on Component-Oriented Programming*, Jyväskylä, Finland, June 9, 43-49.

Dhillon, G. (1997). *Managing Information System Security*. London: Macmillan.

EU Data Protection Directive. (1995). (95/46/EC). On the protection of individuals with regard to the processing of personal data and on the free movement of such data. *Official Journal of the European Community*, 281, 31-50, November 23.

EU-US. (1997). Joint EU-US statement on electronic commerce 5th of December 1997.

Fayed, M. E. and Schmidt, D. C. (1997). Object-oriented application frameworks. *Communications of the ACM*, 40(10), 32-38.

France, E. (1998). *An Introduction to the Data Protection Act 1998*, October.

Hart, P. and Saunders, C. (1997). Power and trust critical factors in the adoption and use of electronic data interchange. *Organization Science*, 8(1), 23-41.

Helm, R., Holland, I. M., and Gangophyay, D. (1990). Contracts: Specifying behavioural compositions in object-oriented systems. *ACM SIGPLAN Notices*, 25(10), 169-180.

Hunt, A. (1998). Data protection–Meet the new guard. *In Accountancy Age* 23, April.

Johnson, R. E. (1997). Frameworks = (Components + Patterns). *Communications of the ACM*, 40(10), 39-42.

Johnston, D. (1999). Global electronic commerce-realizing the potential. In Leer, A. (Ed.). *Masters of the Wired World*, 228-237. London: Financial Times Pitman Publishing.

Kruchen, P. B. (1995). The 4 + 1 view model of architecture. *IEEE Software*, 12(6), 42-50.

Latour, B. (1987). *Science in Action.* Harvard University Press, MA: Cambridge.

Nicolle, L. (1998). The next big issue. *The Computer Bulletin*, November.

Nierstrasz, O. and Dami, L. (1995). Component-oriented software technology. In Nierstrasz, O. and Tsichritzis, D. (Eds.). *Object-Oriented Software Composition*, Prentice Hall, Englewood Cliffs, NJ, 3-28.

Nierstrasz, O. and Meijler, T. D. (1995). Research directions in software composition. *ACM Computing Surveys*, 27(2), 262-264.

Poulymenakou, A. and Holmes, A. (1996). A contingency framework for the investigation of information systems failure. *European Journal of Information Systems*, 5(1), 34-46.

Ratnasingham, P. (1998). The importance of trust in electronic commerce. *Internet research: Electronic Networking Applications and Policy*, 8(4), 313-321.

Reagle, J. and Cranor, L. F. (1999), The platform for privacy preferences. *Communications of the ACM*, 42(2), 48-55.

Sauer, C. (1993). *Why Information Systems Fail: A Case Study Approach.* Henley-on-Thames: Alfred Walled Limited.

Sessions, R. (1998). *COM and DCOM: Microsoft's Vision for Distributed Objects.* John Wiley and Sons, New York.

Sparling, M. (2000). Lessons learned through six years of component-based development. *Communications of the ACM*, 43(10), 47-53.

Steyaert, P., Lucas, C., Mens, K. and De Hondt, T. (1996). Reuse contracts: Managing the evolution of reusable assets. *ACM SIGPLAN Notices*, 31(10), 268-285.

Swanson, E. B. and Beath, C. M. (1989). Maintaining Information Systems in Organizations, Chichester: Wiley.

Swire, P. P. and Litan, R. E. (1998). *None of your business. World Data Flows, Electronic Commerce, and the European Privacy Directive*, Brookings Institution Press, Washington, D.C.

Szyperski, C. (1998). *Component Software - Beyond Object-Oriented Programming.* Addison-Wesley, Harlow, Essex.

Warren, P. (1998). Protect and survive. *Business and Technology*, September, 29-32.

Weck, W. (1997). Independently extensible component frameworks. In Mühlhäuser, M. (Ed.), *Special Issues in Object-Oriented Programming: Workshop Reader of the 10th European Conference on Object-Oriented Programming ECOOP '96*, Linz, July, dpunkt.verlag, Heidelberg, 177-183.

Wilson, S. (1997). Certificates and trust in electronic commerce. *Information Management & Computer Security*, 5(5), 175-181.

Chapter V

Internet Privacy: Interpreting Key Issues

Gurpreet S. Dhillon and Trevor T. Moores
University of Nevada, Las Vegas, USA

INTRODUCTION

The Internet has transformed the way in which goods are bought and sold. Forrester Research predicts retail sales on the Internet to grow from less than 1% in 1999 to 6% by 2003. According to Gartner Group, convenience and time saved are two of the main incentives for users to buy online. At the same time, however, research conducted by Price Waterhouse Coopers suggests that during the 1999 Christmas season, 18% of all customers who purchased online were "dissatisfied" with their experience. A Business Week/Harris Poll (see *Business Week*, March 20, 2000) survey reported that 41% of online shoppers were very concerned over the use of personal information. Among the people who go online but have not shopped, 63% were very concerned. Clearly, as Keeney (1999) suggests, maximizing privacy is a fundamental objective related to Internet commerce.

The purpose of this paper is to identify issues related to maximizing Internet privacy. The paper is organized into five sections. Following a brief introduction, Section 2 explores the notion of Internet privacy and how various researchers have attempted to understand the concept. Section 3 presents the study design. Section 4 is a discussion of research findings. Section 5 presents the conclusions.

This chapter originally appeared in the Information Resources Management Journal, Vol. 14, No. 4.
Copyright © 2001, Idea Group Publishing.

INTERNET PRIVACY

Internet privacy can be defined as the seclusion and freedom from unauthorized intrusion. The key word in the definition is "unauthorized." Although we may not like that our personal information regarding our purchases and habits to be monitored and stored in databases around the country, we are at least usually aware that it's happening. However an unauthorized intrusion to collect personal data marks the beginning of privacy infringement. Various opinion polls have shown increasing levels of privacy concerns (Equifax, 1990, 1992). The 1992 Equifax study reports a survey indicating nearly 79% of the Americans being concerned about personal privacy and 55% suggesting that security of personal information was bound to get worse by year 2000. Indeed this has happened. Fairweather and Rogerson (2000) report that it is technically easier than ever before to gather and search vast amounts of personal data. Hence it has become easy to track individuals across the globe as they leave the data shadow behind–through the use of gas stations, cash machines, logging on to check email.

A March 1999 Federal Trade Commission (FTC) survey of 361 Web sites revealed that 92.8% of the sites were collecting at least one type of identifying information, such as an address. Furthermore 56.8% of the sites were collecting at least one type of demographic information. The FTC study also found that over one third of the sites did not have a privacy disclosure notice on the site. Even in cases where the privacy disclosure notice had been posted, only 13.6% were following the FTC's fair information practice guidelines.

Previous literature on privacy--not necessarily Internet privacy--has critiqued the majority of opinion surveys based on the assumption that information privacy is not a unidimensional construct, i.e., focusing on the level of concern alone, rather than understanding the nature of concern. In response, Smith et al. (1996) suggest four dimensions of the construct "individuals" concerns about organizational practices in managing information privacy." These factors were: collection, unauthorized secondary use, improper access, and errors. Smith et al.'s (1996) research, although providing a very useful instrument to measure individuals' concern about information privacy, does not necessarily consider privacy issues in relation to Internet use. Clearly the use of the Internet to conduct business has gained prominence in recent years and the converging trends, competitive and technological, pose interesting privacy challenges (cf. Culnan & Armstrong, 1999).

There are two reasons for an increased importance of Internet privacy concerns, as opposed to simple information privacy issues relevant to any brick-and-mortar business. First, the increasingly competitive business environment is forcing companies to collect a vast amount of personal information. Many a time there is good intent in doing so, since many businesses may seriously want to customize their products and services for the benefit of the consumer. However the security of personal data and subsequent misuse or wrongful use without prior permission of an individual raise privacy concerns and often end up in questioning the intent behind collecting private information in the first place. Second, the advances in information technology have not only made it possible to record personal information at the point of sale, but also map the patterns of online behavior. Although this is a useful marketing ploy (Bessen, 1993; Glazer, 1991), it certainly overwhelms the customer and hence there are numerous privacy concerns. Similar issues about overwhelming the customer through excessive use of technology have been voiced in the literature (see Dhillon & Hackney, 1999; Ciborra, 1994).

With respect to the two reasons identified above, the question of fairness in collecting personal information needs to be understood adequately. Fairness, with respect to Internet commerce, can be considered at two levels. As Glazer (1991), and Milne & Gordon (1993) contend, fairness could either be a component in the "social contract" or related to the procedure followed for a particular activity (Lind & Tyler, 1988; Folger & Bies, 1989). When individuals willingly disclose personal information for nonmonetary gains, such as higher quality service, privacy concerns are limited as long as the concerned organization upholds its side of the social contract. Individuals will clearly continue engaging in the social contract as long as the benefits exceed the risks, to a point where an individual begins trusting the organization. This is evidenced by many of the new generation Internet businesses. Barnesandnoble.com and Yahoo, for example, have clear-cut privacy policies, thereby facilitating in developing trust over a period of time. On the other hand, ediets.com believes in overwhelming the customer with emails and offers once personal details have been recorded.

Fairness is also linked to the procedure that might be followed in a particular activity. Clearly fairness of the procedure, as opposed to the nature of the outcome (Lind & Tyler, 1988), is a clear determinant of the level of privacy concern an individual might have. Some Internet businesses are now beginning to place importance on procedural fairness. In many cases the Web sites first give a notice as to why personal information is being collected, its usefulness and the manner in which it would be kept secure, then the consent is sought as to the manner in which an individual's personal information would be used. As would be evident, procedural fairness is closely coupled with social contract and trust. If an individual feels, that in spite of procedural fairness, the social contract in the exchange of private information is not maintained, it would clearly lead to loss of trust and integrity of the organization. On the other hand if an individual willingly gives private information in lieu of some social or economic benefit, but the procedure used in collecting and maintaining the information is not fair, again it would lead to concerns about privacy infringement, trust and integrity of the process.

Given an understanding of various aspects of Internet privacy, as discussed in the literature, our intention is to understand the various issues that could be of potential concern for individuals. The next section describes the multi-method adopted to identify such issues.

STUDY DESIGN

In identifying issues related to individual's concerns about Internet privacy, we set out to use a combination of two methodological approaches. The first relates to steps 1 and 2 as described by Schmidt (1997) while the second is related to the identification of means and fundamental objectives as described by Keeney (1999). A combination of these two approaches helped us to generate a list of issues that are of significant concern for individuals with respect to Internet privacy. Further research would enable us to validate the preliminary list and develop an instrument that would be useful in assessing the level of Internet privacy concern for an individual with respect to a particular online business.

This study was designed to span two main phases. Phase one followed Schmidt's (1997) approach to (a) discover relevant issues and (b) determine the most important issues. Phase two of the study followed Keeney (1999) in identifying the fundamental Internet privacy objectives of individuals and means objectives in achieving the fundamental Internet privacy objectives. Essentially Keeney's concepts were used to classify the output of Schimidt's second step.

Keeney (1999) stresses the importance of defining a decision context when identifying the objectives. He contends that the fundamental objectives together with the decision context provide a decision frame. Furthermore a decision context defines the alternatives to consider for a specific decision situation. In our study the decision context was the maintenance of individual privacy with respect to Internet use. We defined our overall objective as maximizing Internet privacy for individuals. According to Keeney, the decision context would imbed in itself a number of means objectives. These would be objectives that individuals would have with respect to maximizing Internet privacy. Our task was to not only identify fundamental Internet privacy objectives, but also all possible means objectives. We also wanted to rank all objectives in order of importance.

Phase 1

Our first step in Phase 1 was to unearth as many issues as we could from a panel of experts. Panel members, 11 in total, were invited to a brainstorming session and were asked to identify all possible objectives they would have in maximizing Internet privacy. The actual elicitation of objectives followed a 40-minute general discussion on Internet privacy issues and was moderated by the first author. The panel was representative of various experts in the field. There was one attorney, one formerpoliceman, one network administrator, one sales and marketing professional, one software engineer, one dot-com entrepreneur, two full-time students and three ardent Internet users who had considerable experience in purchasing online.

The brainstorming session lasted little over an hour and the panelists identified 144 concerns/objectives. At this stage it was hard to differentiate whether these were merely concerns or were in fact Internet privacy objectives. Following the data collection exercise, the authors consolidating the list of objectives and posted it on their Web site. The consolidation process produced 70 objectives. The panelists were invited to visit the Web site to refine, add to or suggest deletions from this list. An online bulletin board was used to capture the responses. The respondents added another 15 objectives to the consolidated list to produce a total of 85 objectives.

Our second step was to determine the most important issues. We presented our list of 85 objectives to a group of 16 IS executives. These executives represented five different industries: government, hotel, pharmaceutical, health care, and IS consulting. The average work experience of the IS executives was five years. The group was asked to rank the top 10 issues from the list of 85 objectives. We followed the guidelines of selecting at least 10%, following Schmidt (1997). No ties were allowed. The results were consolidated and presented once again to the group. Open discussion resulted in clearly identifying the top five objectives. These objectives appear in Table 1 in rank order.

Phase 2

Phase 2 involved the identification of means objectives with respect to maintaining Internet privacy. The argument used in identifying the means objectives was that any objective that was not a top issue of concern clearly contributed in some way to one of the top issues. The remaining 80 issues from Phase 1 were subjectively evaluated with an intent to formulate means objectives. This was a two-step process. First, issues with a similar meaning were clustered together. Second, a judgment was made whether an issue had merit to be a means objective on its own or was merely a part of a larger means objective. This process resulted in 18 means objectives. The majority of the remaining 62 issues were condensed into one of the 18 means objectives. Others did not necessarily relate to our overall objective and were hence not included. The means objectives (in no particular order) appear in Table 2.

DISCUSSION OF RESEARCH FINDINGS

This section presents a discussion of key Internet privacy issues. The intent is to provide an explanation of the top issues identified by respondents in this study in light of the literature and the means objectives.

Table 1: The top five Internet privacy issues

Rank #	Issue stated as objective
1	Companies should not sell personal information.
2	Adequate measures should be in place to prevent theft of personal information by a third party.
3	Eliminate the chance of "losing" personal files.
4	Maximize security to deter "hackers" from destroying the data.
5	Eliminate spam.

The top issue is the potential for a Web site to sell the details of online consumers to a thirdparty. While the use of personal information to further the cause of businesses has become a competitive necessity, the issue raised here suggests that the burden resides with online businesses to ensure that confidentiality of personal information collected is maintained. As identified in Section 2 of this paper, individuals may be willing to provide their personal information as long as they are receiving some benefit, i.e., increased customer service. This means that online businesses need to ensure "procedural fairness" (Culnan & Armstrong, 1999). Individuals may not be interested in giving out personal information on first contact with an online business, but a trust may develop over a period of time. Hence, as identified in this research (see Table 2), it is important for businesses to self-determine what they should divulge to a thirdparty. Moreover providing personal information online should be discretionary. Such actions would go a long way to enhance the credibility and integrity of online businesses and enable them to remain competitive ethically.

Establishing adequate measures to prevent identification theft is another critical concern identified by this research. This issue can be addressed at two levels: (1) the security of personal information once it has been collected and (2) establishing tougher laws to prevent consumer ID theft. When dealing with security of information internally, establishment of a security policy and a general culture of trust and high integrity will be beneficial (Dhillon & Backhouse, 2000), as well as other organizational issues that are beyond the scope of this paper (see Dhillon, 1997, for details). There is also a need to have tougher Internet privacy laws, such that violators could be adequately prosecuted. At the present time, there is no doubt that US and European governments are responsive to Internet privacy demands. Research has shown that increased levels of privacy regulation are a function of the level of data processing environment in a particular country and increased government involvement in privacy protection (see Milberg et al., 2000; Flaherty, 1989).

Table 2: Internet privacy means objectives

Increased awareness to have firewall protection	Boycott companies who do not have a privacy policy
Provide credit card security assurance by third parties	Use encryption in email communications
Provide guarantees from shopping sites	Online businesses should not collect personal information
Enact stronger laws to protect consumer privacy	Watch children online
Tougher laws to protect consumer ID theft	Strict penalties for violators of personal privacy
Facilitate self-policing the Internet community	Establish international standards on privacy
Prosecute violators of laws	Check authenticity of an online business prior to purchase
Make spam illegal	Increase self determination in providing personal information online
Businesses should be required to have a privacy policy	Providing personal information online should be discretionary

Several of the fundamental issues identified by the respondents in this research related to establishing adequate measures to protect information, from inappropriate sale (issue #1), but also from accidental loss (issue #3), and from deliberate attack by "hackers" (issue #4). In the US, the FTC has also given due credence to the protection of personal financial information. The onus however has been placed on individual organizations to ensure responsible data manipulation, implementing encryption standards and maintaining secure servers. Although many online businesses, especially banks, have security very high on their agenda, many other businesses with an aspiration to develop customer confidence have turned to third parties for "seals of approval." In recent years, one means has been the Web Assurance Seals. Organizations such as the Better Business Bureaus, Certified Public Accounting Firms, and/or organizations devoted to security, privacy or dispute resolution award seals of assurance to Web sites that meet certain criteria. The seals of assurance cover such areas as privacy, security, transaction integrity/ completeness, business disclosures, quality control processes, and consumer recourse. These seals often highlight the close relationship between privacy and security issues. Clearly there were concerns with maintaining privacy of personal information when connected through a cable modem, from viruses to Trojan horses. Whether deliberate or accidental, the issue raised here is that any data provided to a Web site must be protected.

An issue related with electronic communication is that of spam. Receiving unsolicited email is certainly an invasion of privacy. Some businesses feel that inundating consumers about their products and services is going to increase their sales. However the converse may be true. Unsolicited emails are irritating and our respondents seemed to have a very strong opinion about them. Some of the popular Internet email services such as Hotmail and Yahoo! now include a "spam guard" that detects bulk mail and automatically directs the spam to the Trash folder. There are now also facilities to block mail from the more technically savvy spammers that do not use bulk mail addresses in their email header. According to the respondents in this study, spam email is seen as a sufficiently irritating phenomenon that there are calls to make spam illegal.

In this section we have discussed various aspects of Internet privacy which our respondents considered to be fundamental concerns. Clearly there are no simple answers to the issue of Internet privacy, but our fundamental issues would help in starting a dialogue.

CONCLUSION

This paper has identified an individual's concerns with respect to Internet privacy. Five fundamental and 18 means objectives were identified, essentially suggesting that in order to adequately manage the fundamental concerns, concrete steps have to be taken with respect to the means objectives. While the governments and organizations gear up their resources to tackle Internet privacy concerns, it is prudent to engage in self-regulation. A way ahead could be through the creation of private rights of action for individuals who have been harmed. Following on from research presented in this paper, work is needed to develop measures to assess the extent to which individuals are comfortable with Internet privacy within the context of a particular business. This would help businesses to create new policies and reassess existing ones.

REFERENCES

Bessen, J. (1993). Riding the marketing information wave. *Harvard Business Review*, September-October, 71(5), 150-160.

Ciborra, C. (1994). Market support systems: Theory and practice. In Pogorel, G. (Ed.), *Global Telecommunications Strategies and Technological Changes*, 97-110. Amsterdam: North-Holland.

Culnan, M. J. and Armstrong, P. K. (1999). Information privacy concerns, procedural fairness, and impersonal trust: An empirical investigation. *Organization Science*, 10(1), 104-115.

Dhillon, G. (1997). *Managing Information System Security*. London: Macmillan.

Dhillon, G. and Backhouse, J. (2000). Information system security management in the new millennium. *Communications of the ACM*, 43(7), 125-128.

Dhillon, G. and Hackney, R. (1999). IS/IT market support systems: augmenting UK primary care groups. *Topics in Health Information Management*, 20(2).

Equifax. (1990). *The Equifax Report on Consumers in the Information Age*. Atlanta, GA: Equifax Inc.

Equifax. (1992). *Harris-Equifax Consumer Privacy Survey*. Atlanta, GA: Equifax Inc.

Fairweather, N. B. and Rogerson, S. (2000). *Social Responsibility in the Information Age*. Leicester, UK: De Montfort University, CCSR.

Flaherty, D. H. (1989). *Protecting Privacy in Surveillance Societies*. University of North Carolina Press, Chapel Hill.

Folger, R., and Bies, R. J. (1989). Managerial responsibilities and procedural justice. *Employee Responsibilities and Rights Journal*, 2(2), 79-90.

Glazer, R. (1991). Marketing in an information-intensive environment: Strategic implications of knowledge as an asset. *Journal of Marketing*, 55(4), 1-19.

Keeney, R. L. (1999). The value of Internet commerce to the customer. *Management Science*, 45(4), 533-542.

Lind, E. A. and Tyler, T. R. (1988). *The Social Psychology of Procedural Justice*. Plenum Press, New York.

Milberg, S. J. et al. (2000). Information privacy: Corporate management and national regulation. *Organization Science*, 11(1), 35-57.

Milne, G. R. and Gordon, M. E. (1993). Direct mail privacy-efficiency trade-offs with an implied social contract framework. *Journal of Public Policy & Marketing*, Fall, 12(2), 206-215.

Schmidt, R. C. (1997). Managing Delphi surveys using nonparametric statistical techniques. *Decision Sciences*, 28(3), 763-774.

Smith, H. J. et al. (1996). Information privacy: Measuring individuals' concerns about organizational practices. *MIS Quarterly*, June, 167-196.

Chapter VI

Privacy and the Internet: The Case of DoubleClick, Inc.

Scott Chapman and Gurpreet S. Dhillon
University of Nevada, Las Vegas, USA

With growing frequency, information about how you use the Web–the sites you visit, search terms and other queries you make, online purchases, "click through" responses to advertisements–is being captured by advertising networks or "profiling companies." With the permission of the Web site, but not your permission, these companies place a tag on your computer. This tag–or identifier–is then used to track your movements as you surf the Web. In addition to long lists of collected information, a profile may contain "inferential' or "psychographic" data–information that the company infers about you based on your surfing habits. From this amassed data, elaborate inferences may be drawn, including your interests, habits, associations and other traits.

-The Center for Democracy and Technology (CDT, 2000)

INTRODUCTION

With the advent of the Internet, a number of issues have surfaced that are affecting our society positively, negatively and confusingly at breakneck speeds. The issues surrounding an individual's right to privacy on the Internet are one such example. Affording an individual a right to privacy is most definitely a unique right preserving the quality of the Constitution of the United States. Certainly the Internet has blurred an already gray line that courts have fought hard and long to preserve and define over the past 225 years.

Once it was thought that one could not legally invade another person's privacy without a specific consenting act on the part of the invaded party, barring court order. However, since the Internet has come into common use, the question now comes before us, "Is access to the Internet an act of giving up one's right to privacy?" or "Are we still afforded the same rights to privacy as traditionally held?" Surely, these questions are not answered simply and, in fact, approach so many different levels that the questions themselves does not even accurately frame the issue. Instead, the stage is still forming and the actors are just coming forward. The discussion in this chapter merely attempts to better define some of the blurry issues, bringing us closer to an understanding of how this new technology should fit into our traditional beliefs in a right to privacy.

The Internet has become a new locus for social interaction and communication on a global basis. The Internet by its nature is decentralized, open and interactive. It allows users to publish information, engage in commerce, communicate, research and even interact on levels only previously imagined in private and intimate settings. There are no barriers to geography, society and political community. As the Internet continues to grow and allows for fully integrated voice, data and video transfer at optimal rates of speed, it will quite literally become a virtual face-to-face social, commercial and political environment.

As for today, the Internet exists within social, technological and political arenas. The technology is progressing to a point where entities can gain access to information at their every whim. Implementation of such technological advances raises significant concern by all involved. Assuredly, everyone that interacts with the Internet has concerns of privacy. Whether it is a government that worries about national security, a bank that worries about financial record accuracy, a business that worries about balancing economic potential with anticompetition impulses or an individual sitting at home desiring to maintain anonymity while e-shopping, the concerns about privacy on the Internet are pervasive and remain unanswered.

As a result of all the technological advances, individuals and entities around the nation and across the globe are organizing efforts to understand and generate some kind of context in which to protect privacy. Governments are struggling to identify their role in this new environment, businesses are under pressure to be aware of certain limitations, and individuals are rushing to maintain their protections. As a result, we have a dynamic combination of governmental solutions, business solutions, industry solutions, advocate solutions and individual user solutions. It is difficult to make sense of these different efforts to solve a common problem and even more difficult to combine them for a focused solution. What's more, the future for protection of privacy on the Internet is completely uncharted and reveals an unwritten chapter in this nation's history. One thing is certain: The various constituencies that make up the Internet are all pushing toward new technologies and rules that provide greater control over information and privacy.

The following discussion takes a close look at DoubleClick and how they have experienced conflict and legal battles as they have apparently attempted to push the limits on an individual's right to privacy. In order to gain a better perspective on these issues, the discussion then continues by analyzing specific legal, technological and societal issues and giving specific recommendations and solutions for the future of "right to privacy" issues on the Internet.

THE CASE OF DOUBLECLICK, INC.

Summary of DoubleClick Legal Actions

DoubleClick, a leading provider of comprehensive Internet advertising solutions for marketers, was incorporated as a Delaware corporation on January 23, 1996. Currently the company maintains over 30 offices globally with 1,800 employees and over 7,000 customers. Recently DoubleClick also acquired Abacus Direct, the country's largest catalog database firm. The new organization combined technology, media and data expertise and used it to develop a centralized planning, execution, control, tracking and reporting system for online media campaigns. However there were growing concerns about the manner in which consumer privacy issues were being addressed. On February 10, 2000, a complaint against DoubleClick was filed with the Federal Trade Commission (FTC) by the Electronic Privacy Information Center (EPIC).

EPIC's complaint alleged that with the merger of DoubleClick and Abacus Direct and the subsequent consolidation of their two databases, there were concerns and possible violations of the company's assurances that the information it collects on Internet users would remain anonymous. This amounted to the data collection being unfair and deceptive (EPIC, 2000a). EPIC also claimed that DoubleClick had failed to follow its revised privacy policy, which EPIC felt was also unfair. The allegations center around a practice known as "online profiling." DoubleClick is alleged to be tracking the online activities of Internet users by devices known as "cookies" and combining surfing records with detailed personal profiles contained in a national marketing database. In their complaint EPIC asked for relief in destruction of all records wrongfully obtained, assessment of civil penalties for the behavior, and injunctive relief enjoining DoubleClick from violating the Federal Trade Commission Act.

The executive director of EPIC states that this complaint was filed in order to test "the current state of privacy protection in the United States" (EPIC, 2000b). It is hoped that the FTC will bring accountability to those that make promises regarding privacy and then collect personal information unfairly and deceptively.

Shortly prior to EPIC filing suit with the FTC, DoubleClick was sued in California, Superior Court, Marin County, on January 27, 2000, by Hariett Judnick seeking to represent the public in the state of California. The lawsuit alleged that DoubleClick employs "sophisticated computer tracking technology, known as cookies, to identify Internet users and collect personal information without their consent as they travel around the Web" (Junnarkar, 2000). According to the lawsuit, DoubleClick has represented to the public that it was not collecting personal and identifying information and that it gives privacy interests of Internet users paramount importance. Judnick sought relief in an injunction to stop such behavior and destruction of all information wrongfully obtained without knowing consent.

On February 29, 2000, EPIC's complaint was accompanied by the Center for Democracy and Technology's (CDT) filing a statement of additional facts and grounds for relief with the FTC. Their statement similarly alleged that sensitive information including "video titles, salaries, and search terms are being passed to DoubleClick" (Junnarkar, 2000). Additionally, they asked for the FTC to stop "DoubleClick and other businesses from tying individuals' names and addresses to information collected online" (Junnarkar, 2000).

In an effort to ease public concern over the complaint, on March 2, 2000, Kevin O'Connor, CEO of DoubleClick stated that, "We commit today, that until there is agreement between government and industry on privacy standards, we will not link personally identifiable information to anonymous user activity across Web sites" (Blum, 2000).

DoubleClick's Position

DoubleClick submitted a new company policy, just after the merger, stating that it plans to use the information compiled to build a database that profiles consumers. The database will include consumers' names; addresses; retail, catalog ad online purchases histories; and demographic data. Prior to this, DoubleClick's policy had been to not connect personal information with its widespread cookies. DoubleClick now feels that it's "warning" to the public is enough notice of the act. However, "Even if DoubleClick provides warnings, such warnings give no protection to many unsophisticated Web surfers," states Ira Rothken, an attorney representing Judnick (Junnarkar, 2000).

Early on in the controversy, DoubleClick stated that it had used sensitive online data on building profiles and had no plans to do so in the future. The company had also claimed that it was their policy to only merge personally identifiable information with nonpersonally identifiable information for profiling, after providing clear notice and choice (Reuters, 2000a). Looking back to 1996, when the company was first formed, Kevin O'Connor is known to have stated that DoubleClick would not be connecting its database to names, addresses and the like unless it was totally "voluntary on the user's part, and used in strict confidence. We are not going to trick people or match information from other sources" (Gillmor, 2000).

When DoubleClick joined with Abacus, it acquired a database of more than 2 billion consumer catalog transactions. This gave a clear opportunity that more than 11,500 sites that belong to DoubleClick network could feed into the new database, which could correlate with personal information (Macavinta, 2000). The stance adopted by DoubleClick in year 2000 marked the complete reversal of the policy advocated by Kevin O'Connor since the company's inception. In the new environment, it was considered adequate if the consumers were told that their information will be shared with other parties and if they were given a notice and choice for opting out.

Opponent's Position

The interesting part of this argument is that privacy advocates (for example, Jason Catlett, founder of Junkbusters and quoted in Macavinta, 2000) have been stressing that the marketers will turn the Internet into a gigantic data-gathering machine for junk mail, telemarketing and advertising. Since it has now become a reality, companies such as DoubleClick, with limited or no consideration towards personal privacy, characterize the "data collection machinery" as based on choice and opting out rather than opting in.

There are also problems with DoubleClick's "opt-out" claim. First, one will need to do it for every browser used on each and every computer. Second, the notion of trusting a trading partner and establishing a social contract with an online business gets questioned. In the case of DoubleClick, the process used to collect personal information follows three steps. DoubleClick sends a cookie to a browser and gives it a unique ID number. It then sends the same ID number on to the site that knows an individual's identity. This site (or company) then sends back the data that DoubleClick needs to look up an individual in the Abacus database. This enables DoubleClick to know who the individual is. The fact that Abacus contains names, addresses and retail information on 90% of American households creates a highly likely chance that they will be able to match the information quickly and efficiently. Much of the information on the Internet that is collected by others "is invisible to the consumer, which raises serious questions of fairness and informed consent" (EPIC, 2000a).

The act of DoubleClick really becomes disingenuous and fraudulent when the chance to opt out comes only in the form of a few lines of text placed in the privacy policies of participating Web sites. Since such policies are usually buried a few levels down, it's rare for the consumers to find out if their personal information is being collected or their identity is being established, let alone them having a chance to opt out. Clearly this is not permission, but as David Banisar, deputy director of Privacy International, states, it is "fraudulent on its face" (Rodger, 2000). The issue becomes even more complex when DoubleClick refuses to divulge the names of the participating Web sites in an attempt to maintain "confidentiality of violators of privacy."

Status of the Case

As a result of the filings with the FTC, the FTC filed its third report to Congress making specific recommendations relevant to online privacy and online profiling. While the commission praised the efforts of the private sector for addressing the issues of online privacy, they state that the number of Web sites meeting basic standards for privacy protection is "far too low," endangering consumer confidence in the "fast-growing, pro-consumer marketplace." The report recommends that Congress enact legislation that ensures minimum levels of privacy protection for online consumers. The FTC recommends "basic standards of practice for the collection of information online" and a requirement that "consumer-oriented commercial Web sites that collect personal identifying information from or about consumers online" be forced to comply with the "four widely-accepted fair information practices: notice, choice, access and security" (see FTC recommendation of May 22, 2000). The FTC believes that the proposed legislation, in conjunction with self-regulation, will provide sufficient context for Internet commerce to reach its full potential. This would allow consumer confidence to blossom, facilitating full participation in the Internet marketplace.

Commentary on the DoubleClick Cases

Generally when a party files a lawsuit in any given situation, it is looking for some type of monetary damages because they have been harmed. However, in rare instances, lawsuits are filed for broader reasons, viz. to stop a certain behavior. The lawsuits filed against DoubleClick are an example of such actions. The individuals have not been affected by any real monetary damages. They are fighting to protect their rights and generate precedent. This is the quickest way for an individual to protect their rights, albeit it is also the most expensive.

Typically, in order to change certain implementation and remedy social concerns, the legislator is petitioned by the people or by advocates for the people to enact legislation on the issue. However, this is likely to be a long, drawn-out process that could take several sessions to pass, if ever even passed at all. Thus, individuals can attack certain actions of business on a constitutional basis to have the action heard immediately and receive quick resolve through the courts. The legislature can then, later, turn around and enact legislation that follows the court's ruling or legislation that opposes the ruling.

In the case at hand, we not only have individual actions against DoubleClick for violations of constitutional rights, we have private consumer and citizen protection groups (i.e., the CDT and the EPIC) filing complaints with governmental agencies in an effort to influence legislation on the issue. This sends a message to Congress that there is a problem and the citizens desire to have legislation enacted for their protection. The pleas to the FTC and to the Department of Commerce have not fallen on deaf ears and those administrative governmental agencies have submitted reports to the federal legislative bodies to increase protection of the citizens' right to privacy through proposed legislation.

In a nutshell, the process is working. It is likely that the lawsuits will bear similar fruit, but in a more timely fashion. We have already seen the statement from DoubleClick claiming that they will "await clear industry standards before" deciding the future direction of new products and that they will not be implementing a plan to associate names with other personally identifiable information and Internet user activity (see Blum, 2000).

The procedural matter is moving full steam ahead and appears to be achieving its objectives. This is yet to be seen in full from legislation and court proceedings in the future.

DISCUSSION: RIGHT TO PRIVACY AND THE INTERNET

While the procedural issues seem to be running smoothly, there are still substantive issues that need to be researched, discussed, debated and analyzed so that an efficient and effective method can be created to protect the privacy of the citizens of the United States, while still allowing capitalism to flourish. The process is only the forum for approach to the substantive issues. This section presents a brief discussion of the issues that appear to be of significant relevance and that must receive consideration for any legislative body to draft effective laws and for any court to issue effective rulings.

Though not approached in this discussion nor approached in the DoubleClick actions, access to information regarding our children, our finances, and our medical history are so valuable they cannot be ignored while discussing privacy concerns. While we merely discuss Internet access to browsing habits, loosening of privacy laws can lead to dissemination of information regarding our most valuable private matters.

With regard to children, suffice it to say that on October 20, 1999, the United States Congress passed a law that went into effect on April 21, 2000. The act requires that "commercial Web sites and other online services directed at children 12 and under, or which collect information regarding user's age, to provide parents with notice of their information practices and obtain parental consent prior to the collection of personal information from children" (CDT, 2000a). It also requires those sites to provide the parents with the ability to analyze and correct their information about the child. The act is designed so that a child's ability to speak, seek out information and publish would not be adversely affected by these pages. Whether this will be of significant help is yet to be seen.

Medical and financial records are among the most personal information that an individual possesses. The transition of the American health industry from "fee-for-service" health care to the dominant managed care (i.e. HMO, PPO, etc.) has generated a demand for an "unprecedented depth and breadth of personal information" by an ever increasing number of players (CDT, 2000b). The ability of these entities to join forces, pool information and share records has reached an unprecedented level and will only be increasing in the future. Congress has taken efforts to regulate health privacy rules in recent sessions, however, has failed to meet its self-imposed deadlines. The Clinton Administration imposed an initiative listing out federal privacy rules that require consumer consent before companies share medical data or detailed information about spending habits. However, this remedy is limited, as many medical providers simply require signature of consent in order to sign up with the managed health care entity.

The basic point remains that the development of the issues is in its infancy and there are a number of very pressing concerns with regard to technology and an individual's right to privacy. The issues surrounding DoubleClick and user profiling are only the tip of the iceberg. Other issues regarding Internet privacy include national privacy and consumer groups, U.S. government agencies, industry groups, various publications, privacy services, technologies and databases, "snoop" technologies, online books, articles, papers and reports, employer access to email, ISP access to information, and government control of full and free access. The issues pointed out below deal with general concerns and solutions that are approached in the DoubleClick case. They are all related, however, because as the door opens ever wider, more and more rights escape, even if it is all in the name of free enterprise; don't be fooled, freedom is eroded slowly.

Technological Issues

The primary dispute, as noted in the DoubleClick case, involves "user profiling." User profiling is made possible by a technology that places identification codes on a user's computer and allows access to that information by other Web sites. This technology is known as a "cookie." According to Netscape, "cookies" are no longer a small treat to have with milk just prior to bed. They are a mechanism that server-side connections, such as CGI scripts, can use to store and retrieve information on the client side of the connection. And the addition of a client-side state significantly extends the capabilities of Web-based client/server applications.

Cookies are embedded in the HTML code that is generated by a site and flows back and forth between the server and the user's computer. The cookies are utilized in a two-stage process: First, the cookie is stored on the user's computer without their consent or knowledge–the Web server then creates a specific cookie defining certain preferences of the user in a string of text stored on the user's computer in a file called the cookie list; second, the cookie is automatically transferred from the user's computer to a Web server whenever the user brings up a specific page on the Web browser–the Web browser transmits the cookie (which contains personal information) to the server, without the knowledge of the user. In order to be warned of these cookies, the Web browser must be programmed by the user to warn of the cookies, a task not commonly known to the user. It should also be noted that the warnings only ask the user whether they consent to a cookie being deposited; if the user has no frame of reference they are clueless (Mayer-Schönberger, 1997). A current cookie may read something like this:

> The server adlink.exchange.com wishes to set a cookie that will be sent back to any server in the domain .linkexchange.com. The name and value of the cookie is: SAFE_COOKIE=33ee55190305260c. This cookie will persist until Tue, Nov. 09 15:59:59: 1999.

Recently the Energy Department's Computer Incident Advisory Capability (CIAC) issued a report deeming the use of cookies as being "ok." however, they stressed concern because at times cookies may be used for tracking an individual's browsing habits, which may make a lot of people really uncomfortable. Clearly the original intent of using cookies was to assist the user as they accessed their favorite sites by storing passwords and the like. However, it is now being utilized far beyond that scope.

The technological interchange of this information between numbers of networked entities over time could easily result in a system similar to what we presently call the "credit bureau." Currently the three largest credit bureaus cannot verify most of the information in their databases, which are regularly used to decide whether individuals receive credit loans, mortgages and other financing. Clearly, the Internet could become tomorrow's credit report for all to see. Consider the following scenario (Cookie Central, 2000):

> ... if you visited a number of sites that advertise alcohol ... and you end up on a list that your insurance company purchases. The list compiled from a variety of Internet sites shows your name as someone who frequents sites that promote alcohol, or at least as someone who is a prime prospect for alcohol sales. They raise your premiums on a profile that has been built about you based upon the sites you visit on the Internet. Someone assumes this is an accurate profile ... and acts upon this erroneous assumption. ... This scenario may never happen but the door has been opened. ... Just ask anyone who has been victimized by an inaccurate credit report.

The problem that we are now facing surrounds the ability of the technology to change in an instant. While we are spending so much time and effort to stop what we *know* is invading our privacy, we have not yet approached what will be developed tomorrow that will be invading our privacy. The job of the legal community in this country is to have the foresight and the knowledge to develop a system that can regulate known and unknown technologies: a task proven to be impossible. The technology in and of itself is a living and breathing thing. It is all we can do to protect ourselves from it, no matter how much it benefits us. The balance of the benefit and the protection is unfortunately a constant battle.

Legal Issues

The United States Constitution does not explicitly utilize the word "privacy" in any of the sections traditionally referred to as the "Privacy Amendments." However, the following constitutional amendments provide an array of protection of privacy that throughout history has been defined over and again:[1]

First Amendment: protects the freedom of expression and association, protecting information about those with whom we associate and materials that we generate.

Fourth Amendment: safeguards individuals in their persons, homes, papers and effects from unreasonable searches and seizures; limits government intrusion into people's private lives.

Fifth Amendment: grants a privilege against self-incrimination protecting the autonomy of our bodies, thoughts and beliefs.

Ninth Amendment: pursuant to rulings by the US Supreme Court, this protects the privacy of the family and reproductive lives.

Fourteenth Amendment: limits state intrusions into the freedom and privacy of intimate decisions that affect our sexual, family and reproductive lives, as defined by the Supreme Court.

The United States legislature has in recent years passed a number of laws for the protection of privacy. Initiatives issued by both the administrative branches of government, such as the FTC, and the Executive Office of the President have significantly increased over the last decade. "Internet privacy" has become an official international topic on the agenda at international government round tables throughout the world. What does this mean? Clearly Internet privacy is on the mind of government. The concern for the US is how they balance the interests of capitalistic democratic business, yet protect the interests of the citizens as per the Constitution.

In 1973, the standard was essentially set in the *Code of Fair Information Practices* (Berman, 2000). This code was set forth in the Secretary's Advisory Committee on Automated Personal Data Systems, Records, Computers, and the Rights of Citizens, US Department of Health, Education and Welfare. The code sets forth four primary requirements for entities gathering information. Essentially, they translate into five commonly accepted standards with which even Internet sites must comply. Unfortunately, while the number of sites meeting this standard has doubled–from 10% in 1999 to 20% in 2000–it still falls even shorter than that, as the fair information practices are largely sealed and self-regulatory by nature (Berman, 2000). The standard includes (FTC, 1998):

Notice/Awareness: Consumers should be given notice of an entity's information practices before personal information is collected from them. The decision must be an informed decision.

Choice/Consent: Choice means giving consumers options as to how any personal information collected from them may be used, specifically relating to secondary uses of the information.

Access/Participation: This refers to an individual's ability to both access data about him/herself and to contest that data's accuracy and completeness: this includes timely and inexpensive access, simple means for contesting, a means for verification and a means for correction of the data.

Integrity/Security: Collectors of data must take reasonable steps in gathering the data, such as using only reputable sources, providing consumer access to data, destroying untimely data; this includes both managerial and technical measures to protect against loss of the data, unauthorized access to the data, destruction, or disclosure.

Enforcement/Redress: The core principles of privacy can only be effective if a mechanism is in place to enforce them. Absent the enforcement, the Code is only suggestive; thus, self-regulation, private remedies and government penalties are all necessary.

The problem that we are now facing is no enforcement and failure to comply with the first four requirement standards. Even a novice can tell from the description of how the "cookie" works that it violates nearly every level of the standards. The notice that is given is not "informed," there is no explanation as to how the information will be used, the user has no access to the data that is being compiled and the data is readily transferred between entities without thought of whether the user has even given consent. Clearly, the legislature must enact enforcement measures to combat the blatant disregard for privacy in this technology. Every area of this technology violates an individual's right to privacy. It took the federal government over a decade to enact laws governing the credit bureau's actions and they have still run amuck. It is hard to say if they will ever be able to get a handle on the infringement of rights on the Internet.

Solutions to Consider

Technological
There are a number of ways to combat the cookie through technological advances in the browsers. For advanced users, there is a new Platform for Privacy Preferences Project (P3P) recently developed by the World Wide Web Consortium (W3). On June 21, 2000, certain major Internet companies offered a first look at this platform (W3C, 2000). Essentially this platform provides an industry standard and a simple automated way for users to gain more control over the use of personal information on Web sites. The platform is a standardized set of multiple-choice questions covering all major aspects of Web sites' privacy policies. The browser will then take a snapshot of the information on the Web site and compare it to the users information on their computer to better inform the user of the site's intentions. The industry is actively trying to find some sense of self-regulation through development of this technology.

Legal
Federal and state legislatures are currently working on a number of bills in an effort to solve the problem. The discussion of the issues that must be considered has not even been fully formulated. However, because of the public's outcry for protection of privacy, the legislators move forward and instead generate piece-meal bills that are hard to pass and difficult to implement as law, not to mention the fact that they largely cater to special interest groups that sponsor the legislation. A solution through this channel will be cumbersome, expensive, slow to formulate and most likely be completely ineffective.

Self-Regulation
It may indeed take a very long time for the legislature to formulate an effective privacy strategy. Hence self-regulation by individuals using the Internet may be an option. Infringement of privacy could be avoided by considering the following suggestions (CDT, 2000a):
- Look for the privacy policies and Web assurance seals on the Web sites.
- Utilize a separate email account for personal email. It should not be the same as work email.
- Teach children that giving out personal information online is like talking to strangers.

- Clear your memory cache after browsing.
- Make sure that online forms are secure.
- Reject unnecessary cookies (place your browser on warn).
- Use anonymous re-mailers.
- Encrypt your email.
- Use anonymizers while browsing.
- Optout of third-party information sharing.

Of course, this does not mean that one would have all problems solved. Even Internet businesses should proactively consider the following issues, without totally excluding their ability to know who visits their sites:

- Sites should display privacy policies in conspicuous places and they should be stated simply.
- Give the user a choice by offering a clearly written, prominently displayed opt-out box, without any of the usual "trickery-type" language.
- Allow the user to inspect the recorded data at their whim to check for accuracy.
- Finally, enforcement is a must. Whether by a self-imposed monitoring authority joined by all Web sites or whether government imposed, there must be accountability for those that utilize deceptive practices and illegally track users.

CONCLUSION

Privacy on the Internet has emerged as a significant issue. Because of the technological advances, the issue of privacy goes beyond the relatively straight-forward issues of seeking consent and giving choice to opt in or opt out. This chapter has brought to the fore some of the privacy concerns related to Internet commerce as evidenced by the DoubleClick case. Clearly there are ethical issues related with the use of technology, and marketers in the information age need to give due consideration to various aspects of social responsibility. An ability to collect personal data and relate it to another piece of data collected with a different intent does not necessarily account for an ethical action. As has been suggested in this chapter, good laws coupled with technological means to forewarn consumers and uniform third-party assurances would go a long way in curbing the invasion of privacy in the information age.

ENDNOTE

1 United States Constitution; including case law: Katz v. U.S., Supreme Court (1967); Griswald v. Connecticut, Supreme Court (1965); Whalen v. Roe, Supreme Court (1977).

REFERENCES

Berman, J. (2000). The Federal Trade Commission's report to congress–Privacy online: Fair information practices in the marketplace. *CDT's Testimony, Speeches and Filings*, May 25. Retrieved November 30, 2000 on the World Wide Web: http://www.cdt.org/testimony/000525berman.shtml.

Blum, J. (2000). Statement from Kevin O'Connor, CEO of DoubleClick, Company press release. *Business Wire*, New York, March 2, 1.

Center for Democracy and Technology. (2000). News Web Site. Retrieved November 30, 2000 on the World Wide Web: http://www.cdt.org/privacy/issues/profiling.html.

Cookie Central. (2000). Cookies and Internet Privacy. Internet Privacy, November 11, 2000. Retrieved November 30, 2000 on the World Wide Web: http://www.cookiecentral.com/ccstory/cc3.htm.

Electronic Privacy Information Center. (2000a). EPIC files FTC complaint against DoubleClick, alleges 'Deceptive and unfair trade practices' in online data collection. *Electronic Privacy Information Center*, February 10 News Release. Retrieved November 30, 2000 on the World Wide Web: http://www.epic.org/privacy/internet/ftc/DCLK_comp_pr.html.

Electronic Privacy Information Center (2000b). The Cookies Page. Retrieved November 30, 2000 on the World Wide Web: http://www.epic.org/privacy/internet/cookies.

Federal Trade Commission. (2000). Statement of Chairman Pitofsky, Privacy Online: Fair Information Practices in the Electronic Marketplace. May 22. Retrieved November 30, 2000 on the World Wide Web: http://www.ftc.gov/reports/privacy2000/pitofskystmtonlineprivacy.htm.

Federal Trade Commission. (1998). Privacy Online: A Report To Congress, Section III. *Fair Information Practices Principles*, June 1998. Retrieved November 30, 2000 on the World Wide Web: http://www.ftc.gov/reports/privacy3/toc.htm.

Gillmor, D. (2000). DoubleClick does double take on Web privacy. *SiliconValley.com News*, January 27. Retrieved November 30, 2000 on the World Wide Web: http://www0.mercurycenter.com/svtech/columns/gillmor/docs/dg012800.htm.

Junnarkar, S. (2000). DoubleClick accused of unlawful consumer data use. *CNET News.com*, January 28. Retrieved November 30, 2000 on the World Wide Web: http://news.cnet.com/news/0-1005-200-1534533.html.

Macavinta, C. (2000). Privacy fears raised by DoubleClick database plans. *CNET News.com*, January 25. Retrieved November 30, 2000 on the World Wide Web: http://news.cnet.com/news/0-1005-200-1531929.html?dtn.head.

Mayer-Schönberger, V. (1997). The Internet and privacy legislation: Cookies for a treat? *West Virginia Journal of Law and Technology*, 1(1). Retrieved November 30, 2000 on the World Wide Web: http://www.wvu.edu/~wvjolt/Arch/Mayer/Mayer.htm.

Reuters. (2000a). DoubleClick defends data practices. *ZDNET News*, February 17. Retrieved November 30, 2000 on the World Wide Web: http://www.zdnet.com/zdnn/stories/news/0,4586,2439228,00,html?chkpt=zdnntop.

Reuters (2000b). DoubleClick sued over privacy. *ZDNET News*, January 28. Retrieved November 30, 2000 on the World Wide Web: http://www.zdnet.com/zdnn/stories/news/0,4586,2429053,00.html?chkpt=zdnnrla.

Rodger, W. (2000). Activists charge DoubleClick double cross. *USA Today.com*, June 7. Retrieved November 30, 2000 on the World Wide Web: http://www.usatoday.com/life/cyber/tech/cth211.htm.

World Wide Web Consortium. (2000). Platform for Privacy Preferences (P3P) Project. June. Retrieved November 30, 2000 on the World Wide Web: http://www.w3.org/P3P/.

Chapter VII

Electronic Commerce and Data Privacy: The Impact of Privacy Concerns on Electronic Commerce Use and Regulatory Preferences

Sandra C. Henderson, Charles A. Snyder and Terry Anthony Byrd
Auburn University, USA

Electronic commerce (e-commerce) has had a profound effect on the way we conduct business. It has impacted economies, markets, industry structures, and the flow of products through the supply chain. Despite the phenomenal growth of e-commerce and the potential impact on the revenues of businesses, there are problems with the capabilities of this technology. Organizations are amassing huge quantities of personal data about consumers. As a result, consumers are very concerned about the protection of their personal information and they want something done about the problem.

This study examined the relationships between consumer privacy concerns, actual e-commerce activity, the importance of privacy policies, and regulatory preference. Using a model developed from existing literature and theory, an online questionnaire was developed to gauge the concerns of consumers.

The results indicated that consumers are concerned about the protection of their personal information and feel that privacy policies are important. Consumers also indicated that they preferred government regulation to industry self-regulation to protect their personal information.

Electronic commerce (e-commerce) is revolutionizing the way we conduct business. It is changing economies, markets, and industry structures; the flow of products and services through the supply chain; as well as consumer segmentation, values, and behavior (Drucker, 1999). "It is redefining commerce, transforming industries, and eliminating the constraints of time and distance. There is not a market on the face of the earth which will be ignored (PwC, 1999a)."

Despite the phenomenal growth of e-commerce, two studies recently released by the Wharton School indicated that while total spending was up, the average number of dollars spent per consumer was down. The researchers found that the concern about privacy and an unwillingness to trust online businesses with private data are the two biggest factors contributing to the decline in the dollar amount of sales per consumer (Garfinkel, 2000). According to PricewaterhouseCoopers, without privacy protection, there is no consumer confidence in e-commerce (PwC, 1999b).

This paper reports the results of a study that explored consumers' concern about the privacy of their personal information and their perceived importance of privacy policies. We also looked at consumer preferences for the alternative regulatory approaches to protecting privacy–government regulation or industry self-regulation.

In the following sections, we first discuss the existing literature on both e-commerce and privacy. We then follow with a theoretical model that links consumer attitudes toward privacy with the different regulatory options. Details of the study's methodology and results are followed by a discussion of the findings. We conclude with a discussion of the implications for both researchers and managers.

E-COMMERCE

Definitions of e-commerce vary widely, but in general e-commerce refers to all forms of commercial transactions involving organizations and individuals that are based upon the processing and transmission of digitized data, including text, sound, and visual images (OECD, 1997; US DOC, 2000). In its most basic form, e-commerce includes technologies such as telephones, facsimile machines, automated teller machines (ATMs), electronic funds transfer (EFT), and electronic data interchange (EDI). More often, though, e-commerce is simply thought of as the buying and selling of goods and services through the Internet, particularly the World Wide Web (WWW). The two most common forms of e-commerce are labeled business-to-consumer (B2C) and business-to-business (B2B) e-commerce.

B2C e-commerce may be thought of as the basic type of e-commerce because it was first exploited by retail "e-businesses" such as Amazon.com, eTrade, and eBay that were created as Internet-only versions of traditional bookstores, brokerage firms, and auction houses. These e-businesses could deliver almost unlimited content on request and could react and make changes in close to real time because of the freedom from the geographic confines and costs of running actual stores

(Buckley, 1999). These factors soon caused traditional "brick and mortar" stores to launch their own online stores (e.g., Barnes and Noble, Merrill Lynch, Southebys).

B2B e-commerce has many of the same advantages that hold for B2C e-commerce organizations such as the ability to increase the services they can offer their business customers. Internet technology has helped create new relationships and to streamline and augment supply-chain processes. The roles of logistic and financial intermediaries (e.g., FedEx, UPS, American Express) are expanding as these changes are occurring (Buckley, 1999).

E-commerce is not without risks or barriers. Market conditions constantly change as new competitors can easily enter the market with new business models. Customer loyalty is fleeting, as competitors are only a mouse click away. Competitive advantage is short-lived, as traditional barriers are rendered irrelevant by technological advances (Oracle, 1999). One risk that has received a lot of attention recently concerns the privacy and security of personally identifiable information (PII) transmitted over the Internet and stored by the organization collecting the data (Hoffman, Novak, & Chatterjee, 1993).

PRIVACY

According to Westin (1967), privacy is "the claim of individuals, groups or institutions to determine for themselves when, how, and to what extent information about them is communicated to others." Information privacy can be thought of as "the ability of the individual to personally control information about one's self" (Stone, Gardner, Gueutal, & McClure, 1983). Personal information privacy has become one of the most important ethical issues of the information age (Culnan, 1993; Mason, 1986; Smith, 1994).

Data privacy is a major issue facing nearly every business in every country in the world. Over the past several years, many surveys have found consistently high levels of concern about privacy (Cranor, Reagle, & Ackerman, 1999; Culnan, 1993; GVU, 1998; Harris Louis and Associates & Westin, 1991, 1994, 1996; Louis Harris & Associates, Inc., 1999; Milberg, Burke, Smith, & Kallman, 1995; Smith, Milberg, & Burke, 1996). This attention to the data privacy issue has been brought about, in part, by the increasing impact of information technologies (IT) such as the Internet on daily life and by recent media attention (Smith, 1993).

The European Union's (EU) Data Protection Directive also has contributed to the concern over the protection of an individual's data privacy. The directive was enacted to protect European citizens from privacy invasions. One of the major provisions of the directive prevents the transfer of personal data to countries whose privacy laws or policies do not measure up to those of the EU.

The United States is especially concerned about the implications the directive will have on trade with Europe (Santosus, 1998). The 2-year negotiations between the US Department of Commerce and the European Commission's (EC) Internal Market Directorate resulted in the EC finally accepting the US "safe harbor" principles, which are supposed to meet the test of the European directive in protecting personal data (LaRussa, 2000; Mogg, 2000).

Even with the satisfactory outcome of the EU and US negotiations, consumers and the Federal Trade Commission (FTC) have pushed and will continue to focus on the issue of data protection in the US as rumors surface that the FTC is ready to recommend new regulations to protect online privacy (Schwartz, 2000). This is a complete turnaround from their prior position that self-regulation is the method of choice.

Online Privacy

There have been several recent studies that addressed the issue of online privacy. The FTC conducted three studies between 1998 and 2000. These studies found that most Web sites collected personal information from consumers and most had not implemented the fair information practice principles originally outlined by the 1998 study (FTC, 1998, 1999, 2000). Culnan (1999a, 1999b) conducted two studies that revealed that once again most Web sites collected personal information while only a limited percentage implemented all of the fair information practice principles.

What these studies do not show, however, is how consumers view efforts to protect their personal data on their behalf. This study examines the variables that affect consumer views of privacy, the importance of privacy policies, and whether governmental or self-regulation is more desirable.

RESEARCH MODEL AND HYPOTHESES

The research model proposed for this study is shown in Figure 1. The model considers the interrelationships among several factors based on the literature. The following sections describe each component of the proposed model and develop associated hypotheses.

Figure 1: Research Model

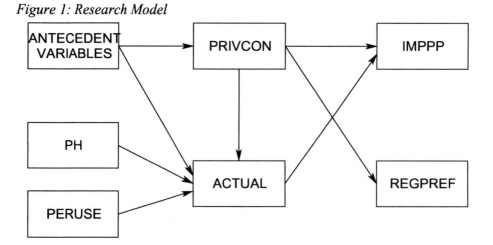

PRIVACY CONCERNS

Privacy is a multidimensional concept. Agranoff (1991) defined information privacy in terms of three issues: data collection, data accuracy, and data confidentiality. Smith et al. (1996) identified four dimensions that constitute the construct "individual privacy concerns" (PRIVCON). The four factors are: collection, unauthorized secondary use, improper access, and errors.

The collection dimension involves concern that extensive amounts of PII are collected and stored in databases. Unauthorized secondary use deals with information that is collected for one purpose but is used for another, secondary purpose (internally within the organization collecting the PII) without authorization from the individuals. Improper access is concerned with data about individuals that are available to people without proper authorization from the individual (i.e., information sold or rented to a third party). The last area of concern involves inadequate protections against deliberate and accidental errors in personal data (Smith et al., 1996).

The results of several studies, governmental, industry and academic, show that individuals are concerned about the privacy of their personal information (Cranor et al., 1999; Culnan, 1993; Harris et al., 1991, 1994, 1996; Louis et el., 1999; Milberg et al., 1995; Milberg, Smith & Burke, 2000; Smith 1993, 1994; Smith et al., 1996; Stone et al., 1983).

ACTUAL E-COMMERCE ACTIVITY

Prior research suggests that individuals with higher levels of concern about their information privacy may be more likely to refuse to participate in activities that require them to provide personal information (Smith et al., 1996; Stone et al., 1983). Understanding the behaviors that cause individuals to accept or reject computers and systems has been one of the most challenging issues in information systems (IS) research (Swanson, 1988). Previous IS research has used intention models from social psychology as the basis for research on the determinants of user behavior (Davis, Bagozzi, & Warshaw, 1989; Swanson, 1982).

In the research model proposed for this study we did not use the behavioral intention, but we used the individuals' perceptions of their actual e-commerce activity. The research model posits that privacy concerns (attitude) have a direct impact on a consumer's actual e-commerce activities. Previous research indicates that individuals may take a variety of different actions based on their levels of concern, such as having no intention to provide personal information (Culnan, 1993; Stone & Stone, 1990). Therefore, we hypothesized:

H1: Higher levels of privacy concerns will result in lower levels of actual e-commerce activity.

The research model in Figure 1 also captures the effect of perceived usefulness (PERUSE) on actual e-commerce activity. The following was hypothesized:

H2: Higher levels of perceived usefulness result in higher levels of actual e-commerce activity.

Culnan (1993) included a variable to measure whether the respondents had shopped by mail or phone during the previous year. This study also used a variable that gauges a consumer's proclivity to purchase merchandise (PH) sight unseen. Thus the following hypothesis was proposed:

H3: The more likely a consumer is to purchase merchandise or services via mail, telephone or over the Internet during the past year, the higher the level of actual e-commerce use.

IMPORTANCE OF PRIVACY POLICY

Several studies have looked at the privacy policies of Web sites (Culnan, 1999a, 1999b; FTC, 1998, 1999). In addition, the FTC issued its report, "Privacy Online: Fair Information Practices in the Electronic Marketplace," as a result of the previous studies (FTC, 2000). Neither study looked at how consumers feel about privacy policies. However, the IBM Multi-National Privacy Survey did examine the relationship between consumers and privacy policies (Louis et al., 1999). This study also examined the relationship between privacy concerns and the importance of privacy policies (IMPPP). Thus, the following hypothesis was proposed:

H4: The higher the level of privacy concern, the higher the perceived importance of privacy policies.

None of the previous studies have examined the impact of e-commerce usage on the perceived importance of privacy policies (IMPPP). The more PII consumers provide over the Internet, the more vulnerable their data becomes. Thus, the following was hypothesized:

H5: The higher the level of actual e-commerce activity, the more important a consumer will view an organization's privacy policy.

REGULATORY PREFERENCE

How well corporations manage privacy often drives the desire for government regulation (Milberg et al., 2000). Several studies suggested that consumers' perceptions of how their personal data is handled by organizations impact their propensity to complain about privacy concerns and to demand governmental involvement (Harris et al., 1991, 1994, 1996; Stone & Stone, 1990). Milberg et al. (2000) found a positive direct relationship between privacy concerns and regulatory preferences (REGPREF). Thus, the following hypothesis was proposed:

H6: There is a positive direct relationship between consumer privacy concerns and regulatory preferences.

ANTECEDENTS

Because life experiences tend to shape attitudes toward privacy, two antecedents were also included in the research model: (1) prior privacy invasion experience (PIE) (Culnan, 1993; Harris et al., 1991; Smith et al., 1996; Stone & Stone, 1990) and (2) technology knowledge (TK). Culnan (1993) did not find prior privacy experiences to be significant. However, Smith et al. (1996) found that persons having been the victim of personal information misuse should have stronger concerns regarding information privacy. Thus, we proposed the following hypotheses:

H7a: Privacy concerns are higher if an individual has experienced a prior privacy invasion.

H7b: An individual's actual e-commerce activity decreases if the individual has experienced a prior privacy invasion.

Prior research has established a positive relationship between experience with computing technology and a variety of outcomes such as affect towards computers and computing skill (Harrison & Rainer, 1992; Levin & Gordon, 1989). Agarwal and Prasad (1999) did not find that prior experience with similar technologies had a significant impact on attitude or behavior intentions. The Agarwal and Prasad (1999) study also did not test technology experience on actual system use. The IBM study found that groups that use computers and access the Internet to the greatest extent have relatively greater levels of confidence in companies that do business on the Internet (Louis et al., 1999). We propose that there is a significant effect of technology knowledge on the actual e-commerce activity. Thus, the following was hypothesized:

H8a: Higher levels of technology knowledge increase the privacy concerns of an individual.

H8b: Higher levels of technology knowledge increase the levels of actual e-commerce use.

Demographics such as gender, age, and education play a role in an individual's privacy concerns. Nickell and Pinto (1986) found that males tend to have more positive computer attitudes. Harrison and Rainer (1992) found that males exhibited significantly higher computer skill levels than females. Previous research has found evidence of a negative relationship between age and acceptance of technological change (Harrison & Rainer, 1992; Nickell & Pinto, 1986). One study posited that education is negatively related to computer anxiety (Igbaria & Parsuraman, 1989). The IBM study found that the younger, more educated, more affluent consumers are most likely to take steps to protect their privacy (Louis et al., 1999). Therefore, the following was hypothesized:

H9a: Gender, age, and education have a direct impact on the level of privacy concerns.

H9b: Gender, age, and education have a direct impact on the level of actual e-commerce activity.

METHOD

Sample and Procedure

The study was conducted during the spring and summer of 2000 to investigate the consumer privacy concerns and the relationships with behavioral intention to provide PII, actual e-commerce activity, and regulatory preferences. Since the research topic dealt with e-commerce over the Internet, the authors decided to put the questionnaire on the Internet. A study conducted by Brigham Young University's assessment office found that with electronic surveys, the response rate is better than with traditional mail surveys, the turnaround time is quicker, and data validity is nearly identical to mail surveys (Lindorf & Wygant, 2000).

Information on the survey was sent via email to the faculty and staff of the Department of Management at a large university in the southeast United States. In addition, a request for participants was announced in a few selected undergraduate management classes. While many criticize the use of students for business and social science research, other studies found students are adequate surrogates for decision makers (Hughes & Gibson, 1991; Remus, 1986). In this case, students are consumers who have to make decisions concerning their use of e-commerce over the Internet and providing PII to those Web sites. An unexpected group of respondents came from several participants contacting the authors for permission to give the survey URL out to people who would be interested in the study.

A total of 172 usable responses were submitted. Respondents were 63% men and 37% women. Sixty-two percent of the respondents were in the 18-29 age group; 26% were in the 30-49 age group; 12% were in the 50 and over age group. The respondents reported their education level as follows: 5% have a high school education or less, 42% have some college, and 53% are college graduates.

Questionnaire Development

The questionnaire was developed from scales and techniques used in prior research. Each section was coded in hypertext markup language (HTML), JavaScript, and Active Server Pages (ASP). JavaScript was used to ensure that certain responses were completed. ASP was used to select a random Web page for the respondent to examine and to submit the responses from the completed questionnaire to the database used to collect the data.

Once the questionnaire was completed, several colleagues reviewed it to check for completeness and understandability. Several other individuals (outside academia) were asked to test the questionnaire by completing the survey online and provide comments concerning any problems. The responses confirmed that the questionnaire was clear and understandable. Internal consistency of the appropriate scales was calculated using Cronbach's alpha. The alpha for PRIVCON was 0.72, 0.88 for IMPPP, and 0.92 for TK. All the alphas were above the cutoff value suggested by Nunally (1978) of 0.70 for hypothesized measures of a construct. The questionnaire items can be found in the appendix.

Measures

Several measures were required to evaluate the hypotheses. The following section describes each scale and the variable it measures.

Privacy Concern. Measurement of an individual's privacy concern (PRIVCON) was obtained by using items taken from existing scales (Culnan, 1993; Louis et al., 1999; Smith et al., 1996). Respondents scored all items on a 5-point Likert-type scale, with Strongly Disagree to Strongly Agree.

Actual E-Commerce Activity. The respondent's actual e-commerce activity (ACTUAL) was obtained by using a scale adapted from a previous study (Louis et al., 1999). Respondents were asked questions concerning e-commerce activities during the past year. For each item, the respondent chose between the following responses: Never, 1-2 times, 3-5 times, 5-10 times, and Over 10 times.

Importance of Privacy Policy. The perceived importance of a Web Site's privacy policy (IMPPP) was measured using a scale adapted from a previous study (Louis et al., 1999). The respondents rated the importance of components of an organization's privacy policy on a 5-point Likert-type scale ranging from Not At All Important to Absolutely Essential.

Regulatory Preference. Regulatory preference (REGPREF) was assessed by using a similar method to Milberg et al. (2000). Respondents were asked to indicate their agreement or disagreement (using a 5-point Likert-type scale, with Strongly Disagree and Strongly Agree as the endpoints) with the following questions: "the government should enact additional laws in order to protect the privacy of individuals..." and "Industries should rely on self-regulation in order to protect personal information collected..." The difference between the two measures (preference rating for governmental intervention minus preference rating for industry self-regulation) was used to indicate the degree to which the respondent preferred government regulation to industry self-regulation (Milberg et al., 2000).

Purchasing Habits. A consumer's propensity to purchase (PH) merchandise without the benefit of seeing and touching the item(s) before purchasing them was assessed using two items used by Culnan (1993). These items assessed whether the consumer had purchased items by mail or phone during the past year. Another item that covers Internet purchases was added. The respondents chose between the following responses: Never, 1-2 times, 3-5 times, 5-10 times, and Over 10 times.

Perceived Usefulness. Perceived usefulness (PERUSE) was assessed by asking the respondents how strongly they agree or disagree with a question concerning benefits of using the Internet as opposed to any potential privacy problems. Respondents rated the item on a 5-point Likert-type scale anchored by Strongly Disagree and Strongly Agree.

Prior Privacy Invasion Experience. Respondents were asked whether they had ever had a prior privacy invasion experience (PIE). The respondent checked either yes or no. A space was provided for an explanation of the privacy invasion experience.

Technology Knowledge. Technology knowledge (TK) was assessed by asking the respondent to rate the level of expertise with computer and Internet technology. For each item, the respondent chose between the following responses: Not at all knowledgeable, Somewhat knowledgeable, Knowledgeable, Very knowledgeable.

Demographic Items. Respondents were asked three demographic items: gender, age, and education. The range of responses for age was as follows: 18-29, 30-49, and 50+. Education was assessed using the following possible responses: High school or less, Some college, and College graduate.

RESULTS

Method of Analysis

EQS was used to determine the relationships among the variables shown in the path diagram shown in the model in Figure 1. EQS, a structural equation modeling software developed by Bentler (1990), implements a general mathematical and statistical approach to the analysis of linear structural equations. Using EQS, the researcher is able to check the overall goodness of fit of the proposed model and to compare the relative goodness of fit of competing models, thereby assessing the need for, and strength of, different path models (Bentler, 1990; Hartwick & Barki, 1994).

Overall Goodness of Fit

There is not one generally accepted measure of overall model goodness of fit, or even a set of optimal tests. Thus, we must rely on the use of multiple fit criteria. In this study, four goodness of fit indices were used. The first is the Π^2 statistic, which tests the proposed model against a fully saturated model–meaning that all variables are correlated (Bentler, 1990; Hartwick & Barki, 1994). A nonsignificant Π^2 value indicates good fit. However, the Π^2 is sensitive to sample size. In large samples, the Π^2 is almost always significant.

A better measure using the Π^2 statistic is to divide it by its degrees of freedom. In this case, the smaller the value, the better the fit. The literature gives several thresholds for reasonable fit: 5.0 or less (Wheaton, Muthen, Alwin, & Summers, 1977) and 3.0 or less (Carmines & McIver, 1981) and between 1.0 and 2.0 (Hair, Anderson, Tatham, & Black, 1998).

The most widely used overall goodness of fit indices are the goodness of fit index (GFI) and the adjusted goodness of fit index (AGFI). GFI measures the absolute fit of the measurement and structural models to the data. AGFI adjusts the value of the GFI to the degrees of freedom in the model. Thresholds for these indices are above 0.90 and above 0.80, respectively Chin and Todd, 1995, and Segars and Grover, 1993. A more restrictive threshold of above 0.90 for AGFI is often cited in IS research (Chin & Todd, 1995; Hair et al., 1998).

Another measure of goodness of fit is the comparative fit index (CFI), which is appropriate for all sample sizes and is thought to provide a more stable estimate than some of the other fit indices (Bentler, 1990; Hartwick & Barki, 1994). Values greater than 0.90 reflect acceptable fit.

Finally, the root mean square error of approximation (RMSEA) index measures the discrepancy in the population between the observed and estimated covariance matrices per degree of freedom. Thus, RMSEA is not affected by sample size (Garver & Mentzer, 1999). RMSEA is acceptable if the value is 0.08 or less (Hair et al., 1998).

The initial measurement model did not fit the data adequately (Π^2 = 123.54, GFI = 0.88, AGFI = 0.79, CFI = 0.61, RMSEA = 0.12) as illustrated in Table 2. Thus, the model was altered using the modification index provided by the LM test. The LM test represents the expected Π^2 decrease due to model modification (Bentler & Chou, 1993). The modifications based on this index are shown in Figure 2. The following were added to the model: covariances between some of the antecedent variables and direct paths between GENDER and IMPPP, between TK and IMPPP, and between PERUSE and REGPREF. The covariances added are supported by the significant correlations between the antecedent variables (see Table 1). Previous studies showing that gender and technology skills/knowledge have an impact on computer attitudes provide support for the direct paths that were added to the model (Agarwal & Prasad, 1999; Harrison & Rainer, 1992).

The final model fit the data quite well (Π^2 = 49.71, GFI = 0.95, AGFI = 0.89, CFI = 0.91, RMSEA = 0.06), as illustrated in Table 2, giving evidence that the model is supported. Table 3 illustrates the standardized coefficients and t-values for the paths between the antecedent variables and the PRIVCON and ACTUAL variables. All the covariances between the antecedent variables were significant (see Table 4).

Tests of Hypotheses

As with prior research, consumers are concerned about the protection of their personally identifiable information. The mean of the privacy concern measure was 3.76, where 1 = Strongly Disagree and 5 = Strongly Agree. The first four items of the measure resulted in more concern than the remaining three. The mean for the first four questions was 4.28, indicating a stronger concern with the protection of consumer personal information.

A list of the hypotheses and results can be found in Table 5. H1 was not supported (coefficient = -.056, t = .804). Higher levels of privacy concerns negatively impact actual e-commerce activity, however the results were not significantly significant. H2 was supported (coefficient = .145, t = 2.257). Support for H2 indicates that if the consumer feels that the benefits of using the Internet are sufficient, he or she will provide personal information and continue to participate in e-commerce activities despite any privacy concerns. There was strong support for H3 (coefficient = .425, t = 6.597). The results indicate that if a consumer is likely to buy goods and/or services sight unseen, it does not matter if the medium is the telephone, the mail, or the Internet.

Figure 2: Final model

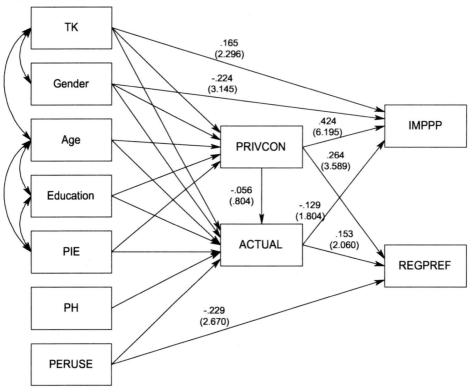

H4 was supported (coefficient = .424, t =6.195), indicating that as consumers are more concerned with the vulnerability of their personal information, the greater they perceive the importance of privacy policies. An additional finding from the final model shows a significant negative relationship between gender and the perceived importance of the privacy policy (coefficient = -.224, t = 3.145). The IBM study found that males place more importance on an organization's privacy policy (Louis et al., 1999). Technology knowledge was also found to impact the importance of privacy policies (coefficient = -.165, t = 2.296). H5 was not supported (coefficient = -.129, t = 1.804). Actual e-commerce usage does not significantly impact the perceived importance of an organization's privacy policy.

The findings indicate that H6 was supported (coefficient = .264, t = 3.589). As consumers become more concerned with the protection of their personal data, they become more likely to prefer governmental regulation to industry self-regulation. Another finding that was not hypothesized was the significant relationship between the actual e-commerce activity and regulatory preferences (coefficient = .153, t = 2.060). This possibly indicates that if a consumer provides personal information to a Web site, he or she would prefer stronger laws–as opposed to self-regulation–to ensure that the personal information is protected.

Table 1:Correlation matrix with standard deviations

	TK	GENDER	AGE	EDU	PIE	PH	PERUSE	PRIVCON	ACTUAL	IMPPP	REGPREF
TK	(1.496)										
GENDER	.271**	(.485)									
AGE	-.220**	-.061	(.687)								
EDU	.110	.046	.276**	(.591)							
PIE	.015	.058	.194**	.304**	(.431)						
PH	.171*	.101	.131*	.215**	.194**	(2.184)					
PERUSE	.067	.136*	.041	.024	-.099	.176*	(1.110)				
PRIVCON	-.041	.051	.164*	-.011	.310**	-.014	-.168*	(3.769)			
ACTUAL	.346**	.255*	-.113	.171*	.029	.480**	.265**	-.130*	(5.089)		
IMPPP	.040	-.189**	.102	-.050	.128*	-.146*	-.206**	.421**	-.197**	(2.574)	
REGPREF	-.059	.085	.010	.069	.149*	-.016	-.222**	.285**	.061	.212**	(1.774)

Note: Standard deviations enclosed in parentheses.

* Correlation significant at the 0.05 level; ** Correlation significant at the 0.01 level.

Table 2: Goodness-of-fit indices for the initial and final models

Measure	Initial Model	Final Model
Π^2 (d.f.)	123.543 (38)	49.712 (30)
p-value	<0.000	0.013
Π^2 / d.f.	3.251	1.657
GFI	0.878	0.948
AGFI	0.789	0.886
CFI	0.613	0.912
RMSEA	0.119	0.064

Table 3: Standardized coefficients and t-values for final model

	PRIVCON	ACTUAL	IMPPP	REGPREF
TK	-.011(.141)	.185(2.681)	.165(2.296)	
GENDER	.066(.884)	-.166(2.475)	-.224(3.145)	
AGE	.170(2.154)	-.145(2.035)		
EDUCATION	-.170(2.130)	.107(1.506)		
PIE	.333(4.332)	-.038(.522)		
PH		.425(6.597)		
PERUSE		.145(2.257)		
PRIVCON		-.056(.804)	.424(6.195)	.264(3.589)
ACTUAL			-.129(1.804)	.153(2.060)

Table 4: Coefficients and t-values for covariances between antecedent variables

Covariance	Coefficient	T-Value
TK - GENDER	.256	3.255
TK - AGE	-.232	3.128
AGE - EDUCATION	.284	3.589
AGE - PIE	.205	2.635
EDUCATION - PIE	.313	3.811

Table 5: Hypotheses and results

	Hypotheses	Results
H1:	Higher levels of privacy concerns will result in lower levels of actual e-commerce activity.	Not supported
H2:	Higher levels of perceived usefulness result in higher levels of actual e-commerce activity.	Supported
H3:	The more likely a consumer is to purchase merchandise or services via mail, telephone, or over the Internet during the past year, the higher the level of actual e-commerce use.	Supported
H4:	The higher the level of privacy concern, the higher the perceived importance of privacy policies.	Supported
H5:	The higher the level of actual e-commerce activity, the more important a consumer will view an organization's privacy policy.	Not supported
H6:	There is a positive direct relationship between consumer privacy concerns and regulatory preferences.	Supported
H7a:	Privacy concerns are higher if an individual has experienced a prior privacy invasion.	Supported
H7b:	An individual's actual e-commerce activity decreases if the individual has experienced a prior privacy invasion.	Not supported
H8a:	Higher levels of technology knowledge increase the privacy concerns of an individual.	Not supported
H8b:	Higher levels of technology knowledge increase the levels of actual e-commerce use.	Supported
H9a:	Gender, age, and education have a direct impact on the level of privacy concerns.	Age – Supported Education – Supported Gender – Not supported
H9b:	Gender, age, and education have a direct impact on the level of actual e-commerce activity.	Age – Supported Education – Not supported Gender - Supported

One of the two parts to H7 was supported. H7a was supported (coefficient = .333, t = 4.332), indicating that if an individual has experienced a privacy invasion experience, he or she will be more concerned with the protection of their personal data. H7b was not supported (coefficient = -.038, t = .522), indicating that even a privacy invasion experience will not keep an individual from participating in e-commerce over the Internet.

Only one of the two-part H8 was supported. H8a (coefficient = -.011, t = .141) was not supported. Increased technology knowledge did not have a significant effect on privacy concerns. However, higher levels of technology knowledge do tend to significantly increase actual e-commerce use (H8b; coefficient = .185, t = 2.681).

H9a was partially supported. Age and education had a significant effect on the level of privacy concerns (coefficient = .170, t = 2.154; coefficient = -.170, t = 2.130; respectively). Gender did not significantly impact the level of privacy concern (coefficient = .066, t = .884). H9b was also partially supported. Education does not have a significant impact on the actual level of e-commerce activity (coefficient = .107, t = 1.506). Age and gender did impact the level of actual e-commerce activity (coefficient = -.145, t = 2.035; coefficient = .166, t = 2.475; respectively). Younger individuals tend to use the Internet more than older individuals and males tend to use the Internet more that females.

DISCUSSION

A specific research objective in this study was to examine the relationship between an individual's privacy concerns and e-commerce use. More specifically, the purpose was to ascertain whether privacy policies have an impact on actual e-commerce activities and whether privacy concerns impact an individual's preference for government regulation or industry self-regulation for protection of personal information. To this end, we proposed and tested a model based on existing theories.

In general, the findings of the study were consistent with theoretical expectations, as most of the hypotheses were supported. The most surprising finding was that higher levels of privacy concern (H1) did not have a significant impact on actual e-commerce activity. This finding coupled with the perceived usefulness (H2) could possibly indicate that consumers will continue using the Internet if they feel the benefits and convenience of the Internet outweigh any privacy problems. In addition, consumers who have privacy invasion experiences are more concerned about privacy (H7a) issues but do not necessarily decrease actual e-commerce usage (H7b). Again, this can help explain the continued rise in e-commerce use in the face of parallel increased privacy concerns.

It is clear that individuals are concerned about the privacy of their personal information. Numerous surveys over the years have indicated a high percentage of respondents are very concerned about this issue (GVU, 1998; Harris et al., 1991, 1994, 1996; Louis et al., 1999). High levels of concern over the privacy issue have led many to express a desire for regulatory control. Our findings concerning the relationship between privacy concerns and regulatory preferences (H6) are consistent with those found by other studies (GVU, 1998; Milberg et al., 2000). The findings showed that consumers prefer government regulation to industry self-regulation with regards to the protection of their personally identifiable information.

Individuals who have higher levels of privacy concerns feel that privacy policies are important (H4). However, the negative relationship (marginal) between actual e-commerce activity and the importance of privacy policies indicates that consumers who use the Internet more place less importance on those policies. This finding suggests that high-level Internet users feel that privacy policies are either inadequate or ineffective.

Limitations

Although previous research provides support that students are acceptable surrogates for decision makers (Hughes & Gibson, 1991; Remus, 1986), other researchers criticize the use. The use of students in this study was justified due to the subject nature and the fact that they are consumers. Since students are usually comfortable Internet users they should be suitable subjects.

Implications and Directions for Future Research

The findings of this study have regulatory, organizational, and research implications. Now, more than ever, it appears that consumers are ready for government intervention in order to protect their personal information. This affects organizations because their efforts at self-regulation did not work well enough according to the FTC (2000). While great strides were made towards protecting the personal information of consumers, self-imposed privacy policies did not get the job done (FTC, 2000). It appears that laws will be passed (Schwartz, 2000), organizations will have to make changes in order to be in compliance, and this may necessitate a change in business models for many e-commerce organizations.

There are many opportunities to develop and extend models dealing with the privacy issue. Further research could include a study to align the attitudes of consumers in relation to behavioral intentions and actual use utilizing the TRA and TAM models. Researchers could also expand the antecedent variables to gain a better understanding of the underlying issues surrounding privacy concerns, behavioral intention, and actual use of e-commerce or the Internet in general.

Another avenue of research would be to determine why consumers are indicating a preference for government regulation for protection of their personally identifiable information. Focus groups could be set up to determine why high-level Internet users feel that industry self-regulation is not as desirable as government regulation for this issue.

CONCLUSION

Research on the issue of privacy, while not new, has recently become a hot topic. The Internet and the EU Data Protection Directive have played a large role in this interest. In addition, media attention has made the consumer very aware of the data privacy issue. They have become very aware of just how vulnerable their personal information is and they want something done about it.

Relatively speaking, e-commerce is new and not fully understood. E-commerce is growing faster than anyone expected and, of course, will experience growing pains such as the backlash stemming from the ability to invade the privacy of Internet users and the lack of data protection against any invasions. Research such as this study should help organizations understand just how critical the privacy issue is and allow adjustments to their business models to accommodate the concerns of consumers. In the long run, protecting the data privacy of consumers will help ensure success and longevity for organizations in this new economy.

APPENDIX
Questionnaire (adapted from the online version)
Instructions: Read each question carefully and either click on the button indicating your answer or type in your answer in the space provided.

Privacy Concerns

How strongly do you agree or disagree with the following statements?

	Strongly Disagree	Disagree	Unsure	Agree	Strongly Agree
a. Companies should never share personal information with other companies unless it has been authorized by the individuals who provided the information.	O	O	O	O	O
b. Companies should take more steps to make sure that unauthorized people cannot access personal information in their computers.	O	O	O	O	O
c. Companies are collecting too much personal information about me.	O	O	O	O	O
d. Consumers have lost all control over how personal information is collected and used by companies.	O	O	O	O	O
e. Most businesses handle the personal information they collect about customers in a proper and confidential way.*	O	O	O	O	O
f. Existing laws and organizational practices in the U.S. provide a reasonable level of consumer protection today.*	O	O	O	O	O
g. Business Web sites seem to be doing an adequate job providing notices and informing visitors how any personal information collected will be used.*	O	O	O	O	O

Regulatory Preferences

How strongly do you agree or disagree with the following statements?

	Strongly Disagree	Disagree	Unsure	Agree	Strongly Agree
a. The government should enact additional laws in order to protect the privacy of individuals using the Internet.	O	O	O	O	O
b. Industries should rely on self-regulation in order to protect personal information collected on Internet sites.	O	O	O	O	O

Importance of Privacy Policies

Many individuals and organizations feel that companies should adopt privacy policies. Indicate how important it is for a company to adopt and communicate or provide the following to its customers.

	Not At All Important	Somewhat Important	Important	Very Important	Absolutely Essential
a. An explanation to customers of what personal information is collected about them and how it will be used.	O	O	O	O	O
b. A choice to consumers not to have their name passed along to other companies for their marketing purposes.	O	O	O	O	O
c. A procedure allowing customers to see what personal information the company has stored about them and to make any needed corrections.	O	O	O	O	O

Internet Activity

During the past year, have you personally...

	Never	1 - 2 Times	3 - 5 Times	5 - 10 Times	Over 10 Times
a. Visited a Web site to get information?	O	O	O	O	O
b. Provided personal information to a Web site such as your date of birth, your age, or your address?	O	O	O	O	O
c. Used a credit card to pay for information purchases on the Internet?	O	O	O	O	O
d. Used a credit card to pay for goods or services purchased on the Internet?	O	O	O	O	O
e. Conducted home banking online (i.e., checking balances or paying bills online)?	O	O	O	O	O
f. Invested in the stock market or traded stocks online?	O	O	O	O	O
g. Participated in an online auction as a seller?	O	O	O	O	O
h. Participated in an online auction as a buyer?	O	O	O	O	O

Purchasing Habits

During the past year, have you personally...

	Never	1 - 2 Times	3 - 5 Times	5 - 10 Times	Over 10 Times
a. Bought something from a catalog or brochure sent to your residence?	O	O	O	O	O
b. Bought any product or service offered to you by a telephone call to your residence?	O	O	O	O	O
c. Bought any product or service through a Web site on the Internet?	O	O	O	O	O

Perceived Usefulness

How strongly do you agree or disagree with the following statement?

	Strongly Disagree	Disagree	Unsure	Agree	Strongly Agree
a. The benefits of using the Internet to get information, send e-mail, and to shop far outweigh the privacy problems that are currently being worked on.	O	O	O	O	O

Prior Privacy Invasion Experience

As far as you know, as a consumer...
Have you personally ever been the victim of what you felt was an
improper invasion of privacy by a business or organization?   ☐ No   ☐ Yes

Technology Knowledge

How knowledgeable would you say you are when it comes to...

	Not At All Knowledgeable	Somewhat Knowledgeable	Knowledgeable	Very Knowledgeable
a. Computer technology?	O	O	O	O
b. Internet technology?	O	O	O	O

Demographic Information

Gender   O Female
         O Male

Age   O 18 - 29
      O 30 - 49
      O 50+

Education   O High school or less
            O Some college
            O College graduate

REFERENCES

Agarwal, R. and Prasad, J. (1999). Are individual differences germane to the acceptance of new information technologies? *Decision Sciences*, 30(2), 361-191.

Agranoff, M. H. (1991). Controlling the threat to personal privacy: Corporate policies must be created. *Journal of Information Systems Management*, 8, 48-52.

Ajzen, I. and Fishbein, M. (1980). *Understanding Attitudes and Predicting Social Behavior*. Englewood Cliffs, NJ: Prentice-Hall.

Bentler, P. M. (1990). Comparative fit indexes in structural models. *Psychological Bulletin*, 107(2), 234-246.

Bentler, P. M. and Chou, C.-P. (1993). Some new covariance structure model improvement statistics. In Bollen, K. A. and Long, J. S. (Eds.), *Testing

Structural Equation Models. Newbury Park, CA: Sage.

Buckley, P. (1999). The emerging digital economy II, *US Department of Commerce*. Retrieved February 1, 2000 on the World Wide Web: http://www.ecommerce.gov/ede/chapter1.html.

Carmines, E. G. and McIver, J. P. (1981). Analyzing models with unobserved variables: Analysis of covariance structures. In Bohrnstedt, G. W. and Borgatta, E. F. (Eds.), *Social Measurement: Current Issues*. Newbury Park, CA: Sage.

Chin, W.W. and Todd, P.A. (1995). On the use, usefulness, and ease of use of structural equation modeling in MIS research: A note of caution. *MIS Quarterly*, 19(2), 237-246.

Cranor, L. F., Reagle, J. and Ackerman, M. S. (1999). Beyond concern: Understanding net users' attitudes about online privacy. *AT&T Labs-Research Technical Report TR 99.4.3*. Retrieved February 1, 2000 on the World Wide Web: http://www.research.att.com/library/TRs/99/99.4/99.4.3/report.htm.

Culnan, M. J. (1993). How did they get my name? An exploratory investigation of consumer attitudes toward secondary information use. *MIS Quarterly*, 17(3), 341-363.

Culnan, M. J. (1999a). *The Georgetown Internet Privacy Policy Survey*. Retrieved December 1, 1999 on the World Wide Web: http://www.msb.edu/faculty/culnanm/gippshome.html.

Culnan, M. J. (1999b). Privacy and the top 100 Web sites: A report to the Federal Trade Commission. *The Online Privacy Alliance*. Retrieved December 1, 1999 on the World Wide Web: http://www.msb.edu/faculty/culnanm/gippshome.html.

Davis, F. D., Bagozzi, R. P. and Warshaw, P. R. (1989). User acceptance of computer technology: A comparison of two theoretical models. *Management Science*, 35(8), 982-1003.

Drucker, P. F. (1999). Beyond the information revolution, *The Atlantic Monthly*.

Fishbein, M. and Ajzen, I. (1975). *Belief, Attitude, Intention and Behavior: An Introduction to Theory and Research*. Reading, MA: Addison-Wesley.

FTC. (1998). Privacy online: A report to congress. *Federal Trade Commission*. Retrieved on the World Wide Web: http://www.ftc.gov/privacy.

FTC. (1999). Self-regulation and privacy online: A report to Congress. *Federal Trade Commission*. Retrieved December 1, 1999 on the World Wide Web: http://www.ftc.gov/privacy.

FTC. (2000). Privacy online: Fair information practices in the electronic marketplace. *Federal Trade Commission*. Retrieved June 21, 2000 on the World Wide Web: http://www.ftc.gov/reports.

Garfinkel, S. (2000). Protecting your privacy concerns about third-party monitoring putting a damper on e-commerce. *Boston Globe*, January, C4.

Garver, M. S. and Mentzer, J. T. (1999). Logistics research methods: Employing structural equation modeling to test for construct validity. *Journal of Business Logistics*, 20(1), 33-57.

GVU. (1998). GVU's 10th WWW user survey. *Georgia Tech Graphics, Visualization & Usability Center*. Retrieved on the World Wide Web: http://www.gvu.gatech.edu/user_surveys.

Hair, J. F., Jr., Anderson, R. E., Tatham, R. L. and Black, W. C. (1998). *Multivariate Data Analysis* (5th ed.). Englewood Cliffs, NJ: Prentice Hall.

Harris Louis and Associates and Westin, A. F. (1991). *Harris-Equifax Consumer Privacy Survey 1991*. Atlanta, Georgia: Equifax, Inc.

Harris Louis and Associates and Westin, A. F. (1994). *Equifax-Harris Consumer Privacy Survey 1994*. Atlanta, Georgia: Equifax, Inc.

Harris Louis and Associates and Westin, A. F. (1996). *The 1996 Equifax-Harris Consumer Privacy Survey*. Atlanta, Georgia: Equifax, Inc.

Harrison, A. W. and Rainer, R. K., Jr. (1992). The influence of individual differences on skill in end-user computing. *Journal of Management Information Systems*, 9(1), 93-111.

Hartwick, J. and Barki, H. (1994). Explaining the role of user participation in information system use. *Management Science*, 40(4), 440-465.

Hoffman, D. L., Novak, T. P. and Chatterjee, P. (1993). Commercial scenarios for the Web: Opportunities and challenges, *Journal of Computer-Mediated Communication*, 1.

Hughes, C. T. and Gibson, M. L. (1991). Students as surrogates for managers in a decision-making environment: An experimental study. *Journal of Management Information Systems*, 8(2), 153-166.

Igbaria, M. and Parsuraman, S. (1989). A path analytic study of individual characteristics, computer anxiety, and attitudes toward microcomputers. *Journal of Management*, 15(3), 373-388.

LaRussa, R. S. (2000, June 9). Cover letter to U.S. organizations. *Acting Under Secretary for International Trade Administration*. Retrieved on the World Wide Web: http://www.ita.doc.gov/td/ecomm/LaRussaLetJune2000.htm.

Levin, T. and Gordon, C. (1989). Effect of gender and computer experience on attitudes towards computers. *Journal of Educational Computing Research*, 5(1), 69-88.

Lindorf, R. and Wygant, S. (2000). Surveying collegiate surfers-Web methodology or mythology? *Quirks Marketing Research Review*. Retrieved June 20, 2000 on the World Wide Web: http://www.surveynetwork.com/surveys.asp.

Louis Harris & Associates Inc. (1999). *IBM Multi-National Consumer Privacy Survey*. New York, NY: IBM Global Services.

Mason, R. O. (1986). Four ethical issues of the information age. *MIS Quarterly*, 10(1), 4-12.

Milberg, S. J., Burke, S. J., Smith, H. J. and Kallman, E. A. (1995). Values, personal information privacy, and regulatory approaches. *Communications of the ACM*, 38(12), 65-74.

Milberg, S. J., Smith, H. J. and Burke, S. J. (2000). Information privacy: Corporate management and national regulation. *Organization Science*, 11(1), 35-57.

Mogg, J. F. (2000, July 27). Letter from Commission Services transmitting the European Commission's adequacy finding, European Commission Internal Market Director-General. Retrieved September 7, 2000 on the World Wide Web: http://www.ita.doc.gov/td/ecom/EUletter27JulyHeader.htm.

Nickell, G. S. and Pinto, J. N. (1986). The computer attitude scale. *Computers in Human Behavior*, 2, 301-306.

Nunally, J.C. (1978). *Psychometric Theory*, 2nd ed., McGraw-Hill: New York.

OECD. (1997). OECD Policy Brief No. 1-1997: Electronic commerce. *Organization for Economic Co-operation and Development*. Retrieved March 7, 2000 on the World Wide Web: http://www.oecd.org/publications/Pol_brief/9701_Pol.htm.

Oracle. (1999). The Internet changes everything. *CIO*.

PwC. (1999a). Electronic Business Outlook. *PricewaterhouseCoopers LLP*. Retrieved July 13, 2000 on the World Wide Web: http://www.e-business.pwcglobal.com/pdf/PwCPrivacy.pdf. C:\MyFiles\ECPrivacy.wpd.

PwC. (1999b). Privacy...A weak-link in the cyber-chain: Privacy risk management in the information economy. *PricewaterhouseCoopers LLP*. Retrieved July 13, 2000 on the World Wide Web: http://www.e-business.pwcglobal.com/pdf/PwCPrivacy.dbf.

Remus, W. (1986). Graduate students as surrogates for managers in experiments on business decision making. *Journal of Business Research*, 14, 19-25.

Santosus, M. (1998). Too much ado about nothing. *CIO*, August.

Schwartz, J. (2000). FTC to propose new online privacy rules. *The Washington Post*, E1.

Segars, A. H. and Grover, V. (1993). Re-examining perceived ease of use and usefulness: A confirmatory factor analysis. *MIS Quarterly*, 17(4), 517-525.

Smith, H. J. (1993). Privacy policies and practices: Inside the organizational maze. *Communications of the ACM*, 36(12), 105-122.

Smith, H. J. (1994). *Managing Privacy: Information Technology and Corporate America*. Chapel Hill, NC: University of North Carolina Press.

Smith, H. J., Milberg, S. J. and Burke, S. J. (1996). Information privacy: Measuring individuals' concerns about organizational practices. *MIS Quarterly*, 20(2), 167195.

Stone, E. F., Gardner, D. G., Gueutal, H. G. and McClure, S. (1983). A field experiment comparing information—privacy values, beliefs, and attitudes across several types of organizations. *Journal of Applied Psychology*, 68(3), 459-468.

Stone, E. F. and Stone, D. L. (1990). Privacy in organizations: Theoretical issues, research findings, and protection mechanisms. In Rowland, K. M. and Ferris, F. R. (Eds.), *Research in Personnel and Human Resources Management*, 349-411. Greenwich, CT: JAI Press.

Swanson, E. B. (1982). Measuring user attitudes in MIS research: A review. *OMEGA*, 10, 157-165.

Swanson, E. B. (1988). *Information System Implementation: Bridging the Gap Between Design and Utilization*. Homewood, IL: Irwin.

US DOC. (2000). Defying definition. *U.S. Department of Commerce*. Retrieved March 7, 2000 on the World Wide Web: http://www.ecommerce.gov/6.htm.

Westin, A. F. (1967). *Privacy and Freedom*. New York: Atheneum.

Wheaton, B. B., Muthen, B., Alwin, D. F. and Summers, G. F. (1977). Assessing reliability and stability in panel models. In Heise, D. R. (Ed.), *Sociological Methodology*. San Francisco: Jossey-Bass.

Chapter VIII

Aggression on the Networks: An Australian Viewpoint

William Hutchinson
Edith Cowan University, Australia

Matthew Warren
Deakin University, Australia

This chapter examines the attitudes of Australian IS/IT managers to the concept of cyber-vigilantism. Also, it explores the policies and procedures which have been set in place by various organizations to cope with concerted attacks on their systems. It finds that although a majority of managers do approve of the concept of "striking back', only a minority are prepared for this eventuality. There appears to be complacency about the threats posed by organized, offensive attackers.

INTRODUCTION

This exploratory research was undertaken to establish a general impression of the attitudes of professionals in business and government to the concept of cyber-vigilantism. It was undertaken as an initial project to provide the context for a larger, formal international survey. Cyber-vigilantism is the proactive process of responding to information attacks by hackers (from whatever source) with corresponding attacks on them. In short, it is hacking the hackers. The military and intelligence services have developed much of the technology for this. It is bringing the military concept of "information warfare' (Schwartau, 1996; Dearth, Williamson, 1996; Knecht, 1996; Waltz, 1998; Denning, 1999) into the civilian world. The survey was based on an initial, informal survey carried out by Schwartau (1999) using an

Internet site to gauge the attitudes of (mostly) American managers toward non-passive strategies against hackers. The survey described in this paper, attempts to specifically seek out the attitudes of Australian IT managers to this "offensive" method of information security. To obtain as wide a range as possible, the sample included organizations of as many sizes and industry types as could be found.

BACKGROUND

Cobb (1998) has outlined the potential threats to the Australian economy from information warfare attacks. In a world, where hackers claim they can easily crash the whole Internet (Mosquera, 1998), "hackivists' manipulate the Web sites of companies to discredit them (Goldberg, 1999), and the American Army's director of information systems says that the military does not "have a prayer or hope defending ourselves" against hacker attacks (Elvin, 1999), then there is potentially a very serious security problem for management. Wray (1999) feels that "electronic civil disobedience" will increase in volume and effectiveness. Many types of organizations can be targets of interest groups, for example, government departments (numerous issues), mining (environmental issues), pharmaceutical companies (animal rights issues), and banks (various issues). This list is easily expanded. As this is a new source of threat, it appears that many Australian businesses and government departments have not seriously considered it. The level of "passive" security is highly developed, but the potential for concerted, organized, and aggressive attacks from other than sole hackers has not been included in management thinking. The survey results outlined below tend to support this assertion.

A problem with the area of computer crime in Australia is ambiguity of the law. This is also confused by the potential international legal implications of foreign attacks. For instance, in the state of New South Wales, the Crimes Act 1900 (NSW), Section 310, states it is illegal to "destroy, erase, insert, or alter data in a computer system or interfere with, interrupt, or obstruct the lawful use of a computer" (Internet Law Bulletin, 1998, p.14). However, it is rare for these offenses to be detected, prosecuted, or proven.

Schwartau (1999, p.1) outlines the frustration of management in the American context and lists the following as the main causes:
- hacking events are increasing by huge numbers;
- the assaults are becoming more aggressive and hostile;
- the attack tools are automated and require few technical skills;
- political and social motivations have invited civil disobedience;
- investigation of hacking events is very difficult;
- law enforcement is not up to the task of investigating cyber crimes for lack of manpower, resources, and interest;
- corporate America distrusts law enforcement to prosecute and keep any investigations secret.

At this point, the definition of a "hacker' should be introduced. This has been the subject of debate in computing circles. Caelli et al. (1989) provide two

explanations of the term:
1. In programming, it denotes a computing enthusiast. The term is normally applied
   to people who take a delight in experimenting with system hardware (the
   electronics), software (computer programs) and communication systems
   (telephone lines, in most cases).
2. The popular view of data (information) security, an unauthorized user who tries
   to gain entry into a computer or computer network by defeating the computers'
   access and/or security controls.

Table 1 illustrates the extent of the hacking problem, based upon figures taken
from a series of surveys concerned about all forms of IT abuse conducted by the UK
Audit Commission (Audit Commission 1990, 1994, 1998). These surveys consider
the general problem of computer abuse, encompassing various types of incidents
(including hacking, viruses, fraud, sabotage and theft) across a number of indus-
tries/sectors (including government, healthcare, banking, retail and education). The
table indicates the consequences of the incidents in terms of financial losses (which
may have occurred directly or indirectly as a result of the incidents). However, it is
likely that other, less measurable consequences may also have occurred as a result
(e.g., disruption to operations, breaches of personal privacy or commercial confidentiality, etc.).

As an aside, it is worth noting that the significant increases in the "total
incidents" figures in the 1994 and 1998 surveys are largely accounted for by the
widespread emergence of the virus problem. It should also be noted that these
figures only refer to the reported incidents–it is frequently speculated that the true
figures may be much higher than this, but organizations are choosing to remain silent
in order to avoid adverse publicity and the like (Nycum and Parker, 1990).

Research from around the world also back ups these findings. Within the USA
national surveys (CSI/FBI, 1999) showed that 51% of the total number of respondents acknowledged losses due to IT abuse; however, only 31% could quantify the
damage. Nevertheless, the dollar amount represent by that loss represented US$124
million.

Australian national research surveys (Deloitte Touche Tohmatsu/Victoria
Police, 1999) showed of the total number of respondents only 8% had experienced
attacks that resulted in losses over AU$10,000 and 4% of which the losses were over
AU$100,000, resulting in a overall minimal loss of AU$168,000.

It is with this background that the survey was designed and implemented.

Table 1: Reported incidents of computer hacking

	1990	**1994**	**1998**
Total abuse incidents reported	180	537	510
No. hacking incidents	26	15	56
Hacking as % of total	14%	3%	11%
Resulting loss (£)	£31,500	£16,220	£360,860

Rationale and Drawbacks of Cyber-Vigilantism

The concept of retaliation to an information attack must be considered in relation to the benefits to the organization. One motivation may be "vengeance." However, this personal and subjective rationale has no meaning in organizational terms unless it is coupled with "deterrence." The idea that any attacker who can be identified will be subjected to the same sort of aggression might be a deterrent to that particular attacker and others in general. However, as many of the comments below indicate, it might be a trigger to some attackers to re-attack. Hence, a vicious cycle of attack and retaliation may develop. This is not the stuff of rational management, although in many competitive environments it is present.

Another major inhibitor to the practice is that of legal liability and public relations. Hacking a hacker puts the organization in the same legal position as the original attacker. Whilst the chance of getting prosecuted may be the same, the likely financial penalties may not. The chance of destroying equipment and/or data of an innocent whose address has been used illegally might be a public relations nightmare if an organization were caught.

Forno and Baklarz (1999, p.54) state, "… The goal of Information Warfare is not to symbolically 'kill' the intruder but to fend off his every attempt to penetrate the system." This implies a dynamic but passive approach. However, this approach is the very reason why the attacker might always hold the initiative.

Attacks on the systems can have positive outcomes. The lessons learned about security weaknesses can make the protective system much more effective. Keeping the potential for aggressive attack in the forefront of security management can also revitalize such things as access monitoring.

METHODOLOGY

The survey was sent out to 528 IT managers in two states of Australia (Western Australia and Victoria). This figure does not include 38 surveys, which were returned because of closure of businesses, etc. The names of the organizations

Table 2: Responses by organization type

Organizational type	Responses	Percentage
Finance	11	10
Manufacturing	10	9
Mining	5	5
Wholesale	7	6
Retail	5	5
Government	28	25
Education	12	11
Other	33	29
Total Replies	111	100

Table 3: Responses by organization size (respondents were asked to pick the largest size option that was applicable to them)

Organization size	Responses	Percentage
<10	13	12
>10	5	5
>20	6	5
>50	10	9
>100	16	14
>250	14	13
>500	8	7
>1000	18	16
>5000	13	12
>10000	8	7
Total Replies	111	100

surveyed were obtained from business telephone directories and databases of IT managers held at Deakin and Edith Cowan universities. The responses were anonymous. Each survey form was supplied with a prepaid envelope, and names of individuals or organizations were not required. As some of the questions were of a sensitive nature, this anonymity was thought to add to the validity of the data. The survey was sent out in February and March 1999. There were 111 valid responses, giving a response rate of 21% (61 from Western Australia and 50 from Victoria). Information on the variety of respondents by type of organization is shown in Table 2, and the size (determined by employee numbers) in Table 3.

Rationale for Each Question

Table 4 lists the questions and the results for each. Each question had space for more specific comments. Also, there was an area for overall comments at the end of the questionnaire. Each of the questions was designed to discover either an attitude toward aggressive responses to information attack or to find the level of organizational awareness for a particular aspect. The questions mentioned in this section can be found in Table 4.

Question 1 "sets the scene" and partially establishes the respondent's attitude. Questions 3, 4, and 5 develop this by establishing the attitude toward their own situation (Question 3), the level of attack to which it is appropriate to respond (Questions 4a–4e), and to see if there was any contradiction (Question 5, which asks if it is more appropriate for the "authorities" to respond rather than themselves).

Question 2 ascertains the respondent's knowledge of previous attacks. Questions 8 and 9 establish if any policies have been established in relation to hacker attacks. This was also to investigate if those organizations which had been attacked were more likely to have policies for these events.

Question 6 was designed to establish the respondent's attitude toward the right of an organization's system to exist. It is coupled with Question 7, which establishes the attitude toward their own system's "rights."

Question 10 has the purpose of establishing the level of perceived threat from competitors.

RESULTS AND DISCUSSION

All results were tested for significance at the 5% and 1% levels of probability (p=0.05 and p=0.01). The analysis treated the results of each question as a binomial set. The "Undecided" answers were collapsed into the smallest number of answers in the "Yes" or "No" categories. For instance, for Question 1, the 4% of "Undecided" answers were added to the 23% of "No" answers. This was then tested for significance at the two levels of probability. All results were found to be significant at the 5% level, and all but two sets were significant at the 1% level. The results not found to be significant at the 1% level were those for Questions 5 and 8.

Also, the research was interested in the textual answers to each question as they added richness to the responses, enabling a greater understanding at this preliminary stage.

Attitude Toward Aggressive Response

Table 4 contains the basic answers. The first question established that a significant majority of respondents (73%) agreed, in principle, with someone else (the Pentagon) "striking back" to an attack. There was no pattern in the written comments to this question. Comments ranged from concern about legality ("Seems appropriate but is it legal") to a satisfaction that something is being done ("One for the good guys"). When asked about their **own** responses to an attack (Question 3), the respondents seemed less sure. Although a majority (65%) agreed it was appropriate to respond, it was less than that for others to retaliate. This may have been a reflection of the example (the Pentagon), where some respondents perceived "national security" as being an overriding element. The majority of comments expressed concern about the legality of the action, for example:

- "I would have to seek legal advice before I attack back";
- "May be a problem legally";
- "Must stay within the legal system."

Others reinforced the need for some sort of response:

- "Certainly there needs to be a response level";
- "History has shown that being passive is only an invite to do it again."

By and large, the comments showed support for striking back over and above other considerations:

- "Two wrongs do not make it right versus protection of my space and property. The latter wins."

Table 4: Survey questions and percentage responses

Question	Answers (% of total)		
	Yes	No	?
1.Recently, the Pentagon responded to a series of hacker attacks by striking back with software, which disabled the attackers' browsers. Do you think this was a valid and appropriate response?	73	23	4
2.To your knowledge has your organisation ever been the victim of an attack?	14	80	6
3.Do you feel that your organisation has a right to respond to an attack in this manner?	65	30	5
4.When do you think it is valid to respond to an attack? a. Someone attempts to enter your network? b. Someone reads some of your system data? c. Someone reads some of your applications data? d. Someone attempts to alter data? e. Someone tries to destroy a part of your system?	70 80 81 90 93	24 16 16 9 6	6 4 4 1 1
5.Is it more appropriate to allow the authorities and the legal system to deal with hackers?	60	26	14
6.Do people have the right to attack child pornography and other 'controversial' web sites?	23	64	13
7.Do you feel that your organisation has the right to expect others to respect the integrity of your sites?	98	0	2
8.Has your organisation developed a policy about dealing with such things as hacker attacks?	33	60	7
9.Has your organisation investigated offensive software?	20	73	7
10.Do you believe an attack from a competitor organisation is a real threat?	30	66	4

Question 4 investigates the trigger point for retaliation. The question presents events of increasing damage to a system. As the potential damage increases, the support rises, going from 70% to 93%. There seems a slight contradiction in these answers. Although only 65% of respondents supported actively responding to an attack in Question 3, 70% support a response for an attempt to enter a network in Question 4. Strangely, the comments are also much more aggressive and assertive in tone (for example, "Any attack should not be tolerated," "Entry without prior advice or authority equals trespass"). However, despite the overwhelming (93%) agreement to response to an attempt to destroy a part of the system, there still appears to be trepidation present:

- "Yes, but only after a warning has been given, otherwise it may be an innocent browser":

- "How do you distinguish an attack from something else?";
- "Respond in the sense of stopping the attack, not striking back."

Contradiction in the responses is also exposed in the answers to Question 5, which deals with the appropriateness of the "authorities" to deal with hackers. Schwartau (1999) contends that frustration with the legal process and other official channels has a large influence on American management's support of strike back options. However, the respondents to this survey showed support for preferentially using the authorities to solve the problem (60%). This seems to conflict with the answers to Questions 3 and 4, where there is majority support for organizational response. It is perhaps reflective of the desired state of affairs rather than the practical aspects of the situation. For instance, Question 3 asks for support in principle of striking back, and, although it did get majority support, this was not as high as when the specifics of Question 4 were outlined. The comments for Question 5 also expose some interesting views, for example:

- "Needs a dual approach";
- "Both needed. Authorities determine their own priorities based on dollar value of damage done. Not appropriate";
- "What authority? What time frame? What stops the hacker in the meantime?"

Expanding on this last comment, many of the others also reflect on the time element of official response, for example:

- "Ineffective and too slow--How can they react in time?";
- "Too slow and uncertain."

Other comments expose the enormity of effective official response, for example:

- "Are you kidding? Across international borders and with no ability to establish definite proof";
- "They may have no way of tracing the offender after the event";
- "They won't get their act together in time."

However, the contradictions may not be as wide as stated. Only 34 respondents answered "yes" to both Questions 3 and 5. Of these, 47% who thought it right to respond themselves also thought it more appropriate that the authorities do so (54% of those who thought it appropriate for the authorities also thought it was alright for themselves to retaliate). From this, it can be established that about one half had the conflicting opinion that they should retaliate themselves and it was more appropriate for the authorities to do so.

Organizational Awareness, Threats and Response

It appears from Question 2 that the majority of respondents (80%) have not experienced (or have knowledge of) an attack on their systems. This may reflect effective security. Paradoxically, it can also expose a weak monitoring system. Whatever the reasons, it gives no real incentive to research or produce policies and procedures to deal with attacks, except at the general risk management process within the organization. This is reflected in the answers to Question 8, where 60% of the respondents declare they have no policy for dealing with hackers.

Most comments to Question 8 declare "passive" security measures, for example:
- "We have firewalls, etc. Preventive rather than attack";
- "In a sense, as we have installed firewalls, system security, and access control."

The perceived lack of attacks could also account for the majority of respondents not investigating "offensive software." A small number of the respondents confused the context of the word "offensive," assuming it to mean such things as pornography or viruses. If there is no perceived need for a product why investigate it, or even know what it means?

The threat of an organized attack from a competitor (Question 10) does not appear to be a concern for the majority of respondents (66%). Some do not even recognize that they have competitors, for example:
- "Government agency. No competitors";
- "Charity providing services to clients";
- "No, not in our business."

These responses may be derived from a narrow view of what a competitor is, but do imply a lack of thought about potential aggressors. For example, comments such as "Perhaps, but not yet possible," and "Not competitors but malicious individuals" indicate that the threat is not thought to be great. A number of respondents did comment that the idea of using system attacks, as a competitive tool was a novel one, for example:
- "Had not thought of that angle. Interesting thought."

Of those that had registered an attack (that is, saying "yes" to Question 2), 53% (8 out of 15) did not think that they had anything to fear in this area from their competitors. Of those who did not recognize a threat from their competitors (73), only 11% had registered an attack.

The impression given is that, at this moment in time, ethical business practice and/or the legal system will stop competitors from these aggressive acts. Of course, it could be lack of exposure to the techniques which has caused little consideration of the possibilities.

System Integrity

Not surprisingly, 98% of the respondents thought that others should respect the integrity of their own site (Question 7). The main thrust of the comments was that their "property rights" were sacrosanct, for example:
- "It is property the same as physical property";
- "Most definite on this";
- "Yes, as I have the right to expect for any of my property."

There was no confusion in these replies. However, the responses to Question 6 revealed some contradictions.

Whilst 64% of respondents did feel that controversial sites should have their integrity respected, 23% said it was a right to attack them (13% did not know). Strangely, the small number (5) from the retail industry almost all (4) said that it is permissible to attack these sites. Most comments expressed the opinion that the authorities should deal with this type of site, for example:

- "Law should stop these sites";
- "The law should cover these issues."

There seems to be a dilemma here. Many comments expressed the view that Internet sites should be free to all opinions and that without this the system would be compromised. For example:

- "Must protect freedom of speech. This is up to authorities not individuals";
- "What is controversial? Who is the umpire that can ensure political, racial, religious, etc. overtones are not used to stop Web sites?";
- "No but I understand how they feel."

However, the contrast between the answers to Questions 6 and 7 does show potential dilemmas and justifications to attack certain sites.

General Comments

The general comments from respondents illustrate other issues. Some respondents put the onus on the victim, for example:

- "Organizations with poor security have no right to use retaliation as a deterrent. This is no different to booby trapping your car in case someone steals it ...";
- "Hacking is an invasion of one's private business and needs to be harshly treated by the law. It is up to us to protect ourselves but not to take the law into our own hands."

Others reflect that hacking is wrong no matter who does it:

- "I believe that there needs to be a complete understanding that hacking is not a justifiable course of action for anyone to take";
- "If a burglar breaks into my house, can I attack him? Could I attack his house in a similar way? Probably not."

Another response puts an interesting slant on semantics:

- "The word attack is an emotive word. If access was simply the question, the answer may be different."

Recent Events in Australia

The Australian Security Intelligence Organization (ASIO) has received approval to hack into personal computers and bug online communications under new legislation (Tebbutt, 1999).

The Australian Security Intelligence Organization Legislation Amendment Bill 1999 (Parliament of the Commonwealth of Australia, 1999), gives the ASIO a range of new powers:

- authorizing ASIO officers to use a computer or other electronic equipment found on a subject's premises to access computer data relevant to national security;

- authorizing ASIO officers to copy, add, delete or alter data in a computer or other electronic equipment;
- authorizing ASIO officers to modify protection mechanisms in a computer or other electronic equipment;
- authorizing ASIO officers to obtain remote access to data held in a computer;
- authorizing ASIO officers to undertake anything reasonably necessary to conceal the fact that any thing has been done by ASIO officers.

This range of new powers will allow the ASIO to engage in offensive online activities to protect the national interest of Australia. Perhaps the most important point is whether the protection of Australia's interests includes protection of Australia's business interests. Question 5 of the survey indicates that 60% of the organizations interviewed would support the role of authorities to take actions against hackers; within Australia this action could take the form of direct action against hackers by government organizations.

CONCLUSION

Whether we find it acceptable or not, modern society has a significant (and increasing) dependence upon information technology. Because of this dependence, the impact of hackers can be significant. However, the threats are still perceived by managers to come from individuals, whereas more significant dangers may come from organized groups. This chapter has sought to suggest that, as a result of this, we face a number of immediate and long-term threats that need to be recognized in order for protective action to be taken. But who should take this action?

This chapter describes an introductory investigation into the attitude of Australian management towards hackers and the rights that businesses have to proactively defend themselves against attacks. As the research was only a preliminary investigation to assess the level of awareness and concern in Australian IT management, there can be no firm conclusions drawn. A further, formal survey will be undertaken in the year 2000 and will include responses from Australia, the United States, and the United Kingdom. Attitudes to and the practice of cyber-vigilantism in each of these countries will be compared.

REFERENCES

Caelli, W., Longley, D. and Shain, M. (1989). *Information Security for Managers*. Stockton Press, New York, USA.

Cobb, A. (1998). *Thinking About the Unthinkable: Australian Vulnerabilities to a High-Tech Risks*. Research paper 18 1997-98. Department of Australian Parliamentary Library, Canberra, Australia.

CSI/FBI. (1999). *Computer Crime and Security Survey*, Computer Security Institute, USA.

Dearth, D. H. and Williamson, C.A. (1996). Information age/information war. In Campen, A. D., Dearth, D. H. and Goodden, T. R. (Eds). *Cyberwar: Security, Strategy, and Conflict in the Information Age*. AFCEA International Press, Fairfax, USA.

Deloitte Touche Tohmatsu/Victoria Police. (1999). *Computer Crime & Security Survey–1999*. Australia.

Denning, D. E. (1999). *Information Warfare and Security*. Addison-Wesley, New York, USA.

Elvin, J. (1999). You want it, you got it. *Insight on the News*, 15(18), 34.

Forno, R. and Baklarz R. (1999). *The Art of Information Warfare*–second edition, Universal Publishers, USA.

Goldberg, A. (1999). The dangers of hactivism. *Upside*, 11(5), 38.

Internet Law Bulletin. (1998). Guilty plea on inserting data charge. *Internet Law Bulletin*, 1(1).

Knecht, R. J. (1996). Thoughts about information warfare. In Campen, A. D., Dearth, D. H. and Goodden, T. R. (Eds.), *Cyberwar: Security, Strategy and Conflict in the Information Age*. Fairfax, USA: AFCEA International Press.

Mosquera, M. (1998). Hackers claim capability to crash the net. *Internetweek*, 718, 3.

Parliament of the Commonwealth of Australia. (1999). Australian Security Intelligence Organization Legislation Amendment Bill 1999, Federal Australian Government, Australia.

Schwartau, W. (1996). *Information Warfare*–second edition. Thunder's Mouth Press, New York, USA.

Schwartau, W. (1999). *Corporate Vigilantism Survey Results*. December. Retrieved on the World Wide Web: http://www.infowar.com.

Tebbutt, D. (1999). Australia: Canberra gives spies hack power. *The Australian Australia*, November 30.

Waltz, E. (1998). *Information Warfare–Principles and Operations*. Artech House, Norwood, USA.

Wray, S. (1999). On electronic disobedience. *Peace Review*, 11(1), 107.

Chapter IX

Cyberspace Ethics and Information Warfare

Matthew Warren
Deakin University, Australia

William Hutchinson
Edith Cowan University, Australia

INTRODUCTION

We have seen a rise in computer misuse at a global level and also the development of new policies and strategies to describe organized computer security attacks against the information society–these strategies are described as being "information warfare." This is very different from the traditional view of attack against computers by the individual, determined hacker, a cyber warrior with a code of conduct to follow. Today the threats come from individuals, corporations, government agencies (domestic and foreign), organized crime and terrorists. This new world of conflict in the electronic ether of virtual cyberspace has brought with it a new set of ethical dilemmas.

COMPUTER HACKERS

In the beginning, there were hackers. A group of what seem now to be a simple case of technocentric juveniles out to challenge their wits against the system. The term "computer hacker" usually denotes those who try to gain entry into a computer or computer network by defeating the computers' access (and/or security) controls. Hackers are by no means a new threat and have routinely featured in news stories during the last two decades. Indeed, they have become the traditional "target" of the media, with the standard approach being to present the image of either a "teenage whiz kid" or an insidious threat. In reality, it can be argued that there are different degrees of the problem. Some hackers are malicious, while others are merely naive and hence do not appreciate that their activities may be doing any real harm. Furthermore, when viewed as a general population, hackers may be seen to have numerous motivations for their actions (including financial gain, revenge, ideology or just plain mischief making). However, in many cases it can be argued that this is immaterial as, no matter what the reason, the end result is some form of adverse impact upon another party.

Steven Levy's book *Hackers: Heroes of the Computer Revolution* (1984) suggests that hackers operate by a code of ethics. This code defines main key areas:

- Hands-on imperative: Access to computers and hardware should be complete and total. It is asserted to be a categorical imperative to remove any barriers between people and the use and understanding of any technology, no matter how large, complex, dangerous, labyrinthine, proprietary, or powerful.

- "Information wants to be free." This can be interpreted in a number of ways. Free might mean without restrictions (freedom of movement = no censorship), without control (freedom of change/evolution = no ownership or authorship, no intellectual property), or without monetary value (no cost).

- Mistrust of authority. Promote decentralization. This element of the ethic shows its strong anarchistic, individualistic, and libertarian nature. Hackers have shown distrust toward large institutions, including, but not limited to, the state, corporations, and computer administrative bureaucracies.

- No bogus criteria: Hackers should be judged by their hacking, not by "bogus criteria" such as race, age, sex, or position.

- "You can create truth and beauty on a computer." Hacking is equated with artistry and creativity. Furthermore, this element of the ethos raises it to the level of philosophy.

- Computers can change your life for the better. In some ways, this last statement really is simply a corollary of the previous one. Since most of humanity desires things that are good, true, and/or beautiful.

During the 1980s and 1990s this pure vision of what hackers are was changed by the development of new groups with various aims and values. Mizrach (1997) states that the following individuals exist in cyberspace:

- Hackers (Crackers, system intruders)–These are people who attempt to penetrate security systems on remote computers. This is the new sense of the term, whereas the old sense of the term simply referred to a person who was capable of creating hacks, or elegant, unusual, and unexpected uses of technology.

- Phreaks (phone phreakers, blue boxers)–These are people who attempt to use technology to explore and/or control the telephone system.

- Virus writers (also, creators of Trojans, worms, logic bombs)–These are people who write code which attempts to a) reproduce itself on other systems without authorization and b) often has a side effect, whether that be to display a message, play a prank, or destroy a hard drive.

- Pirates–Originally, this involved breaking copy protection on software. This activity was called "cracking." Nowadays, few software vendors use copy protection, but there are still various minor measures used to prevent the unauthorized duplication of software. Pirates devote themselves to thwarting these and sharing commercial software freely.
- Cypherpunks (cryptoanarchists)–Cypherpunks freely distribute the tools and methods for making use of strong encryption, which is basically unbreakable except by massive supercomputers. Because American intelligence and law enforcement agencies, such as the NSA and FBI, cannot break strong encryption, programs that employ it are classified as munitions. Thus, distribution of algorithms that make use of it is a felony.
- Anarchists–These are people committed to distributing illegal (or at least morally suspect) information, including, but not limited to, data on bomb making, lock picking, pornography, drug manufacturing, and radio, cable and satellite TV piracy.
- Cyberpunks–Cyberpunks usually have some combination of the above, plus interest in technological self-modification, science fiction, hardware hacking and "street tech."

Mizarch (1997) determined that new groupings with cyberspace had altered the initial code of ethics, which in the late 1990s was more concerned with:

- "Above all else, do no harm." *Do not damage computers or data if at all possible.*
- Protect privacy. *People have a right to privacy, which means control over their own personal (or even familial) information .*
- "Waste not, want not." *Computer resources should not lie idle and wasted. It's ethically wrong to keep people out of systems when they could be using them during idle time.*
- Exceed limitations. *Hacking is about the continual transcendence of problem limitations.*
- The communication imperative. *People have the right to communicate and associate with their peers freely.*
- Leave no traces. *Do not leave a trail or trace of your presence; don't call attention to yourself or your exploits.*
- Share! *Information increases in value by sharing it with the maximum number of people; don't hoard, don't hide.*
- Self-Defense *against a cyberpunk future. Hacking and viruses are necessary to protect people from a possible Orwellian "1984" future.*
- Hacking helps security. *This could be called the "Tiger team ethic": It is useful and courteous to find security holes, and then tell people how to fix them.*
- Trust, but test! *You must constantly test the integrity of systems and find ways to improve them.*

This newer code of ethics is more based upon the view that hackers are helping in the development of the information society and adding to its distinct nature. The ethics of imposing these values on others who are unwilling "victims" does not seem to be questioned.

INFORMATION WARFARE

The advent of the contemporary concept of "information warfare" (see Schwartau, 1994, 2000; Denning, 1999; Waltz, 1998) has raised tampering with computer systems to a new dimension. The individualistic, anarchistic, and rather naive actions of young hackers have been replaced by the determined, methodical, and organized workings of states, corporations, and criminal gangs. Initially, the term "information warfare" was concerned with damaging a country's national information infrastructure (NII) (Schwartau, 1994). For the purposes of this paper, the NII is defined as the physical and virtual backbone of an information society and includes, at a minimum, all of the following (Cobb, 1998):

- government networks–executive and agencies
- banking and financial networks–stock exchanges, electronic money transfers
- public utility networks–telecommunication systems, energy and water supply (military and civil), hospitals, air traffic control and guidance systems, such as the global positioning satellite system and the instrument landing system, both common to commercial aviation
- emergency services networks (including medical, police, fire, and rescue)
- mass media dissemination systems-satellite, TV, radio, and Internet
- private corporate and institutional networks
- educational and research networks.

Information warfare is concerned with the full spectrum of offensive and defensive operations such as electronic warfare, cyber-terrorism, psychological operations and so on (Main, 2000). Mainly it has been associated with the so-called "revolution in military affairs" (RMA), although in the civilian world the increased reliance on information networks and, more specifically, has opened this type of "warfare" to anyone with the motivation to practice it. In some respects information warfare is a subset of the RMA, which is also concerned with the military application of new technologies to the "battlespace" (Cobb, 1998), such as stealth, precision-guided munitions, and advanced surveillance capabilities.

Because of this military aspect of information warfare, its ethics have been associated with those of national conflict. It is a development of the nature of warfare. The development of "total war", arguably started in the actions of Napoleon but certainly present in the Second World War, has been extended by the advent of information warfare. The distinction between military and civilian targets has been blurred. The Kosova conflict illustrated this. The bombing of a television station as a part of the Serbian military machine displayed the importance of the control of information in modern conflict (Ignatieff, 2000). At the state level, there is a tendency to attempt to develop "information superiority" over every competitor. International and national legal systems still have to catch up with this trend.

Increasingly the traditional attributes of the nation-state are blurring as a result of information technology. With information warfare, the state does not have a monopoly on dominant force nor can even the most powerful state reliably deter and defeat information warfare attacks. Increasingly non-state actors are attacking across geographic boundaries, eroding the concept of sovereignty based on physical geography.

There are also ethical implications between developed and less developed countries. In terms of information warfare, each society has its advantages and vulnerability. For instance, the USA has an enormous advantage in digital facilities from fibre optic communications to satellites and sophisticated software production. However, this advantage also adds vulnerability, as digital systems are susceptible to attack. The infrastructure of a "networked" society (e.g., power, water) is very exposed.

Developing countries at a lower level of development have an advantage of slower communication and processing systems, but this lack of sophistication lessens the vulnerability to an information attack.

The advantages of developed societies in the information "struggle" can be summarized as:

- Advanced infrastructure
- Have the intellectual property rights to most advanced developments
- Advanced technologies
- Have control of large corporations
- Advanced networked society possible, reliant on technology but infinitely flexible
- Capable of information dominance strategy
- Dominate perception management industries, e.g., media

The advantages of developing nations can be summarized as:

- Lack of vulnerable electronic infrastructure
- Low entry costs to get into electronic systems development
- Web based systems know no geographic boundaries (in theory), hence neither does "place" of company
- Networked society based on "clans", difficult to penetrate
- Cheap labour, often with an educated elite, eg India.

The implications of interstate behaviours have yet to be fully worked out. Of course, it is questionable whether "ethics" per se are relevant in an environment where international law (which should reflect ethical issues) and national self-interest dominate.

Information warfare has also spilled into the corporate arena. Adams (1998) emphasizes the movement of state aggression from military to economic. However, this conflict can be said to have also moved to corporate to corporate conflict, and even from corporate to individual. The use of information warfare techniques can be seen as just another factor of business behaviour. Grace and Cohen (1998) illustrate the dilemma in business of behaving ethically. They argue that, all too often, arguments are polarized into two choices: behave unethically or fail. For many organizations, business is a form of competitive warfare. Hence, techniques applicable to the military and intelligence services (information warfare) are viewed as feasible choices, although Grace and Cohen assert that it is wrong to assume that competitors' tactics are designed to destroy rivals. However, they do argue for an "international legal and normative infrastructure ... The point is often lost in analogies with war, however, is that a great deal of this infrastructure already exists in private and public international law" (p.181). Whilst this may be the case for general business practices, the advent of cyber-space has created problems of definition and jurisdiction.

However, over the last few years, legislation in America, Europe, and Australia has allowed intelligence and law enforcement agencies to perform these operations. For instance, in 1999, the Australia Security and Intelligence Organization (ASIO) was allowed (with ministerial approval) to access data, and generally "hack" into systems (Lagan & Power, 1999). Therefore, legal hacking is the province of the authorities. Hardly an ethical public stance to take. In fact, it just emphasizes the efficacy of information warfare techniques to others.

The problem with the whole area of computer crime and the ambiguity of the law in this area is also confused by the potential international legal implications of foreign attacks. However, it is rare for these offences to be detected, prosecuted, or proven even within a state. Morth (1998) further argues that although this form of information warfare may be illegal in international law, it is only states that are covered by this, not individuals or companies (for which there is no international law in this area).

The perception of information warfare at the state or corporate level is to obtain as much benefit as possible and cause as much damage as possible to the "enemy." Thus the intent is usually destructive; this is very different from the hacker code of ethics. The reason for this is the emergence of cyberspace attack as the critical ingredient in a new witch's brew of strategic conflict capability. Information warfare tools and techniques allow the potential to destroy communications, information dissemination, and the functioning of critical equipment with no reference to geography or an ability to physically destroy anything in the conventional sense. Such a capability poses a whole new kind of threat to international stability (Molander & Siang, 1998). This destabilizing potential can equally have an organization or individual as its targeted victim.

It is interesting that in a survey of Australian IT managers carried out by the authors in 1999, 66% thought there was no threat from their competitors (Hutchinson & Warren, 1999). In other words, the thinking was that their competitors were ethical; in this area at least. However, the perception of competitor was probably a very narrow one. If the definition is to include "all those who wish to compete with your resource base or market share," then conservationists are competitors of mining companies and animal rights activists are competitors with fur traders. The picture is not so stable if these concepts are brought in.

Some of the comments received in the survey about the likelihood of an attack by competitors illustrate the point:

- "Government agency. No competitors."
- "Perhaps, but not yet possible."
- "Not competitors but malicious individuals."

It is interesting that a government department had the idea that they had no competitors. The impression given is that, at this moment in time, ethical business practice and/or the legal system will stop competitors from these aggressive acts. Of course, it could be lack of exposure to the techniques which has caused little consideration of the possibilities.

SOME SPECIFIC TECHNIQUES IN INFORMATION WARFARE

There are a number of ways information or information systems can be used to gain advantage over (or give a disadvantage to) another organization. Examples of some aggressive tactics are:

- Information can be manipulated or "created" (disinformation) to provide the target or its environment (for example, clients) a perception that develops behaviours detrimental to the target or beneficial to the attacker. At one level, this can be viewed as advertising, and, at another, deliberate deception.
- Information can be intercepted, thus giving the interceptor an advantageous insight into the target's strengths, weaknesses, and intentions.
- Information flows in the target organization can be disrupted or stopped, thereby interfering with the normal processes of the target, producing an advantage for the attacker, for instance, by bringing a server or network down.
- A target organization can be "flooded" with information, thereby slowing or stopping effective processing or analysis of the incoming information.
- Information can be made unavailable to a target organization by destroying the storage medium or cutting off the information source.
- Disrupting the availability of data or making the system produce incorrect/ dubious output can lower the credibility of information systems.
- Confidential or sensitive information can be exposed to the public, clients, government agencies, and so on, thereby embarrassing or in other ways harming the organization.
- Physical attacks on IT or other components of the system can be made.
- Subversion of the people who operate the systems can be attempted.
- Physical destruction of information (erasure or overwrite) without harming the infrastructure components can be effected.
- Logic attacks (malicious code) on system components can be executed.

Obviously, many of these tactics are not pertinent to the contemporary business world (at least, not any ethically based corporate strategy) but they do give an idea of the range of possibilities open to an attacker.

FUTURE TRENDS

Information warfare has shifted the ethical issues from a naive group of technically oriented, young individuals (hackers, etc.) to the organizational arena. The implications of this shift from the relatively benign impact of individual behaviour to that of organized groups has raised the magnitude of the ethical issues surrounding them. They need to be considered at both the legal and policy-making levels of national, international, and corporate institutions before practices become entrenched or cause irreversible damage. However, the future is likely to be even more problematic. Some viewpoints consider that information warfare makes war more thinkable. It does not require that waging information warfare be either destructive or unjust. To the contrary, ethical notions of just war fighting will likely continue to provide a useful guide to behavior well into the information age (Khalilzad, 1999).

If the predictions of those such as Kurzwell (1999) are to be believed, the merging of people and machines will take on a new dimension. Although it can be said that the contemporary developed world is networked, the idea of a cyborg-world gives pause for thought. At the more mundane level, the advent of the wearable computer with its sensory enhancing peripherals makes real individuals the targets, rather than their computer systems. If these individuals with their infraread and hearing sensors, satellite positioning capabilities, face recognition and perceptive software (see Gershenfeld, 1999; Pentland, 2000) become truly networked, then the potential for damage from information warfare can be raised by significant orders of magnitude. Much as some people have become dependent on the mobile telephone, the awesome capabilities of personalized systems will make individuals dependent on them for interpreting every signal from the environment. The potential for perception management and confusion will make the ethical problems of today seem very minor.

To conclude we will look at the earliest research into ethics. Aristotle determined that it is by nature that some people are good, others it is by habit, and others it is by instruction (Aristotle, 1976). In this new information age humankind has developed new, incredible powers. Humankind has the ability to wage total war using the global information infrastructure there is no room left for "goodness."

REFERENCES

Adams, J. (1998). *The Next World War*. London: Hutchinson.

Aristotle. (1976). *The Ethics of Artistotle:The Nicomachean Ethics*. UK: Penguin Books.

Cobb.A. (1998). Australia's Vulnerability to Information attack: Towards a National information Policy, Strategic and Defense Studies Centre working paper No. 310. Australia: Australia National University.

Denning, D. E. (1999). Information Warfare and Security. New York: Addison-Wesley.

Gershenfeld. (1999). *When Things Start to Think*. Hodder and Stoughton, London.

Grace, D. and Cohen, S. (1998) *Business Ethics*–second edition. Melbourne: Oxford University Press.

Hutchinson, W. E. and Warren, M. J. (1999). Attacking the attackers: Attitudes of Australian IT managers to retaliation against hackers. *ACIS (Australasian Conference on Information Systems) 99*, December, Wellington, New Zealand.

Ignatieff, M. (2000). *Virtual War*. London: Chatto & Windus.

Khalilzad, Z, White, J and Andrew W. M. (1999). *MR-1015-AF–Strategic Appraisal: The Changing Role of Information in Warfare*. USA: RAND Publications.

Kurzwell, R (2000). The coming merging of mind and machine. In *Your Bionic Future: Scientific American*, 10(3), 56-61.

Lagan, B. and Power, B (1999). ASIO cleared to hack into computers. *Sydney Morning Herald*, March.

Levy, S. (1994). *Hackers: Heroes of the Computer Revolution*.

Main, B. (2000). Information wrfare: And its impact on the information technology industry in New Zealand. *Proceedings of the NACCQ*. Wellington, New Zealand.

Mizrach, S. (1997). *Is there a Hacker Ethic for 90s Hackers?* Retrieved on the World Wide Web: http://www.infowar.com

Molander, R. and Siang, S. (1998). The legitimization of strategic information warfare: Ethical consideration. *Professional Ethics Report*, 11(4).

Morth, T. A. (1998). Considering our position: Viewing information warfare as a use of force prohibited by Article 2(4) of the U.N.Charter. *Case Western Reserve Journal of International Law*, 30(2-3), 567-600.

Pentland, A. (2000). Perceptual intelligence. *Communications of the ACM*, 43(3), 40-44.

Schwartau, W. (1994). *Information Warfare: Chaos on the Electronic Superhighway*. New York, USA: Thunder's Mouth Press.

Schwartau, W. (2000). *Cybershock. Thunder's Mouth Press*. New York, USA.

Waltz, E. (1998). *Information Warfare–Principles and Operations*. Artech House, Norwood.

Chapter X

Policies for the Prevention of Repetitive Strain Injury Among Computer Users: A Moral Analysis

N. Ben Fairweather
De Montfort University, UK

INTRODUCTION

The chapter starts with a very brief review of the nature of repetitive strain injury (RSI) and some of the less helpful advice about RSI. There is consideration of general issues of employer responsibility for health and safety and mention of the peculiarities of RSI prevention before attention is turned to the balance of individual versus corporate responsibility as shown in policies studied. Attention is then drawn to particular issues of mouse use and then computer games. There is a short discussion of the issues of stress and work pressure, followed by mention of some issues raised by monitoring, and the chapter concludes with a look at the issues raised by consideration of shared workstations.

REPETITIVE STRAIN INJURY (RSI)

The increasing use of information and computer technologies (ICTs) means that an ever-larger proportion of the world's population is exposed to the possibility of RSI from computer use.

RSI is also known as occupational overuse injury or syndrome and cumulative trauma disorder, and in some cases terms such as work-related upper limb disorders, tenosynovitis, thoracic outlet syndrome, and carpal tunnel syndrome are used.

There has been some controversy about whether there are injuries caused by repetitive strain. Some authors such as Lucire (undated) argue that RSI is "an epidemic of a new disorder ... made up of two factors: hysteria in the patients, and impaired medical perception of endemic symptomatology, with the latter a contributing cause to the former." Yet attempts by defendants in RSI compensation cases to argue this are proving unsuccessful (Times, 1999), and research (Greening & Lynn, 1998) has associated RSI of the hands with damage to the median nerve, the major nerve in the hand.

RSI is most closely associated with keyboard use, and there are suggestions that keyboard use might decline, leading to a common assumption that RSI will decline as a problem (e.g., Richardson, 1999). There is also evidence, however, that alternatives to keyboard use can cause RSI in some cases. Mouse use appears to have been a problem for some years (Workers' Compensation Board of British Columbia, 1996), and voice recognition has also been reported as being linked to RSI (Grimshei, 1999). If RSI is associated with technologies that can be expected to supplant keyboard use to some extent, the issues raised will be equally relevant when transferred to the new contexts.

BAD ADVICE

A fair proportion of advice about RSI that is available is out-of-date or poorly focussed. The "RSI checklist" (Hazards, 1993) suggests many things to check that are not of great importance or difficult to change (e.g., 3.d. Has it (the keyboard) a matt surface? or 11.d. Is there street noise?). The University of Wisconsin--Milwaukee (1999) similarly has as few as 26 words about taking breaks, as against well over 1,000 on other issues. The "RSI checklist" (Hazards, 1993) also gives no practical help on how to answer other crucial questions (e.g., 4.b. Is it (desk or working surface) at a suitable height? without any indication of how a suitable height might be determined). It was hardly suitable as the first linked piece of advice on how to avoid causing further injury in a web page (RSI-UK, 1998) for "Dealing With It" when first diagnosed with RSI, and thankfully appears to be no longer.

Many policies studied more obviously suffered from being boring, starting with a section on definitions which would put off many readers who were unsure whether the policy was relevant to them (e.g., University of Glasgow, 1993).

The Responsibility of Employers

Some "free-market" authors (e.g., Machan, 1987, p. 456) argue that there are no special rights for employees, that "As individuals who intend to hire out their skills for what they will fetch in the marketplace, ... Any interference with such trade (in labour) workers (...) might want to engage in, with consent by fellow traders, would violate both the workers' and their traders" (employers') human rights." However, this seems implausible, as the negotiating positions of workers and employers are so unbalanced in most situations as to make the negotiation of fair contracts impossible (although unilateral concession of them by employers is still theoretically possible). As Faden and Beauchamp (1988, p. 278) put it, "in industries where ten people stand up in line for every available position, bargaining for increased protection is an unlikely event."

Given the normally asymmetrical power relationship in employment and the rarity with which individuals can opt out of all employment relationships, there is a need for special responsibilities to be placed on employers over and above any negotiated with the employee.

In the sphere of RSI prevention there are particular issues: regardless of the formal actions of their employers, individuals are to a significant extent able to adopt, or fail to adopt, working practices that reduce the chance of RSI. At the same time, the extent to which the individual worker does so may be determined by factors that are more clearly the responsibility of the employer rather than any individual worker. These factors include the regimes for job security, promotion and pay and such less tangible factors as the culture of the workplace.

By producing materials on RSI prevention, all of the organizations studied implicitly recognize that they have a duty in this sphere.

The Policies

The University of Bristol (undated) is very clear that "it is the responsibility of individuals themselves to ensure that the facilities and equipment are used correctly," rather than the responsibility of managers and supervisors, and makes no mention of training to enable individuals to make such correct use. It later says, "If you think you might have RSI, report it to your Head of Department," without any indication of what heads are expected to do. It continues, "If discomfort persists, stop typing altogether," placing the entire onus on the individual and giving no reassurances at all.

The University of Glasgow (1993) and the University of Tasmania (1998a) policies place responsibility on managers and supervisors. Perhaps the greatest criticism that could be levelled at them in this respect is that they give no guidance to users on possible courses of action if their manager or supervisor fails in their duties. Some further particular deficiencies of each are noted below.

The University of Tasmania (1998a) is also unusual in explicitly mentioning a role for "employee representatives" in determining "realistic and safe work rates."

The University of Wolverhampton (undated) claims its "code of practice" is aimed at "managers and supervisors," but does not explicitly mention such supervisory relationships again except in the context of eye tests, preferring to talk in general terms of "employers." Further, it claims to only apply to "users" and employs an unusually restrictive definition of "user," that I suspect excludes most staff at risk of RSI and, by defining "users" as employees, all students. By its restrictive applicability, this "code of practice" leaves individuals with virtually all responsibility.

The material studied from the Occupational Safety and Health Council (1999) of the Civil Service Bureau of Hong Kong, China, makes no mention of responsibilities of managers and supervisors, and thus implicitly places the onus on the individual.

The University of Wisconsin-Milwaukee (1999) makes no mention at all of managers in its "tips," apparently placing the entire responsibility on the individual.

It should be recognized, however, that the documents studied in these last two cases were not formal policies. Thus the significance of the documents analyzed is less clear than elsewhere.

THE MOUSE

While some sources give specialist advice on working with a mouse, most of those studied do not (e.g., University of Glasgow, 1993; Occupational Safety and Health Council, 1999 University of Tasmania, 1998a, 1998b; University of Wisconsin-Milwaukee, 1999). Given that it is increasingly common for software to be designed with the assumption that the mouse will be the primary method of control, and that mouse use is a particular risk, this is a large failing.

One particular, and almost universal, problem is that the combination of a keyboard with a built-in numeric keypad to the right of the alphabetic keys means that a right-handed mouse needs to be placed some way from the alphabetic keys. This tends to militate against keeping the wrist in-line while using the mouse, yet advice is that the wrist should be kept in-line. One of the few sources of specialist advice on using a mouse (Workers' Compensation Board of British Columbia, 1996) even accidentally illustrates the problem in its illustration of "correct" mouse positioning.

Suppliers should normally avoid shipping keyboards with built-in numeric keypads to the right of the alphabetic keypad at the same time as right-handed mice. A separate numeric keypad is ideal, although keyboards with the numeric keys to the left would be suitable for many users who use the numeric keypad rarely (for right-handed users who make great use of the numeric keypad and rarely use the alphabetic keys, the conventional arrangement may be adequate, provided the keyboard and mouse are correctly positioned for each workmode).

COMPUTER GAMES

Most policies appear not to mention computer games, but where advice does mention computer games, on every occasion I have seen, the advice is not to play the games. Thus Quilter (1998, tip 1) urges people to "Go for a walk or see a movie instead of playing video games." Yet the risks associated with some games appear to be much greater than other games.

The risks are greater with games that require many quick movements and which do not allow the player to stop for a break without losing their place in the game. It is particularly unfortunate that virtually all computers are now supplied with games in which players are encouraged to "beat the clock," and without the possibility of taking a break mid-game. I would strongly recommend that software suppliers stop including this particular type of game "bundled" with other software. I would also recommend that where employers control the software provided and installed on computers used by their employees, they remove the more harmful games from their systems.

A proportion of users is always likely to play games (or waste time in other ways). Given this and the fact that computer games are often available through the Internet or as hidden features of other software (I have heard of a game hidden deep in word-processing software), it may be impossible for employers to stop employees from playing computer games. Taking this realistic perspective, it would be better if employees could be directed towards the less harmful games, which might mean that while more harmful games are removed from systems, less harmful ones are intentionally allowed to remain (perhaps with warnings about the risk of RSI attached to them).

WORK PRESSURE

Workers in the UK have won cases for compensation for RSI caused by working "under intense pressure to perform, with workers achieving four key-strokes per second earning gold stars and more payment" (Frean, 1998). Bad though this is, some sense of proportion is needed: In Japan work pressure that leads to RSI in some has been linked to death among other workers, and policies for the prevention of such deaths, let alone RSI, are "very superficial" (Nishiyama & Johnson, 1997).

Employers in countries with advanced regulation of health and safety may now be persuaded to allow data-entry clerks to pace their own work and take breaks. However, as ICTs spread to less industrialized countries, the high cost of the technology (relative to local incomes) increases the pressure to get maximum use from the equipment.

Not all pressure is so obvious, and I have no reason to believe there is such explicit pressure in the workplaces for which I have studied policies. In these workplaces I expect situations where the individual is given a good degree of flexibility about how to organize their work to be more common. However, even in the many workplaces with flexibility, work pressure can make it difficult to take breaks. This can be because the work environment is highly competitive or because payment, promotion or job security is largely determined "by results," and a culture of working long hours to finish work that is overdue is also unhelpful.

The University of Glasgow (1993), the University of Wolverhampton (un-dated) and the University of Wisconsin-Milwaukee (1999) all fail to recognize the special factors of an academic working environment that may mean breaks are not taken. Mellor (1996?) provides an interesting contrast, with his advice that "Mammoth sessions on that overdue essay or article are a high-risk activity." The University of Tasmania (1998a) is particularly frustrating, mentioning that "Many jobs have predictable peak periods which may result in large variations in job demand. The increased risks generated during these peak periods may be prevented by long term planning of resources and organization of tasks," without relating this to the academic environment and culture.

By contrast, the University of Bristol (undated) makes some implicit recognition of the academic environment (but not that it has duties to students). Despite this, it gives no advice on the practical difficulties that could interfere with its instruction to "Take regular breaks." It again makes no mention of line managers' responsibilities in this regard.

The importance of line managers allowing, enabling, encouraging or enforcing suitable breaks (when all of these may be appropriate in some contexts) is generally not recognized in the policies studied (although the University of Glasgow (1993) and, to a lesser extent, the University of Wolverhampton (undated) are exceptions).

MONITORING

One technically possible method for employers to take responsibility for the prevention of RSI is to electronically monitor keyboard use and other aspects of computer use to ensure that adequate breaks are taken. Network software has existed for many years that enables this. However, such software is more associated with increasing the risk of RSI, because whether intended or not, it is liable to exert psychological pressure to constantly do the types of work that it measures. Few policies mention the possibility of such software existing. Such software also gives rise to serious privacy concerns. (Fairweather, 1999, pp. 41-44).

The University of Wolverhampton's (undated) requirement that "No quantitative or qualitative checking facility may be used without user's knowledge" gives little of the reassurance I suspect it was intended to convey. It gives no indication of what the aims of such monitoring might be, and thus whether it might be used to prevent RSI or in ways that could increase the risk of RSI. Similarly it gives no assurance that privacy will be respected and does not give the individual any opportunity to refuse to be monitored.

A better solution is for each individual to be given the choice about which of a number of non-networked break-reminder programs (CTD Resource Network, 2000) they would like to have installed on their computer.

SHARED WORKSTATIONS

Another possible problem area is when the arrangements for access to ICTs are through the use of "open access" or prebooked workstations. It is common practice in universities to provide such workstations for students and to a lesser extent for staff. However, inherent in such an arrangement is a need for the workstation to be suitable for the "typical" user. This can often preclude proper ergonomic adjustment of the workstation for the individual user, especially where the individual is of a build that is not very close to the mean. For example, a short user may need a footrest (University of Bristol, undated) that is not provided (footrests being essential for many short users to work in comfort with the chair at the correct height to allow for correct positioning of the arms). Yet a tall user could find the same footrest (if it were provided) an obstruction, and the screen too low.

Further, when workstations are prebooked and not plentiful, users will be under pressure to make maximum use of their session, and thus to not take the breaks advised in RSI prevention policies.

An alternative of having no booking system can itself preclude adequate breaks, as the user is often unable to leave and return without risking being unable to find a workstation to use on their return. It is technically possible to secure a workstation to prevent others from using it or interfering with it while the user is away from it, and thus enable the taking of breaks. However, the use of such a facility may be disabled or discouraged to reduce the chance of people wishing to use a workstation having to wait while workstations are not actively being used. Further research is needed on the extent of this problem.

The failure of policies to mention these various issues relating to shared workstations when they are relevant (e.g., University of Bristol, undated; University of Tasmania, 1998a, 1998b; University of Wolverhampton, undated; and University of Wisconsin-Milwaukee, 1999), is a serious flaw.

The various issues related to shared workstations are of particular relevance when considering the spread of ICTs to less industrialised countries, as the high relative cost of them makes it likely that much access will be at shared workstations.

CONCLUSION

This chapter has looked at a number of higher education and workplace repetitive strain injury (RSI) prevention policies, from the United Kingdom, Australia, China and the United States, to morally evaluate them. Evaluations took into account a variety of issues including the balance of corporate responsibility as against individual responsibility. Some of the broader issues of employer responsibility for health and safety were reviewed.

For many policies studied, there is too much weight on individual responsibility, with little or no attention to the context in which the computers are being used, and unrealistic demands on individuals as a result. The chapter also suggests that computer suppliers have a responsibility to supply relatively inexpensive software and equipment to prevent RSI with the computers they are supplying.

RSI is a very real problem and will continue to be unless more widespread attention is paid to it. A number of particular measures to combat it have been suggested. The control of RSI also requires that the attention paid to the problem involves a more realistic appraisal of the amount of responsibility individuals can be expected to bear.

REFERENCES

CTD Resource Network. (2000). *Software: Typing Injury FAQ.* Retrieved September 20, 2000 on the World Wide Web: http://www.tifaq.org/software.html.

Faden, R. R. and Beauchamp, T. L. (1988). The right to risk information and the right to refuse health hazards in the workplace. In Beauchamp, T. L. and Bowie, N. E. (Eds.), *Ethical Theory and Business* 3rd edition, Englewood Cliffs, NJ: Prentice-Hall, as reprinted in Hoffman, W. M. and Frederick, R. E. (Eds.). (1995). *Business Ethics: Readings in Corporate Morality,* New York: McGraw-Hill.

Fairweather, N. B. (1999). Surveillance in employment: the case of teleworking. *Journal of Business Ethics,* 22(1), 39-49

Frean, A. (1998). Bank workers win claim for RSI. *Times* (London), May 23. Retrieved September 20, 2000 on the World Wide Web: http://www.sunday-times.co.uk:80/news/pages/tim/98/05/23/timnwsnws01003.html?1493159.

Greening, J. and Lynn, B. (1998). Vibration sense in the upper limb in patients with repetitive strain injury and a group of at-risk office workers. *International Archives of Occupational and Environmental Health,* 71, 29-34. Retrieved September 27, 2000 on the World Wide Web:: http://www.physiol.ucl.ac.uk/wwwphysiol/research/abstractjg.html.

Grimshei, C. (1999). E-mail to e-mail list. SOREHAND@ITSSRV1.UCSF.EDU, July 21.

Hazards, (1993). Untitled RSI checklist. *Hazards Magazine,* 45(4). Retrieved September 20, 2000 on the World Wide Web: http://www.demon.co.uk/rsi/checklst.txt.

Lucire, Y. (Undated). *Social Iaterogenesis of RSI.* Retrieved September 20, 2000 on the World Wide Web: http://www.ozemail.com.au/~lucire/social_iatrogenesis.htm.

Machan, T. R. (1987). Human rights, workers' rights, and the "right" to occupational safety. In Ezorsky, G. (Ed.). *Moral Rights in the Workplace,* Albany, NY: State University of New York Press, as reprinted in White, T. I. (1993). *Business Ethics: A Philosophical Reader.* New York: Macmillan.

Mellor, N. H. (1996). *Repetitive Strain Injuries (RSIs).* Retrieved September 20, 2000 on the World Wide Web: http://www.leeds.ac.uk/law/it/RSI/rsi.htm.

Nishiyama, K. and Johnson, J. V. (1997). Karoshi-Death from overwork: Occupational health consequences of the Japanese production management. *International Journal of Health Services,* 27, 625-641. Retrieved September 20, 2000 on the World Wide Web: http://www.iro.umontreal.ca/~coter/karoshi.html and http://www.workhealth.org/whatsnew/lpkarosh.htm.

Occupational Safety and Health Council. (1999). Office safety and health series: Repetitive strain injuries. In *Civil Service Newsletter,* 43, English Version. (Hong Kong, China: Civil Service Bureau). Retrieved September 20, 2000 on the World Wide Webt: http://www.hku.hk/hkgcsb/csn/csn43eng/csn19.htm.

Quilter, D. (1998). *Ten Ways to Prevent Repetitive Strain Injury*. Retrieved August 4, 1999 on the World Wide Web: http://www.rsihelp.com/tips.shtml.

Richardson, W. (1999). E-mail to e-mail list. BETS-L@LISTSERV.UIC.EDU, August 16.

RSI-UK. (1998). *Dealing With It*. Retrieved July 4, 1999 on the World Wide Web: http://www.demon.co.uk/rsi/dwi.html.

Times. (1999). Bank fails to reverse RSI cash awards. *Times (London)*, July. Retrieved September 20, 2000 on the World Wide Web: http://www.sunday-times.co.uk:80/news/pages/tim/99/07/23/timnwsnws01017.html?1493159.

University of Bristol. (undated). *Working With Computers-Health and Safety Issues*. Retrieved September 20, 2000 on the World Wide Web: http://www.bris.ac.uk/Depts/SDev/ergo.htm.

University of Glasgow. (1993). *Display Screen Booklet*. Retrieved September 20, 2000 on the World Wide Web: http://www.gla.ac.uk/Otherdepts/SEPS/dsebook.htm.

University of Tasmania. (1998a). *Prevention of Occupational Overuse Syndrome Policy*. Retrieved August 25, 1999 on the World Wide Web: http://silver.admin.utas.edu.au/hr/ohs/poo.html.

University of Tasmania. (1998b). *Guidelines for the Use of Screen Based Equipment*. Retrieved August 25, 1999 on the World Wide Web: http://silver.admin.utas.edu.au/hr/ohs/gus.html.

University of Wisconsin-Milwaukee. (1999). *Tips for Enhancing the Office Environment*. Retrieved September 20, 2000 on the World Wide Web: http://www.uwm.edu/Dept/EHSRM/GENINFO/genergotips.html.

University of Wolverhampton. (undated). *Code of Practice on the Use of Display Screen Equipment*. Retrieved September 20, 2000 on the World Wide Web: http://www.wlv.ac.uk/hs/sm10.html.

Workers' Compensation Board of British Columbia. (1996). How to use, choose and place a computer mouse to prevent injury. *Ergonomics Commentary*, (3), May. Retrieved April 8, 1999 on the World Wide Web: http://www.wcb.bc.ca/resmat/pubs/ergcomm/ergcomm3.htm and September 20, 2000: http://www.worksafebc.com/pubs/brochures/ec/ergcomm3.asp.

Chapter XI

Social Issues in Electronic Commerce: Implications for Policy Makers

Anastasia Papazafeiropoulou and Athanasia Pouloudi
Brunel University, UK

INTRODUCTION

Policy implementation for electronic commerce is a complex process since policy makers, national governments in their majority, have to act in a fast changing environment. They need to balance special national demands with international cooperation (Papazafeiropoulou & Pouloudi, 2000). One of the areas that policy makers have to tackle is dealing with barriers that have been reported in the adoption of electric commerce today. These barriers are mostly derived from factors such as lack of awareness about the opportunities offered by electronic commerce as well as lack of trust to ward network security. Additionally the current legislative framework, drawn before the advent of electronic commerce, is perceived as outdated, thus impeding the expansion of online transactions. Policy makers, therefore, find it increasingly critical to update commerce legislation (Owens, 1999; Shim et al., 2000; the White House, 1999) and take other measures to facilitate the uptake of electronic commerce.

As the need for appropriate policy measures that support the information society is increasing, it is important to prevent a predominantly technical, commercial or legal approach that neglects the broader social issues related to policy making. To this end, this chapter examines social issues related to electronic commerce policy-making and is structured as follows. In the next section we present two fundamental social concerns that are related to policy making in electronic commerce: trust and digital democracy. In Section 3 we discuss these concerns in the light of different policy issues arising from the use of network technologies, and in Section 4 we present their implications for policy making in electronic commerce. The paper concludes with the importance of a holistic approach to policy making and suggestions for further research.

SOCIAL CONCERNS

The introduction of technologies such as the Internet in everyday life has resulted in a debate about its relative merits and disadvantages. Some of the social concerns are illustrated in the study conducted by the Stanford Institute for the Quantitative Study for Society (SIQSS, 2000) concerning the social implications of Internet use. The findings of the study indicate that the Internet is an "isolating technology" that could seriously damage the social fabric of communities as users interact physically with other people less. The social implications of the Internet can be witnessed in organizational processes, the nature of work, learning and education, innovation and competition, electronic democracy, privacy and surveillance (Dutton, 1996). This section considers the social concerns related to the use of Internet technologies by focusing on two of the most frequently discussed social issues in electronic commerce. These are trust, a social issue underlying the business use of the Internet, and digital democracy, a term underlying the use of Internet technology in the society as a whole. The following paragraphs consider each in detail.

Trust

Lack of trust in online transactions is one of the main reasons reported for the relatively low electronic commerce adoption today. Trust is a key issue and its existence among the business community and the end consumers will increase the willingness of trading partners to expand their electronic transactions (e.g., Hart & Saunders, 1997; Miles & Snow, 1992; Ratnasingham, 1998; Wilson, 1997). The low level of trust in electronic commerce can be attributed partly to the lack of face-to-face interaction between trading partners in conjunction with the general uncertainty of users in taking advantage of network technologies (Ratnasingham, 1998). According to Johnston (1999), there are a number of actions that can be taken to respond to user uncertainty. First, users should be educated about privacy and security issues. Second, the necessary legislation framework that protects trading partners must be developed. Third, the perceptions about technology as a tool that can threaten trust need to change to acknowledge that technology can also be applied for the users' protection, for example, through the effective use of encryption mechanisms.

Digital Democracy

Information and communication technologies offer opportunities for governments and citizens to be brought into closer dialogue; they also facilitate political organization and debate (Raab et al., 1996). However, the extent to which the information superhighway can fully enable citizens to participate in this emerging "digital democracy," has been heavily debated. First, at a conceptual level, our understanding of democracy is "as bounded in time as it is rooted in space" (Nguyen & Alexander, 1996, p. 120), which means that the term digital democracy is inherently problematic in "cyberspace." Importantly, there is a concern that if citizens are not able to have access to online services, because they do not have the means or the knowledge to do so, existing patterns of inequalities will be reinforced. The digital democracy is threatened by "information aristocracy" (Carter, 1997). In particular, there is evidence of a gender and race gap in the use of the Internet as well as differences for users with different levels of income and education (Hoffman & Novak, 1999; Kouzmin et al., 1999). While policy makers at an international level are concerned about access to electronic commerce, the burden falls mostly upon local authorities, which are responsible for the provision of access to network facilities through the use of public access centers, kiosks or tele-working centers. At a global level, the penetration of electronic commerce in developing countries is also an outstanding issue related to the "haves" and "have-nots" in cyberspace (e.g., Bhatnagar, 1997; Blanning et al., 1997; Clark & Lai, 1998; Kim & Hong, 1997). Easy global information access, however, is also problematic as it has been described as threatening both cultural identity and the regulatory sovereignty of the state, especially when used in less powerful economies (Shields, 1996). Finally, as privacy protection is a major concern in electronic commerce, there is a concern on whether "cyberspace" can promote democracy while protecting privacy. The free information flow of democracy and the users' need to control the flow of personal data can be seen as zero-sum alternatives that may (or may not) be balanced (Raab, 1997). This generates several policy dilemmas, which are reviewed in the following sections.

EMERGENT POLICY ISSUES

The Internet is the most popular means for the implementation of electronic commerce systems. Its fast expansion in the last decade was exceptional, forcing policy makers to speed up their efforts for its governance and regulation. The policy issues described in this section have to be addressed in order to facilitate the development of a safe and well-defined environment for electronic commerce, addressing the social concerns outlined in the previous section. These policy issues are presented following the six levels of Internet policy architecture including infrastructure, governance, security, privacy, content and commerce. These have been defined by the Global Internet Project (GIP), a group of senior executives from leading companies around the world (Patrick, 1999; www.gip.org). The second part of the section presents the dilemmas in addressing policy issues, leading on to a discussion of the implications for policy makers in the remainder of the chapter.

Policy Issues at Six Levels of Internet Policy

Infrastructure

The infrastructure level aims at addressing "the challenge of meeting the demand for reliable and scaleable access to the Internet" (Patrick, 1999, p. 106). The speed, the quality, the reliability and the cost of the networks used for online transactions are very important factors that can either boost or obstruct evolution of electronic commerce. One of the top priorities of governments is the support of the telecommunication industry so that it can offer better quality services in terms of speed, reliability, continuous access and interconnectivity between subnetworks (Patrick, 1999). The American government, for example, aims at the provision of online services to the majority of American households not only through desktop computers connecting to the Internet but also through devices such as television, cellular phones and portable digital assistants (US Department of Commerce, 1998). The liberalization of the telecommunication market is a relevant directive of the European Union (EC, 1997) and OECD (OECD, 1997b) to their member states. It demonstrates the intention of international policy making organizations to reduce the cost and improve the robustness of the telecommunication infrastructure worldwide.

In relation to the social concerns discussed in the previous section, policies that support the infrastructure level contribute towards better trust in terms of Internet performance. The availability of appropriate infrastructure and the capability to access it, however, as a prerequisite for the digital democracy, are contingent on the resources available within a particular region or country. Thus, global coverage is a major concern for policy makers today (Hudson, 1999). Within a national context, the quality of the telecommunication infrastructure in rural areas is particularly significant, when the accessibility to alternative means of obtaining information is very limited. Overall, as the role of the nation state declines in providing access to telecommunications networks, it may be up to independent bodies to support citizens gaining access to Internet-delivered services (Keenan & Trotter, 1999). At an international level, also, it may be up to independent bodies and international organizations to facilitate the development of Internet and technological infrastructure in developing countries. National governments also take initiatives to improve the take-up and use of information technologies but they do not always succeed (e.g., Walsham, 1999).

Governance

The Internet is characterized by its ability to expand without central governance. The Internet is the "place" where the free economy can blossom and this presents immense opportunities for electronic commerce. It is the intention of the policy makers at an international level to support industry leadership and self-regulation for electronic commerce (The White House, 1999; EC, 1997; OECD, 1997b). Specifically, there is a tendency to minimize government involvement and avoid unnecessary restrictions on electronic commerce.

However, as electronic commerce use becomes mature its international nature creates the need for global governance in certain areas. For example, several legal cases have been reported that involved Web site owners and consumers or other companies. The conflict usually derives from the lack of certainty about where a Web company is physically located and thus under which country's legal system the company works (Aalberts & Townsend, 1998). Taxation is a specific concern for companies that intend to invest in new technologies and for governments that want to control electronic commerce similarly to traditional commerce. There is a wide range of proposals concerning the administration of taxes in electronic commerce (Johnston, 1999; Owens, 1999). At one extreme there is the idea of absolute "tax-free" electronic commerce that has already been implemented for transactions taking place among US states, until February 1998 when the US public administration reaffirmed its commitment to making cyberspace a free-trade zone (Negroponte, 1999). At the other end there are proposals for introduction of special new taxes for electronic commerce. OECD (1997a) proposes an intermediate solution, directing its members to apply existing tax principles in electronic transactions. OECD, in co-operation with the European Union, the World's Customs Organization and the business community, has defined a set of framework conditions to govern the taxation of electronic commerce. These are neutrality, effectiveness and fairness, certainty and simplicity, efficiency and flexibility, factors that are naturally important to traditional commerce as well. Thus it is necessary to define the "rules" that govern electronic commerce and ensure that regulations can be enforced.

Overall, the governance level of Internet policy presents a challenge for national policy makers as they realize it is difficult, if not impossible, to control electronic transactions. Also, it is debatable what is within a specific jurisdiction or how "net-laws" will be enforced or who will pay for enforcement (Shim et al., 2000). Additionally, policy makers are also keen to promote electronic commerce with minimal intervention, as they want to attract investors that will contribute to economic growth. North American countries, the European Union and Japan for example have realized that it is in their best interest to collaborate in order to create market conditions of trust. However, the interests of specific countries may at times prevail, and the compromises reached may be at a cost for digital democracy. A characteristic example is the difference between European and American provisions for personal data protection and its impact on electronic transactions between the two areas. This issue is addressed in further detail at the security and privacy levels in the next paragraphs.

Security

Network security and especially Web security is one of the most sensitive issues identified in the electronic commerce literature (e.g., Crocker, 1996; Kosiur, 1997; Liddy, 1996). A recent survey of Australian firms (Dinnie, 1999), "among the world's earliest adopters" of electronic commerce, reports that network security is a continuing concern and companies are more concerned about external threats. The survey reports that "16% of firms have suffered, or believe they may have suffered, at least one break-in via the Internet" (p. 112). Despite their perceptions of external threats, however, 30% of businesses admitted that their organization had no formal information security policy. More generally, the anxiety about security is expected to increase in coming years as Web-based applications are increasingly used for financial transactions. As the number of computers, networks, data and information multiply every day, the need for better security practices that protect information systems from malicious attacks and at the same time preserve the civil liberties will increase in the future (Hurley, 1999).

Cryptography is put forward as a powerful technological solution to network fraud. At an international level it can be applied with the collaboration of governments, the business community and trusted third parties (Denning, 1996). The required use of public and private keys in cryptography methods raises several public policy issues surrounding the encryption of data and who should hold the keys that unlock the encrypted information (Patrick, 1999; Pouloudi, 1997). Policy makers can play an important role in the implementation of a security policy, acting as trusted third parties or defining the legal framework for such organizations (Froomkin, 1996). There are multiple models concerning the role of governments in security policy. At one extreme, public authorities may have ultimate access to information and, at the other, they may leave the responsibility for security of the data to the information owner (Patrick, 1999). What seems to be urgently required today is better education and awareness of security of information systems and good security practices for companies and individuals (Hurley, 1999).

Privacy

Computer technologies like the Internet facilitate the exchange of personal information that can be collected, aggregated and sold across the world. As companies can easily take advantage of personal information that becomes accessible on information networks, e.g., through direct marketing (Wang et al., 1998), several issues are at stake. The most important concern is whether information is collected, aggregated or sold with the individual's explicit concern. There are several private organizations (Better Business Bureau onLine, BBBOnLine; World Wide Web Consortium, W3C; TRUSTe) that try to address the issue by giving a privacy "seal" to Web sites that are fulfilling some set criteria of privacy protection. These include the responsibility to make visitors to Web sites aware of what data is collected and giving them choice about making this data available to third parties. The TRUSTe white paper (http://www.truste.org/about/about_wp.html) also emphasizes that web sites bearing their privacy seal "must provide reasonable security to protect the data that is collected." Security is seen as the technological aspect of the broader social issues that are related to privacy.

Privacy is particularly important for the protection of sensitive personal data such as medical records, credit records, government data and personal data about children. The US government has taken an untied regulatory approach to protect such information. In other words the aim is to enable Internet users to choose for themselves what level of privacy protection they want (Nelson, 1999). In Europe, in contrast, data protection is stricter and has been articulated at a pan-European level (Allaert & Barber, 1998). In the United States, the EU directive (EC, 1995) has been perceived as being overprotecting for European companies, raising barriers to the free exchange of electronic data between Europe and other countries (Swire & Litan, 1998). Indeed, the European directive on data protection challenged electronic transactions and data exchanges internationally, as it banned the export of personal data from the EU to those countries without strict federal data protection laws. This included the US and resulted in severe trade disputes at an international level, which have been resolved recently with the Safe Harbor Privacy Arrangement. This is a mechanism with which, through an exchange of documents, EU is able to certify that participating US companies meet the EU requirements for adequate privacy protection. Participation in the safe harbor is voluntarily. Privacy advocates, however, argue that privacy is a profound and fundamental concept, hence "it merits extra-ordinary measures of protection and overt support" (Introna, 1997, p. 259).

The political nature of privacy is also evident within national boundaries, in particular in terms of the power that national regulators have: "what we should fear is the growth of government databases" (Singleton, 1998). Privacy therefore clearly raises social concerns in terms of trust, digital democracy as well as employment, particularly in relation to the rights of employers to access or monitor personal information of their employees (ranging from email messages to medical records), often without their explicit consent or even their knowledge. Finally, the difficulties of updating databases and business processes and the challenges to comply at a technical level when using some contemporary information technologies (Lycett & Pouloudi, 2002) signify that privacy protection remains a challenge for policy makers.

Content

As electronic commerce is an international phenomenon it is impossible for policy makers to control the content of the information transferred online. While the exposure to all this information can be beneficial, for example, expanding people's learning horizons (Forcheri et al., 2000), governments and citizens are concerned about the publication of offensive material (Nelson, 1999). As the complaints from parents and educators about the influence of the Internet on children become more frequent, there are several civil liberties organizations devoted to protecting users from exposure to inappropriate online material. Such groups include the Electronic Frontier Foundation (EFF), which supports legal and legislative action to protect the civil liberties of online users, and the Computer Professionals for Social Responsibility (CPSR), which aims to protect privacy and civil liberties. The World Wide Web Consortium (W3C) has developed a technical platform that allows user-defined, customized access to the Internet (Patrick, 1999; www.w3.organisation/PICS) and has enabled the creation of rating services and filtering software for use by concerned parents. While the need for filtering of some information is generally considered as appropriate, there are also attempts at censorship. For example certain

Asian countries place restrictions on the use of the Internet. The use of censorship on the information highway is debatable, both in terms of its technological feasibility but also in terms of its moral foundation (Ebbs & Rheingold, 1997).

Another content-related issues in electronic commerce is the protection of copyright and intellectual property rights. The essence of copyright is to prevent the unauthorized copying, but works stored in a digital format can easily be copied or altered, while they can also be transmitted speedily through electronic networks (Brett, 1999). The practical problems that owners of digital data face are very important for governments trying to apply or extend existing copyright laws to digital means. At an international level the World Intellectual Property Organization (WIPO) facilitates the protection of property rights. According to its general director, Dr. Kamil Idris, the organization's aim is to ensure that "expertise is provided when laws or systems need upgrading to take into account novel areas of invention (such as providing protection for the fruits of genetic research) or of medium (such as the Internet)." As with other policy issues, intellectual property involves multiple stakeholders with different interests (Radcliffe, 1999), which makes it difficult to resolve at a global level.

Underlying the discussion in terms of content are also issues of trust, in terms of access to "suitable" material but also in terms of authenticity, and issues related to the concept digital democracy, depending on who, if any, decides what constitutes "suitable" material.

Commerce

Electronic commerce is at the top of the policy architecture pyramid of the Global Internet Project, as it is perceived to be a critical factor driving the growth of the Internet. Although electronic commerce has revolutionized the way of conducting business, it is still a business activity that has to conform to certain rules and work under specific standards (Negroponte, 1999). The European Union was the first official body that considered a supranational policy on electronic commerce, in its effort to advance the integration process and to create a single market (Mc Gowan, 1998). However, there are several organizations working at a supranational level trying to enable global seamless communication such as the International Organization for Standardization (ISO) and the World Trade Organization (WTO). This is because standardization is recognized as an important issue in electronic commerce, since the establishment of EDI applications (e.g., Chatfield & Bjorn-Andersen, 1998; Faltch, 1998; Sokol, 1995; Tan, 1998). Standardization however can be problematic, as it needs to balance multiple interests in an area where competition has international dimensions and differs considerably from traditional commerce. The extent to which certain stakeholders are privileged has an impact on the role of electronic commerce in facilitating the digital democracy. The importance of trust at this level cannot be understated since, as discussed in section 2, it is one of the main reasons why electronic commerce has not reached its current potential.

The discussion in the previous five levels of the policy architecture demonstrates that issues of trust are relevant at all levels and indeed underpin the development and use of electronic commerce. The problem is that most of these policy issues are related to social concerns and cannot be easily resolved as they bring about conflicts among stakeholder groups and policy dilemmas. These dilemmas are discussed in detail below in the context of electronic commerce policy-making.

Dilemmas in Addressing Policy Issues

Previous research has argued that the policy objective of promoting deregulation and competition is in conflict with other policy priorities, in particular the desire to provide open networks and open access and the aspiration to provide universal service to citizens (Graham, 1995). As electronic commerce expands, the dilemmas for the stakeholders of the information society increase. The review of policy issues at different levels in the previous section has revealed some of the dilemmas that policy makers face today:

- Should governments give priority to the protection of national identity and language or to international compliance?
- Should they promote their own interests or provide assistance to developing countries?
- Is governance about protection or restriction? (For example, at an individual level: is censorship desirable? At a business level: is taxation desirable?)
- Where should priority be given: to the protection of personal data or to competitiveness (to the extent that the free exchange of information and personal data supports electronic transactions and business practices)?
- What is more important, data and intellectual property protection or the free exchange of ideas and data?

These dilemmas relate to the appropriate use of regulation, although in some cases policy makers may have little choice as only some options are realistic (e.g., the Internet is used even though the legal context is unstable). Thus, one important observation is that some dilemmas may no longer be a matter of choice, particularly for less powerful stakeholders, such as individuals, or governments of developing countries. A further observation is that in many cases these dilemmas imply a conflict between the commercial and social interests of various stakeholder groups. However, it is very difficult to draw some general conclusions about when either interest is at stake. Research in management (e.g., Pettigrew, 1985) and information systems (e.g., Walsham, 1993) as well as in law studies (e.g., as evident in the importance of case law) has stressed the importance of context. However, in "cyberspace" the context, whether temporal or spatial, is elusive, making policy making for electronic commerce more challenging. In view of these issues, the following section presents implications for policy makers, with emphasis on the policies that are relevant at the business and the societal level.

IMPLICATIONS FOR POLICY MAKERS

The challenge that policy makers face today in order to implement an efficient electronic commerce policy while addressing the dilemmas outlined above is twofold. Firstly, they need to provide the business community with a robust technical infrastructure and an efficient legislation framework. Secondly, they need to accommodate the social concerns rising from the use of electronic commerce, in order to create a "digital literate" society that will fully exploit the technology at hand while preserving their social interests and cultural identities.

A very important aspect of a national electronic commerce strategy is diffusion of knowledge about the to business and society at large. Damsgaard and Lyytinen (1998) use, in their analysis on the diffusion of EDI (business-to-business electronic commerce), six government strategies defined by King et al. (1994). These are knowledge building, knowledge deployment, subsidy, mobilization, innovation directive, and standard setting. We extend these strategies for the diffusion for electronic commerce, where apart from business individuals are also the targets of the government intervention. Thus, a grid can be created (see Table 1) with the combination of these strategies and their target groups (business, society).

Companies are usually the direct beneficiaries of electronic commerce policies. This is why all the diffusion strategies are applicable (see far right column in Table 1). Policy makers try to persuade enterprises to invest in new technologies and take advantage of the opportunities the new means can offer. The governments may use a great number of the strategies to influence companies and help them in the implementation of electronic commerce technologies and practices. Companies can first be made aware of the new technologies (knowledge deployment), receive financial support for investing in new technologies (subsidy), be encouraged to use technology in the "best way" (mobilization), be provided with examples of electronic commerce use (innovation directive) and finally follow standards (regulation setting). This part of the electronic commerce diffusion practice is related to technical and commercial aspects, which as we will explain in the next paragraph can be conflicting with social issues.

Individuals acting as consumers (such customers of virtual stores) or citizens (as users of online government services) are in need of information. Governments

Table 1: Target groups of an electronic commerce strategy

Policies	Individuals– Societal level	Companies- Business level
Knowledge building	✔	✔
Knowledge deployment	✔	✔
Subsidy		✔
Mobilization		✔
Innovation directive		✔
Standard/regulation setting		✔

can use traditional means such as the media to make their wide audience aware of the usefulness of the new medium and build confidence in electronic commerce transactions. Knowledge deployment and mobilization are the strategies that can best fit government's intention to create awareness about electronic commerce, as well as about the rights of individuals in this new environment. Issues such as awareness about privacy protection and trust towards electronic means should be considered by policy makers when they apply knowledge building and deployment practices. The education of the public, on one hand, can help the electronic commerce marketplace to reach a critical mass of users. On the other hand, a "digital literate" society can use electronic means to perform "electronic activism" and express disappointment about business practices (see, for example Badaracco & Useem, 1997). Additionally, they might refuse the exchange of personal data through electronic means, although this is a practice that is very useful to companies for marketing purposes. Thus, regulators should balance the needs of the business community with the social concerns related to the use of electronic means. It is expected that when the social issues such as trust and digital democracy are addressed satisfactorily, electronic commerce is more likely to become the predominant business practice.

The "education" of individuals within the business environment (business level) is essential. In this field the help of professional bodies such as chambers of commerce and trade associations is essential. While most of policy research concentrates on the role of governments or international organizations, the role of players, such as trade associations, that can act as policy intermediaries is very important: They have knowledge of the local context and thus can complement the general national or international policies. As discussed earlier in the paper, other policy intermediaries that become increasingly involved in policy issues in the information society include independent private organizations as well as civil liberties and professional groups who wish to promote the interest of a particular group or the net-citizens at large. Schools and universities also face pressures to support the "workforce of the future" and try to promote the use of information and communication technologies, thus contributing to knowledge building and deployment strategies. Finally, the Internet empowers individuals to draw their own policies at a micro-level, e.g., choosing as parents which Internet sites they allow their children to access, deciding whether to make their personal information available and so on. While the Internet enables people as citizens and consumers to take action (e.g., Badaracco & Useem, 1997), people are not necessarily aware of the opportunities and risks of cyberspace or they may not have the power and access to make a difference, hence the importance of knowledge building and deployment strategies. Policy makers, whether local or national, government or private, need to recognize the prevalence and importance of social issues and encourage the debate for appropriate policy making among stakeholders.

CONCLUSIONS

Policy makers have recognized the viability of electronic commerce and the opportunities it offers for business and citizens. While several ethical and security issues arise from the use of the new technologies, there is a general consensus that the benefits are substantial and justify the investment in electronic commerce. There are several efforts in this direction by policy makers at a national and international level. The paper has argued that technology alone is not sufficient for the successful implementation of complex electronic commerce strategies, but the examination of social and political issues is crucial for a holistic approach on the subject. Indeed there are several dilemmas related to policy issues, making the role of the policy makers critical. We considered a general framework for policy making that could be used at a national or international level as a starting point for considering social issues in the context of electronic commerce strategies.

Further research in the area may include the investigation of electronic commerce policies implemented in different national settings and social environments since, in practice, different countries have different priorities. The case of developing countries would be of particular interest as technical infrastructure and stakeholder awareness and involvement can be substantially different. Research also needs to be continued in specific areas that are affected by the extensive use of electronic commerce. Because of their social importance, of particular interest are the areas of health and education where issues of Internet use and electronic commerce become increasingly relevant (e.g., through tele-health or distance learning applications). A study of alternative national policies in these areas can lead to an informative debate about the underlying assumptions concerning the duties and social responsibility of policy makers towards different stakeholder groups.

ACKNOWLEDGMENTS

The financial support of EPSRC (grant GR/N03242) is gratefully acknowledged.

REFERENCES

Aalberts, R., and Townsend, A. (1998). The threat of long-arm jurisdiction to electronic commerce. *Communications of the ACM*, 41(12), 15-20.

Allaert, F. A. and Barber, B. (1998). Some systems implications of EU data protection directive. *European Journal of Information Systems*, 7(1), 1-4.

Badaracco, J. L., Jr. and Useem, J. V. (1997). The Internet, Intel and the vigilante stakeholder. *Business Ethics: A European Review*, 6(1), 18-29.

Bhatnagar, S. (1997). Electronic commerce in India: The untapped potential. *Electronic Markets*, 7(2), 22-24.

Blanning, R., Bui, T. and Tan, M. (1997). National information infrastructure in Pacific Asia. *Decision Support Systems*, 21, 215-227.

Brett, H. (1999). Copyright in a digital age. In Leer, A. (Ed.), *Masters of the Wired World*, 162-171. London: Financial Times Pitman Publishing.

Carter, D. (1997). Digital democracy or information aristocracy economic regeneration and the information economy. In Loader, B. (Ed.), *The Governance of Cyberspace*, 136-152. Routledge, London.

Chatfield, A. and Bjorn-Andersen, N. (1998). Reengineering with EDI. A Trojan horse in circumventing non-tariff barriers to trade. In Andersen, K. V. (Ed.), *EDI and Data Networking in the Public Sector*, 155-172. Kluwer Academic Publishers.

Clark, J., and Lai, V. (1998). Internet comes to Morocco. *Communications of the ACM*, 41(2), 21-23.

Damsgaard, J. and Lyytinen, K. (1998). Governmental intervention in the diffusion of EDI: Goals and conflicts. In Andersen, K. V. (Ed.), *EDI and Data Networking in the Public Sector*, 13-41. Kluwer Academic Publishers.

Daniel, J. (1999). The rise of the mega-university. In Leer, A. (Ed.), *Masters of the Wired World*, 333-342. London: Financial Times Pitman Publishing.

Dinnie, G. (1999). The second annual global information security survey. *Information Management & Computer Security*, 7(3), 112-120.

Doukidis, G., Poulymenakou, A., Terpsidis, I., Themistocleous, M. and Miliotis, P. (1998). *The Impact of the Development of Electronic Commerce on the Employment Situation in European Commerce*. Greece: Athens University of Economics and Business.

Dutton, W. H. (Ed.). (1996). *Information and Communication Technologies: Visions and Realities*. Oxford, UK: Oxford University Press.

Ebbs, G., & Rheingold, H. (1997). Censorship on the information highway. *Internet Research: Electronic Networking Applications and Policy*, 7(1), 59-60.

European Commission. (1995). Directive 95/46/EC of the European Parliament and the Council of 24 October 1995 on the protection of individuals with regard to the processing of personal data and on the free movement of such data. *Official Journal of the European Communities*, November, L281, 31.

European Commission. (1997). *A European Initiative in Electronic Commerce* (COM (97) 157 final). Brussels, Belgium.

Faltch, M. (1998). EDI in the public sector: Building on lessons from the private sector. In Andersen, K. V. (Ed.), *EDI and Data Networking in the Public Sector*, Kluwer Academic Publishers.

Forcheri, P., Molfino, M. T. and Quarati, A. (2000). ICT driven individual learning: new opportunities and perspectives. *Educational Technology & Society*, 3(1), 51-61.

Froomkin, A. (1996). The essential role of trusted third parties in electronic commerce. In Kalakota, R. and Whinston, A. (Eds.), *Readings in Electronic Commerce*, Addison-Wesley.

Graham, A. (1995). Public policy and the information superhighway: the scope for strategic intervention, co-ordination and top-slicing. In Collins, R. and Purnell, J. (Eds.), *Managing the Information Society*, 30-44. London: Institute for Public Policy Research.

Hart, P. and Saunders, C. (1997). Power and trust critical factors in the adoption and use of electronic data interchange. *Organization Science*, 8(1), 23-41.

Heldrich Center for Workforce Development. (2000). *Work Trends Survey, Nothing but Net: American Workers and the Information Economy*, 10 February.

Hoffman, D. and Novak, T. (1999). The evolution of the digital divide: Examining the relationship of race to Internet access and usage over time. *Conference on Understanding the Digital Economy: Data, Tools and Research*, May. USA: Washington.

Hudson, H. (1999). Access to the digital economy: Issues in rural and developing regions. *Conference on Understanding the Digital Economy: Data, Tools and Research*, 25-26 May. USA: Washington.

Hurley, D. (1999). Security and privacy laws. The showstoppers of the Global Information Society. In Leer, A. (Ed.), *Masters of the Wired World*, 247-260. London: Financial Times Pitman Publishing.

Introna, L. D. (1997). Privacy and the computer: Why we need privacy in the information society. *Metaphilosophy*, 28(3), 259-275.

Johnston, D. (1999). Global electronic commerce-realizing the potential. In Leer, A. (Ed.), *Masters of the Wired World*, 228-237. London: Financial Times Pitman Publishing.

Keenan, T. P. and Trotter, D. M. (1999). The changing role of community networks in providing citizen access to the Internet. *Internet Research: Electronic Networking Applications and Policy*, 9(2), 100-108.

Kim, E. and Hong, P. (1997). The government's role in diffusion of EC in Korea. *Electronic Markets*, 7(2), 6-8.

King, J., Gurbaxani, V., Kraemer, K., McFarlan, F., Raman, F. and Yap, F. W. (1994). Institutional factors in information technology innovation. *Information Systems Research*, 5(2), 139-169.

Kouzmin, A., Korac-Kakabadse, N. and Korac-Kakabadse, A. (1999). Globalization and information technology: Vanishing social contracts, the "pink collar" workforce and public policy challenges. *Women in Management Review*, 14(6), 230-251.

Lycett, M. G. and Pouloudi, A. (2002). Component-based development: issues of data protection. In Dhillon, G. (Ed.), *Social Responsibility in the Information Age*. Hershey, USA: Idea Group Publishing.

Martin, J. (1999). Building the cyber-corporation. In Leer, A. (Ed.), *Masters of the Wired World*, 324-332. London: Financial Times Pitman Publishing.

Mc Gowan, L. (1998). Protecting competition in a global market: The pursuit of an international competition policy. *European Business Review*, 98(6), 382-339.

Miles, R. and Snow, C. (1992). Causes of failure in network organizations. *California Management Review*, Summer, 53-72.

Murison-Bowie, S. (1999). Forms and functions of digital content in education. In Leer, A. (Ed.), *Masters of the Wired World*, 142-151. London: Financial Times Pitman Publishing.

Negroponte, N. (1999). Being digital in the wired world. In Leer, A. (Ed.), *Masters of the Wired World*, 386-394. London: Financial Times Pitman Publishing.

Nelson, M. (1999). Politics and policy-making in the electronic marketplace. In Leer, A. (Ed.), *Masters of the Wired World*, 261-269. London: Financial Times Pitman Publishing.

Nguyen, D. T. and Alexander, J. (1996). The coming of cyberspacetime and the end of the polity. In Shields, R. (Ed.), *Cultures of Internet: Virtual Spaces, Real Histories, Living Bodies*, 99-124. London: Sage.

Organization for Economic Co-operation and Development. (1997a). *The Communication Revolution and Global Commerce: Implications for Tax Policy and Administration*.

Organization for Econoic Co-operation and Development. (1997b). Global Information infrastructure-Global information society (GII-GIS). Policy requirements.

Owens, J. (1999). Electronic commerce: Taxing times. In Leer, A. (Ed.), *Masters of the Wired World*, 286-295. London: Financial Times Pitman Publishing.

Papazafeiropoulou, A., and Pouloudi, A. (2000). The government's role in improving electronic commerce adoption. In Hansen et al., (Eds.), *Proceedings of the European Conference on Information Systems 2000*, July, 1, 709-716. Austria: Vienna.

Patrick, J. (1999). The opportunity and the challenge to sustain rapid Internet growth. In Leer, A. (Ed.), *Masters of the Wired World*, 105-112. London: Financial Times Pitman Publishing.

Pettigrew, A. M. (1985). Contextualist research and the study of organizational change processes. In Mumford, E., Hirschheim, R., Fitzgerald, G. and Wood-Harper, T. (Eds.), *Research Methods in Information Systems*, 53-78. Amsterdam: Elsevier Science Publishers, North-Holland.

Raab, C. (1997). Privacy, democracy, information. In Loader, B. (Ed.), *The Governance of Cyberspace*, 155-174. London:Routledge.

Raab, C., Bellamy, C., Taylor, J., Dutton, W. H. and Peltu, M. (1996). The information polity: Electronic democracy, privacy, and surveillance. In Dutton, W. H. (Eds.), *Information and Communication Technologies*, 283-299. Oxford, UK: Oxford University Press.

Radcliffe, M. (1999). Intellectual property and the global information infrastructure. In Leer, A. (Ed.), *Masters of the Wired World*, 105-112. London: Financial Times Pitman Publishing.

Ratnasingham, P. (1998). The importance of trust in electronic commerce. *Internet Research: Electronic Networking Applications and Policy*, 8(4), 313-321.

Shade, L. R. (1996). Is there free speech on the Net? Censorship in the global information infrastructure. In Shields, R. (Ed.), *Cultures of Internet: Virtual Spaces, Real Histories, Living Bodies*. London: Sage.

Shields, R. (Ed.). (1996). *Cultures of Internet: Virtual Spaces, Real Histories, Living Bodies*. London: Sage.

Shim, J. P., Simkin, M. G. and Bartlett, G. W. (2000). NetLaw. *Communications of the Association for Information Systems*, 4(4).

Singleton, S. (1998). Privacy as censorship: A skeptical view of proposals to regulate privacy in the private sector (Cato Policy Analysis No. 295).

Sokol, P. (1995). *From EDI to Electronic Commerce*. McGraw-Hill.

Stanford Institute for the Quantitative Study for Society. (2000). *Internet and Society*, February.

Swire, P. P., and Litan, R. E. (1998). None of your business. *World Data Flows, Electronic Commerce, and the European Privacy Directive*. Washington DC, USA: Brookings Institution Press.

Tan, M. (1998). Government and private sector perspective of EDI: The case of TradeNet EDI and Data Networking in the Public Sector, Andersen, K. V. (Ed.), 131-153. Kluwer Academic Publishers.

US Department of Commerce. (1998). *The Emerging Digital Economy*. Washington, USA: US Department of Commerce.

Walsham, G. (1993). *Interpreting Information Systems in Organizations*. Chichester: Wiley.

Walsham, G. (1999). GIS for district-level administration in India: problems and opportunities. *MIS Quarterly*, 23(1), 39-66.

Wang, H., Lee, M. K. O. and Wang, C. (1998). Consumer privacy concerns about internet marketing. *Communications of the ACM*, 41(3), 63-70.

The White House. (1999). *Facilitating the Growth of Electronic Commerce*. Washington DC, USA: The White House.

Wilson, S. (1997). Certificates and trust in electronic commerce. *Information Management & Computer Security*, 5(5), 175-181.

Chapter XII

E-commerce Taxation Issues: A Balanced Perspective and Options for Resolution

Mahesh S. Raisinghani
University of Dallas, USA

Dan S. Petty
North Texas Commission, USA

This chapter is designed to give the reader a balanced perspective on some of the issues surrounding the current discussions related to state and local taxation of Internet access fees and sales transactions on the Internet. It will attempt to describe the issues being discussed and present several viewpoints from interest groups on both sides of the issue. This chapter is being written at an interesting time since the proponents of Internet taxation are searching for technological as well as administrative ways to met their goal. The Advisory Commission on Electronic Commerce released its final recommendations to Congress in April 2000, after its four in-person meetings in Williamsburg, Virginia; New York City, New York; San Francisco, California; and Dallas, Texas. Taxation of Internet access and transactions on the Internet is one of the most complicated public policy issues of our time, affecting over 30,000 state and local taxing jurisdictions and literally thousands of businesses and customers worldwide. The proposal receiving the majority vote of the commissioners is based on the conclusion that existing, internationally accepted tax rules should be applied to e-commerce with no new taxes being levied and with an emphasis on simplification, neutrality, greater certainty and avoidance of double taxation. This chapter will develop a next-steps strategy to be considered by policy makers.

ISSUES IN ELECTRONIC COMMERCE TAXATION

Electronic commerce (e-commerce) has had a profound effect on the way business is conducted worldwide. The impact of the Internet on the economy of the United States has benefited US citizens in all walks of life. The growth of e-commerce has helped create thousands of jobs that are highly skilled and high-paying and this phenomenal growth has provided the consumer with access to goods and services at competitive prices.

Many interest groups such as the Internet Tax Fairness Coalition and the e-Commerce Coalition feel that the growth of the economy has created sufficient taxes to fund the basic needs of state and local governments and that taxation of transactions on the Internet creates an unnecessary burden on business activities (The Internet Tax Fairness Coalition, 2000; e-Freedom Coalition, 2000). These groups point out that state and local governments have provided services to their constituents without Internet transaction taxes and that the Supreme Court of the United States has long held that vendors have a sales tax obligation only when the buyer and seller are in the same state or the seller has a "nexus," or physical presence, in the buyer's state. These coalitions and others feel that the best way to ensure long-term economic prosperity, quality services and the continued growth of Internet business is to continue to support the Internet as the new engine driving the new economy and reduce, not increase, barriers to entry for companies not yet taking advantage of electronic commerce.

The coalitions point out the complexity of the state and local tax systems, with over 30,000 taxing jurisdictions in the United States and the prospect of multiple jurisdictions requiring collection and payment of taxes on transactions. They point out that main-street retailers collect taxes from their customers at a single rate, prepare and file a single tax return, and file tax returns at one place. Taxation of on-line transactions would require the vendor to identify all taxing jurisdictions and send in forms and collections to all relevant jurisdictions. Also, changes in local sales tax rates and the items subject to taxation vary from jurisdiction to jurisdiction, causing a great deal of confusion for the buyer and the seller. The complicated, complex and ever changing maze of state and local tax policies and laws makes application of a sensible, fair and easily understood Internet transaction tax policy virtually impossible under the present circumstances. James Plummer, a policy analyst at Consumer Alert wrote, "Nefarious new taxes and regulations will kill many new start-up e-businesses before they even start up; denying consumers their chance to find the specialized products and services for their needs"(2000).

However the state governors seem to disagree. The antitax community and coalitions mentioned above have a strong adversary in the National Governors Association in that the governors are worried that the brick-and-mortar stores like the main streets and malls of America, are jeopardized by the popularization of Internet commerce, particularly if it is tax-free commerce (National Governors Association, 2000). The governors suggest that if consumers only had to pay taxes when they bought from main street and mall stores but not when they bought goods from Internet stores, that this would discriminate against the main street and mall stores and put them at a competitive disadvantage based solely on government tax policy. Also there has been an argument put forth that while net tax leniency may help spread the Internet more rapidly, it is bad social policy because the people who shop on the Internet disproportionately come from upper rings of the economic ladder and are the least in need of a tax break. Andy Reinhardt claims that tax-free net shopping benefits mostly well-off people and makes the already regressive structure of sales taxes even more unbalanced. It might even be called corporate welfare for tiny start-ups with gigantic market capitalization, while, at the same time, the net-based economy has plenty of traction. In fact, Reinhardt suggests that such a policy seems too generous a helping hand, especially when it's the poor who carry the load (2000). Major brick-and-mortar retailers such as Sears and Wal-Mart are concerned that if the states cannot resolve this issue among themselves quickly, public resistance to taxing e-commerce could grow so strong that a solution may become politically impossible.

THE ADVISORY COMMISSION ON ELECTRONIC COMMERCE

Due to the complex issues and murky state and local policies regarding taxation on the Internet, a bill was enacted by Congress in 1998 entitled the Internet Tax Freedom Act. The act imposed a 3-year moratorium on new Internet taxation. The act also established the Advisory Commission on Electronic Commerce and charged it with the responsibility to address the issues related to Internet taxation (Advisory Commission on Electronic Commerce, 2000).

The Advisory Commission is composed of three representatives of the federal government, eight representatives of state and local governments and eight representatives of the electronic commerce industry. The commission is charged with conducting a thorough study of federal, state, local and international taxation and tariff treatment of transactions using the Internet and Internet access, and other comparable intrastate, interstate, or international sales activities. The commission's recommendations are to be submitted to Congress no later than April 2000. The act also placed a 3-year moratorium on taxes on Internet access in order to give the commission time to review the issues and make its recommendations. The Commission has met three times and is scheduled to have its final meeting March 20-21, 2000, in Dallas. The commission has received volumes of testimony and comments on the issues before it and is reviewing, among other things, barriers imposed in foreign markets on US property, goods or services engaged in the Internet, how such barriers affect US consumers, the collection and administration of consumption taxes on the Internet in the US and abroad, the impact of Internet taxes, model state legislation, the effects of Internet taxation on interstate commerce, and ways to simplify federal, state and local taxes imposed on telecommunications services.

THE NATIONAL GOVERNORS ASSOCIATION'S PERSPECTIVE

Today, 46 states have a sales tax of some sort. All of the 46 states that have a sales tax also have what is called a complementary use tax. The consumer pays both of these taxes. Consumers pay the sales tax when they buy goods and services in their own state. When goods are purchased from out of state, consumers are supposed to pay a use tax. Double taxation is avoided because the consumer only pays the tax in his or her place of residence and taxes are only owed to the state where the consumer lives.

The merchant is responsible for collection of the tax and remitting it to the consumers' state. When the consumer buys from an out-of-state merchant, such as mail order or the Internet, the merchant, under existing law, is required to collect the tax and send it to the consumer's state only if the merchant has a physical presence (nexus) in the consumer's state. A physical presence may be a store, a distribution center, or a sales force. If the merchant does not have a physical presence in the consumers' state, the US Supreme Court has ruled, in the 1967 National Bellas Hess and the 1992 Quill decisions, that the merchant cannot be required to collect the use tax and remit it to the state of residence of the consumer (National Governors Association, 2000). However, the consumer still has the legal responsibility to remit the use tax to the state of his or her residence under present law.

Consumers then are responsible for paying taxes on goods they purchase through mail-order catalogues and over the Internet, just like they are responsible for paying sales taxes on goods bought in main street and mall stores. If consumers only had to pay taxes on goods bought from main street and mall stores and not from goods purchased over the Internet, this would discriminate against the main street and mall stores and put them at a competitive disadvantage based solely on government tax policy. The Governors Association believes that government tax policy should not be picking winners and losers by subsidizing one category of businesses at the expense of their competitors.

The governors have suggested a streamlined sales tax system for the 21st century. The proposed system would retain current law with regard to nexus and move toward a uniform system over the long term (National Governors Association, 2000). Some of the features of the governors' proposed streamlined system include:

- Elimination of the burden for firms to collect state and local sales taxes.
- Maintain the current definitions of nexus.
- Simplify the current system of exemption administration.
- Enact the system by the states without any action by the federal government.
- Offer the system a phased-in approach to all sellers on a voluntary basis.
- Eliminate the cost of compliance, tax returns and payments and tax audits.
- Eliminate tax-rate monitoring and implementation, and eliminate record-keeping requirements for the sellers.
- Eliminate any requirement for sellers to police the intent or status of purchasers asserting special exemptions.
- Eliminate risks for seller exercising reasonable care

The states would implement uniform laws, practices, technology applications, and collections systems to achieve the goals. These goals when implemented would achieve the first step of the streamlined system. The second step would be for all state and local governments to adopt the same classification systems, definitions and audits. In order for states to collect sales taxes, states would have to conform to the uniform nationwide system and those that did not conform would be denied the ability to collect taxes on remote sales until they adopted the uniform system. All merchants should reap the benefits of a uniform system with simple and fair practices.

The overall concept of the streamlined system is to reduce the costs and burden of sales tax compliance for participating sellers through shifting sales tax administration to a technology-oriented business model operated by trusted third parties (TTPs) simplifying sales and use tax laws and administrative procedures and the states assuming responsibilities for the costs of the system whereby a seller would not be charged for participation in the streamlined system. The streamlined system would be implemented by a combination of uniform legislation and multistate agreements among the participating states.

THE E-COMMERCE COALITION PERSPECTIVE

The e-Commerce Coalition is a broad-based national coalition dedicated to providing sound policy information on electronic commerce taxation and includes in its membership AOL, Bank One, Cisco Systems, Accenture, Citigroup, Microsoft, Wal-Mart, Intuit and others (e-Commerce Coalition, 2000).

The coalition believes that sales tax compliance costs result in significant expenses for large and small companies and simplification of the system is crucial if any progress is to be made towards addressing the issues surrounding the taxation of remote commerce, including leveling the playing field for all commerce.

The coalition's goals follow closely those of the National Tax Association. Both organizations suggest that improving the current system was preferred. Improvements should be made through a series of substantive and procedural changes to the existing procedures that an interstate seller uses with each state in which it collects taxes. Each state would be responsible for administration of its own tax system and therefore much could be achieved toward achieving their mutual goals (National Tax Association, 1999).

The coalition urged that simplification of the current sales and use system is absolutely crucial if meaningful progress is to be made towards addressing the many issues relating to e-commerce. Simplification must come before technology can play a major role in a solution. Time is of the essence because of the speed at which this industry is growing and changing. The coalition believes that rather than trying to make a complex and broken existing system fit a new economic environment, that it is time for states and localities to make the sales and use tax system less complex by simplification measures and help level the playing field for all types of commerce.

GOVERNOR JAMES GILMORE'S PERSPECTIVE

Gov. James Gilmore of Virginia is chairman of the Advisory Commission on Electronic Commerce. Governor Gilmore submitted a proposal to the commission on November 8,1999, entitled "No Internet Tax" (Gilmore, 1999).

The governor basically describes the enormous positive impact that the Internet has had on the economy in creating job and new business opportunities. He concludes that the Internet changes everything, including government, and that government must change its policies as well as the way it operates.

Gov. Gilmore's proposal outlines several suggestions for the commission and the Congress to address:

- Congress should prohibit all sales and use taxes on business-to-consumer Internet transactions.
- Congress should protect companies from unfair income and business activity taxes imposed upon them due to their virtual presence in states.
- The Tax Freedom Act should be amended to prohibit all taxes on Internet access.
- Congress should abolish the federal 3% excise tax on telephone service.
- There should be no international tariffs or taxes on e-commerce.
- States should be permitted to spend federal funds for temporary assistance to needy families to buy computers and Internet access for needy families.

The Governor believes that American public policy should embrace the Internet and the borderless economy it creates rather than impose old ways of thinking and antiquated locus-based tax structures upon it.

RADIOSHACK CORPORATION'S PERSPECTIVE

The RadioShack Corporation's perspective was presented to the Advisory Commission on Electronic Commerce at its meeting September 13-15, 1999, in New York City by Ronald L. Parrish, vice president for industry and government affairs (Parrish,1999).

RadioShack's comments were essentially presented in two parts dealing with whether remote sales of goods on the Internet should be subject to sales and use taxes and the subject of taxes on Internet access.

RadioShack supported the passage of the Internet Tax Freedom Act of 1998 and the creation of the Advisory Commission. The issue in RadioShack's eyes is one of equal treatment between retailers who must legally collect taxes on remote commerce and those who do not. Retailers with nexus in many, if not all, states find themselves at a competitive disadvantage to e-tailers and some who even ignore the laws that are on the books. RadioShack believes that no more than one tax rate for each state should be implemented, with uniform classifications of goods subject to taxation. Also, RadioShack believes there is no justification for a federal gross receipts tax, the creation of a new federal agency to collect sales taxes or a private tax clearinghouse to collect taxes.

RadioShack feels that the existing moratorium on Internet access fee taxes should be extended indefinitely. RadioShack's suggested guiding principles for Congress include:

- All retailers of remote commerce should be treated equally, regardless of nexus or lack thereof.
- Sales taxes should be applied to Internet/remote commerce in a manner consistent to brick-and-mortar retailers.
- No more than one sales tax rate per state should be applied to Internet sales.
- The states should adopt uniform principles of taxation for categories of goods to be taxed and exempted.
- No new federal gross receipts tax on Internet sales should be imposed and no new federal agency to collect Internet taxes should be created.
- The current moratorium on Internet infrastructure taxes and access fees should be extended permanently.

INTERNET TAXATION ISSUES IN TEXAS

The e-commerce business community in Texas listened to Lt. Governor Rick Perry, at the first meeting of his newly appointed Advisory Council on the Digital Economy, say that the state should not impose any *new* taxes on the Internet (Stutzt, 2000). There is a widespread assumption in Texas that sales taxes on online sales are illegal for three years because of the federal Internet Tax Freedom Act of 1998. That is a misunderstanding of the federal law, which bars states from imposing *new* taxes on those transactions, but leaves the existing Texas laws in place. If you buy something online from a Texas company, you have to pay sales tax since the seller is located in the state. If you buy something from a company that does not have a physical presence (nexus) in the state, that company does not have to collect the tax or send those taxes to the comptroller's office in Austin. The Texas buyer legally still owes the tax to the state of Texas. However, it is generally felt that most individual buyers probably don't report these types of sales or pay the use tax owed. Most businesses do pay the use taxes. Gov. Perry doesn't seem to want the state to impose a *new* tax on online sales, and he doesn't appear to see a need right now to change the existing state tax law or develop any new interpretations of how that law might be enforced differently.

At the federal campaign level, it appears that President Bush will develop his position on these issues after he has reviewed the final report of the Advisory Commission to Congress (LaGesse, 2000). President Bush does seem inclined to extend the current moratorium.

The Advisory Commission seems to be hung up on how these issues will play internationally. A free-trade cyberspace thrills trade negotiators and at the same time a tax-free cyberspace makes tax collectors miserable. The European Union has worked out a system where all 15 members impose hefty value-added taxes and all retailers must collect the tax for all sales within the union--i.e., an Internet purchase made in Germany by a customer in Portugal gets taxed at the VAT rate for Portugal; the German seller collects it. United States negotiators are working with groups internationally to come to some understanding regarding these complex issues (Landers, 2000).

The governors now want Congress to let the states tax Internet services in a fashion similar to a law passed in Texas in 1999 and signed by then--Gov. George W. Bush. The Texas law applies to monthly Internet access fees greater than $25. per month. The concept of taxing Internet access fees will likely run into serious opposition in Congress. Sen. Ron Wyden and Rep. Christopher Cox say that they would work to extend the e-tax moratorium for five more years and permanently bar all access taxes (*Business Week*, 2001).

On the other side, the taxing entities generally feel that the online retailers should have to collect the same taxes as brick-and-mortar businesses. A number of the states, up to 35 at times, seem to be determined to simplify the tax structure and systems at the state level. They have signed on to the Streamlined Sales Tax Project, whereby they have agreed to pattern their tax system from a model code (*The Wall Street Journal*, 2001). Uniformity is the key and simplicity is essential. Several states are participating in a pilot program in the spring and summer of 2001 with hopes of learning how to work together and streamline their taxation efforts. Four states, California, Massachusetts, Virginia and Colorado, who are leading technology states, put forth the argument that taxing Internet access and commerce would harm the growth sector of their economies and have the effect of reducing income tax collections from their fast-growing technology companies. It is understood that President Bush would be in favor of extending the moratorium and also ban taxes on access fees. Many think Congress will extend the moratorium but there is no way of predicting how long the extension will be for and what elements of Internet access and commerce will be affected.

SUMMARY OF OPTIONS FOR RESOLUTION OF INTERNET TAXATION ISSUES

After reviewing some of the information available on this very complex subject of Internet taxation, it appears that an interim solution might evolve from the final report and recommendations of the Advisory Commission on Electronic Commerce. Any recommendation would probably include an extension of the moratorium on taxes on Internet access.

It must be acknowledged that use of the Internet and transactions on the Internet have precipitated a great deal of dialogue on taxation issues. Although there are serious and complex issues, it appears that a resolution can be constructed that addresses most of the issues and does not disrupt what is clearly one of the most significant economic engines, of modern and perhaps all, time.

A solution or solutions will need to respect the needs of state and local governments, which depend on sales taxes to provide funds for basic state and local governmental services, and, at the same time, support electronic commerce as a mechanism for enhancing our economy and quality of life.

It seems that state and local governments can develop systems with innovative concepts and procedures which allow them to collect taxes due without creating an unnecessary bureaucracy and roadblocks to the normal expansion of the electronic commerce business growth and development.

There can be a combination of workable solutions including technology being applied to the collection process, standardization of tax systems, utilization of private-sector partners and assumption by state and local governments of the responsibility to pay the costs of newly developed and technologically sophisticated collection systems.

A version of the electronic commerce technology for tax administration, developed and operated by a major US company, is being used in Europe to collect transactional value-added taxes at the time of sale (National Tax Association, 2000). This system contains most of the features that states would find necessary for the proper and efficient collection of their taxes. Additional features that would be desirable are within technical reach and are under development by at least one other company. The technology of electronic commerce is itself a major resource for helping solve the long-standing sales and use tax issues.

Another key element of the solution will involve interstate standardization and simplification of key features of sales and use tax systems. State and local governments have acknowledged that their system of sales and use taxes must change in a substantial manner if they are to remain viable in the 21st century (National Tax Association, 2000). Since the Internet is a vast multinational framework comprised of more than 150,000 individual networks and used by more than 304 million people around the world (Advisory Commission on Electronic Commerce, 2000), taxing authorities are now moving toward the development of multistate systems that will help remove complexity and add simplicity to the process. This simplicity movement will provide a foundation for changes in tax laws and procedures necessary to enable the technology for tax administration to work effectively and efficiently for e-commerce. The two most prevalent areas involving simplification are local option taxes and exemption administration.

The United States Supreme Court, in its Quill decision, made it clear that states cannot impose the obligation of use tax collection on remote sellers whose contacts with states are limited in nature because of the burden of collection for those sellers. Thus, it seems if sales and use taxes are to be equitably collected at the time of sale, state and local governments will need to assume the costs and burden of collection for remote sellers who are constitutionally protected. Therefore, state and local governments, working in concert with the private sector, could incorporate the court's direction into a solution for sales and use tax collection issues.

It seems that a new system of sales and use tax administration could be designed around the needs of electronic commerce. What is really required to resolve the sales and use tax issues, more than just technology and simplifications and financing, is leadership among state and local officials, technology companies and interstate marketers that would provide the vision and imagination to move forward in developing a new system of administration. The new system could accomplish the collection of taxes on an equitable and efficient basis without burdening remote sellers. In the end, both state and local governments, the growing electronic commerce industry and the taxpayers and consumers can benefit from the creative genius of the leaders of our time.

CONCLUSION

Seven criteria laid out for use in designing an acceptable cybertax system may form the basis of an effective resolution: The system should be equitable and simple, ensure user confidence, prevent tax evasion and economic distortion, maintain a fair balance among countries, and not introduce a new form of taxation (Kyu Lee & Hwangbo, 2000). Since part of the solution revolves around technology, a growing number of software companies are developing powerful new programs that promise to streamline the collection of sales taxes, both on the Internet and from traditional brick-and-mortar sellers. However, without the assurance of a uniform nationwide approach, even the most sophisticated technological solution will collapse. It is critical to resolve the e-commerce taxation issue by finding a feasible way to implement a multistate system for collecting taxes from literally hundreds of tax jurisdictions across the country. The Streamlined Sales Tax Project has been launched by some 30 state governments "to develop a radically simplified sales and use tax system that eases the burden of state use and tax compliance for all types of retailers, particularly those operating on a multistate basis" (Rankin, 2000). The outcome will have long-term consequences for US retailing and, according to some, for the American system of government itself.

REFERENCES

Advisory Commission on Electronic Commerce. (2000). Report to Congress, April, 7.

Advisory Commission on Electronic Commerce. (2000). Retrieved April 2000 on the World Wide Web: http://www.ecomercecommission.org/FAQs.htm.

e-Commerce Coalition. (2000). joseph.Crosby@ey.com, April.

e-Freedom Coalition. (2000). Retrieved April 2000 on the World Wide Web: http://www.policy.com/news/dbrief/dbrief arc453.asp.

Gilmore, J. III, J. (1999). No Internet Tax Proposal. Advisory Commission on Electronic Commerce, November. Retrieved April 2000 on the World Wide Web: http://www.e-commerceccommission.org/proposal.

Internet Tax Fairness Coalition.(2000). Retrieved April 2000 on the World Wide Web: http://www.nettax.fairness.org/facts.

Kyu, Lee, J. and Hwangbo, Y. (2000). Cyberconsumption taxes and electronic commerce collection systems: A canonical consumer-delivered sales tax. *International Journal of Electronic Commerce*, Winter, 4(2), 6-82.

LaGesse, D. (2000). Governor George W. Bush. *The Dallas Morning News*, January 17, 1D.

Landers, J. (2000). Internet tax issues. *The Dallas Morning News*, January 17, 1D.

National Governors Association. (2000). Retrieved April 2000 on the World Wide Web: http://www.nga.org/internet/overview.asp.

National Governors Association. (2000). Retrieved April 2000 on the World Wide Web: http://www.nga.org/internet/facts.asp.

National Governors Association. (2000). Retrieved April 2000 on the World Wide Web: http://www.nga.org/internet/proposal.asp.

National Tax Association. (1999). *Communications and Electronic Commerce Tax Project Final Report*, September 7, 6-7.

Other tax battleground of 2001: The Internet. (2001). *Business Week*, February 19, 49.

Parrish, R. L. (1999). *Tandy/RadioShack Corporation Comments to Advisory Commission on Electronic Commerce*, September 14-15. ron.parrish@tandy.com.

Plummer, J. (2000). Consumer alert [Interview]. Retrieved April 2000 on the World Wide Web: http://www.policy.com/news.

Rankin, K. (2000). Race against time: Seeking a Net sales tax solution. *ECWorld*, August, 26-28.

Reinhardt, A. (2000). *Business Week*, January 17, 39.

States at odds over Web taxes. (2001). *The Wall Street Journal*, March 7, B3.

Stutzt, T. (2000). Lt Governor Rick Perry. *The Dallas Morning News*, February, 15A.

APPENDIX

State Taxation of the Internet: State-by-state tax treatment of Internet access, sales and software.

Figure 1: State taxation of the Internet

State	Access to Internet	Sales of Goods Over Internet	Downloaded Information/ Software	Canned Software	Custom Software
Alabama	E	T	T	T	E
Alaska	*No state sales tax*				
Arizona	E	T	T	T	E
Arkansas	E	T	E	T	T
California	E	T	E	T	E
Colorado	E	T	T	T	E
Connecticut	T	T	T	T	T
Delaware	*No state sales tax*				
D.C.	E	T	T	T	T
Florida	E	T	E	T	E
Georgia	E	T	E	T	E
Hawaii	T	T	T	T	T
Idaho	E	T	T	T	E
Illinois	E	T	Information - E, Software - T	T	E
Indiana	E	T	Information - E, Software - T	T	E
Iowa	E	T	T	T	E
Kansas	E	T	Information - E, Software - T	T	E
Kentucky	E	T	Undetermined	T	E
Louisiana	E	T	T	T	T
Maine	E	T	T	T	E
Maryland	E	T	E	T	E
Massachusetts	E	T	E	T	E
Michigan	E	T (use tax)	Information - E, Software - T	T	E
Minnesota	E	T	Information - E, Software - T	T	E
Mississippi	E	T	T	T	T
Missouri	E	T	E	T	E
Montana	*No state sales tax*				
Nebraska	E[1]	T	Information - E, Software - T	T	T
Nevada	E	T	E	T	E

* *E - Exempt, T - Taxable*

Figure 2: State taxation of the Internet (continued)

STATE TAXATION OF THE INTERNET

State-by-state tax treatment of Internet access, sales and software

State	Access to Internet	Sales of Goods Over Internet	Downloaded Information/ Software	Canned Software	Custom Software
New Hampshire	*No state sales tax*				
New Jersey	E	T	E	T	E
New Mexico	T	T	T	T	T
New York	E	T	T	T	E
North Carolina	E	T	E	T	E
North Dakota	T	T	Information - E, Software - T	T	E
Ohio	T[2]	T	T - commercial use only	T	T[5]
Oklahoma	E	T	E[4]	T	E
Oregon	*No state sales tax*				
Pennsylvania	E	T	Information - E, Software - T	T	E
Rhode Island	E	T	E	T	E
South Carolina	E	T	E	T	T
South Dakota	T	T	T	T	T
Tennessee	T	T	Information - E, Software - T	T	T
Texas	E[3]	T	T	T	T
Utah	E	T	T	T	E
Vermont	E	T	E	T	E
Virginia	E	T	E	T	E
Washington	E	T	T	T	E
West Virginia	E	T	T	T	T
Wisconsin	T	T	Information - E, Software - T	T	E
Wyoming	E	T	E	T	E

* E - *Exempt*, T - *Taxable*

1 Initial setup taxable if software is provided.
2 Commercial use only.
3 The first $25 of a monthly charge is exempt.
4 Exempt unless purchaser receives a backup copy or manual in addition to downloaded software.
5 Custom"Systems" software sold to a business is taxable, custom "application" software remains nontaxable. Modified canned programs are still considered a sale of canned software if the charge for the modification is no more than half the sale price.

Source: 1999 U.S. Master Sales and Use Tax Guide

Source for Figures 1 and 2: State Taxation Institute

Chapter XIII

Manufacturing Social Responsibility Benchmarks in the Competitive Intelligence Age

James Douglas Orton
University of Nevada, Las Vegas, USA

I am in the competitive intelligence version of a witness protection program. After six years as a spy to the French eye and as a traitor to the American eye, I am becoming comfortable blending back in to the relatively monocultural population of unquestioning Americans. No accents, no suspicions, no guarded words, no misinformation, no handlers, no fauxpas, no culture shock–I have come in from the competitive intelligence cold. Although I can feel myself being reabsorbed into the warm American Emersonian oversoul, I am haunted by the guilt of the double agent. What damage did I do in the last six years?

The Americans believe I sold out the secrets of the American-dominated Fortune 500 for 30 pieces of Parisian silver. Why, they wonder, would a young business school professor (trained in the American heartlands of Utah, Texas, and Michigan) abandon the US economy to go work for another country? When I showed French MBAs, through Harvard Business School cases, that Harley Davidson, Corning Glass, and Caterpillar Tractor had weaknesses that could be skillfully exploited from outside the US, wasn't I being a traitor to my country's economy? When I taught French doctoral students the arcane arts of publishing articles in American business academic journals, wasn't I taking journal space away from American doctoral students? When I taught French executives how Americans built corporate strategies from thousands of small wins, wasn't I aiding and abetting the enemies of America's economic security? Finally, though, when I agreed to teach an elective course to my elite international students on strategic intelligence, didn't I commit the unforgiveable sin of raising up a generation of spies who might torment my country for years to come?

The French believe I was always under the control of CIA handlers. When, every year, I would ask for a raise, the response from senior colleagues would be that I didn't need one, since I already had two salaries: one from the CIA and one from the French business school. The French foreign minister started referring to the United States as a hyperpower. Graffiti started springing up around Paris saying "America dehors l'Europe" (Get America out of Europe). In that context, when I was caught in their libraries, studying their internship reports, and using their Reuters subscription, it was clear to the French that I was an economic intelligence agent for the US government tunneling for information on Totale, Danone, Schneider, Aerospatiale, Air France and Carrefour.

One case study that captures my six years as a competitive intelligence agent involved a meeting of French competitive intelligence officers from 40 large corporations. My French business school employers dipped into their training budget to send me to a seminar in downtown Paris on economic intelligence. For two days, 60 of us listened to 10 presenters explain the state of the art of economic intelligence. A pharmaceutical firm told us how they had transformed their sales network into a business intelligence system by developing electronic contact reports (Thietart & Vivas, 1981). An aerospace company explained how their small intelligence unit was using Web-clipping software to send information to relevant sections of their organization (Gibbons & Prescott, 1996). A big-picture thinker formerly with L'Oreal used Rene Magritte paintings to expand our minds toward the creative use of information. Hubert Lesca presented academic research he has conducted with his doctoral students at the University of Grenoble on removing blockages in the intelligence cycle. Yves-Michel Marti described the elaborate intelligence cycle his consulting firm uses to generate economic intelligence for their clients (Martinet & Marti, 1995). Bernard Besson explained, from his police background, how to conduct counterintelligence operations (Besson & Possin, 1997). Frederic Jakobiak knit the presentations together as a host and commentator.

Early in the two-day conference, one of the presentations came from a part-time instructor at Marne-la-Vallee. The professor explained that a large part of the operation at Marne-la-Vallee involved Internet surfing on the Web sites of American multinationals. They found, though, that some of the American sites were location sensitive, so that a search conducted from an American address would yield different screens than a search conducted from a French address. Furthermore, the young professor was horrified to discover that some of the American multinational Web sites used "sniffers" and "cookies" to try to identify the location and identity of the remote economic intelligence surfers at Marne-la-Vallee. He explained how to create a buffer or indentities by searching through a chain of addresses. He implied that the National Security Agency, the CIA, and IBM were working together to plant viruses, false data, and identification flags on the computers of French economic intelligence agents, and that the French would fight back through viruses of their own, in a spirit of "Cocorico," a French word associated with their national symbol of the rooster, implying "we got you."

In this climate, I found myself at the traditional business meal of eight people sitting around a table eating a salad. All seven of my new colleagues were competitive intelligence officers at French multinationals. After we all introduced ourselves to each other, the woman two seats to my left asked why the National Security Agency had interfered with a contract between the Brazilian government and the French defense company Thomson Electronics. She worked for Thomson Electronics and felt that the US government had interfered in the negotiations by passing on NSA-procured eavesdropping data to the Brazilian government to steer the contract toward the American firm Raytheon. I told the woman that the story I had heard was that the NSA picked up a bribe offer to the Brazilian defense minister and communicated that information to the Brazilian President, who then overruled the Thomson contract in favor of the Raytheon contract. There was silence around the table for a few awkward moments.

The themes explored elsewhere in this volume, on the intersection between information technology and social responsibility, take on new shapes when considered in the context of competitive intelligence. Using the (probably) apocryphal Thomson-Raytheon story as a launching point, this chapter will explore the emergence of social responsibility benchmarks in the competitive intelligence age. This analysis is heavily flavored by my own experiences trying to understand the French approach to competitive intelligence. The paper reviews attempts by competitive intelligence agents in the US and France to manufacture Social Responsibility benchmarks in the contexts of covert operations, competitive strategy, corporate intelligence, economic security, economic intelligence, and economic warfare. The conclusion of the paper will argue that the construction of social responsibility is a local-level human accomplishment, not a global-level rational standard. Furthermore, the paper implies that the burden of social responsibility lies more heavily on the successful economic oppressor than the unsuccessful economic resistance.

COVERT OPERATIONS

Loch Johnson, a political science professor at the University of Georgia, proposed a "partial ladder of escalation for intelligence operations," in reverse order, from "extreme options" through "high-risk options" through "modest intrusions" to "routine operations" (Johnson, 1996, p. 147).

Threshold Four: Extreme Options

38. Use of chemical-biological and other deadly agents
37. Major secret wars
36. Assassination plots
35. Small-scale coups d'etat
34. Major economic dislocations: crop, livestock destruction
33. Environmental alterations
32. Pinpointed retaliation against noncombatants
31. Torture
30. Hostage taking
29. Major hostage-rescue attempts
28. Theft of sophisticated weapons or arms-making materials
27. Sophisticated arms supplies

Threshold Three: High-Risk Options

26. Massive increases of funding in democracies
25. Small-scale hostage rescue attempt
24. Training of foreign military forces for war
23. Limited arms supplies for offensive purposes
22. Limited arms supplies for balancing purposes
21. Economic disruption without loss of life
20. Large increases of funding in democracies
19. Massive increases of funding in autocracies
18. Large increases of funding in autocracies
17. Sharing of sensitive intelligence
16. Embassy break-ins
15. High-level, intrusive political surveillance
14. High-level recruitment and penetrations
13. Disinformation against democratic regimes
12. Disinformation against autocratic regimes
11. Truthful but contentious information in democracies
10. Truthful but contentious information in autocracies

Threshold Two: Modest Intrusions

9. Low-level funding of friendly groups
8. Truthful, benign information in democracies
7. Truthful, benign information in autocracies
6. Stand-off TECHINT against target nation
5. "Away" targeting of foreign intelligence officer
4. "Away" targeting of other personnel

Threshold One: Routine Operations
3. Sharing of low-level intelligence
2. Ordinary embassy-based observing and conversing
1. Passive security measures; protection of allied leaders

In general, this is a list of options that have been used by governments, not corporations. However, there have been reported cases of corporations attempting (25) small-scale hostage rescue attempts (EDS in Iran), (18) large increases of funding in autocracies (ITT in Chile), and (17) sharing of sensitive intelligence (German engineering firms in Iraq). The list of covert operations provides a starting point for our study of the manufacturing of ethics in an age of competitive intelligence. How far up this list will corporations go as they seek to understand and influence their environments? Presumably corporations are more tightly constrained in their actions than governments, and we will see an expansion of types of actions in the first threshold, such as misrepresentation of facts, bribery of competitors' employees, and theft of information.

COMPETITIVE STRATEGY

An understanding of competitive intelligence requires an understanding of the history of competitive strategy. The era of firms lasted from 1500-1865. Firms are small, family-owned, entrepreneur-led businesses with 20 or fewer employees: family farms, small mills, bakeries, grocery stores, shoe cobblers, and blacksmith shops. Firms compete in large, "pure" markets composed of similar firms. The era of bureaucracies lasted from 1865-1944. Bureaucracies were composed of large conglomerations of firms: e.g., General Mills, General Foods, and General Motors. The railroad, telegraph, automobile, and telephone made it economically feasible to coordinate large bureaucracies over long distances. The era of networks lasted from 1944-2001. Networks relied on improved mobility and information technology to create alliances among numerous firms in loosely coupled, organic, international networks composed of autonomous, empowered, intelligent actors. It was not until the era of networks that business operations became complex enough to require the emergence of "competitive strategies."

Herbert Simon and his colleagues shifted the attention away from bureaucratic structures toward network strategies in the 1950s (Simon, 1947, 1955, 1957a, 1957b, 1976). They laid the foundation for later discussions of organizations as organized anarchies (Cohen, March, & Olsen, 1972; March & Olsen, 1976) and loosely coupled systems (Weick, 1976). The case study that made Simon and his colleagues' theories tangible to researchers was the Cuban Missile Crisis, deftly analyzed by Allison through three lenses: rational actor, bureaucratic politics, and organizational processes. During a crisis, a firm moves from the chaotic organizational process model, to the factional Bureaucratic Politics model, to the ordered rational actor model (Allison, 1969, 1971; Allison & Zelikow, 1999). At about the same time as the Cuban Missile Crisis, Kennedy's Harvard rowing team colleague Alfred D. Chandler published an account of bureaucratic changes in the 1920s in a book he labeled *Strategy and Structure*. Chandler used the military strategy metaphor from his teaching at the Naval War College to make sense of the business structural changes he studied in General Motors, DuPont Chemicals, Sears & Roebuck, and Standard Oil (Chandler, 1962). Harvard Business School combined the Allison case with the Chandler cases to create the field of business strategy.

In 1980, Michael Porter crystallized an industrial/organizational economics view of business strategy in his book *Competitive Strategy*. Generations of business students have memorized the five forces model in Chapter 1 of the book, but few students or their professors remember that the five forces model is data-hungry and requires a great deal of competitive intelligence research, described in Chapter 3 and Appendix B:

> Answering these questions about competitors creates enormous needs for data. Intelligence data on competitors can come from many sources: reports filed publicly, speeches by a competitor's management to security analysts, the business press, the sales force, a firm's customers or suppliers that are common to competitors, inspection of a competitor's products, estimates by the firm's engineering staff, knowledge gleaned from managers or other personnel who have left the competitor's employment, and so on (Porter, 1980).

The public, popular side of Porter's work has been the strategy content analyses, but the hidden, dark side of Porter's work is competitive intelligence collection and analysis.

CORPORATE INTELLIGENCE

After Porter, researchers at other schools started to focus on how corporations gather political, technological, cultural, and "violence" intelligence (Eells & Nehemkis, 1984). Columbia professor Richard Eells and UCLA professor Peter Nehemkis described large business organizations as "private governments" and asserted that these "polycorporations" needed intelligence units:

> Without question, in our judgment, the large multinational (or polycorporation, as we call it) should establish well-conceived, effective, professionally-staffed intelligence units within its management structures. It goes without saying that close and effective supervision by the chief executive officer of [the] company's intelligence unit is a sine qua non for its effective and useful operations—operations that are beneficial to the the corporation's own policies and the chief executive's own decision-making (p. 221).

Eells and Nehemkis found that studies of corporate intelligence quickly lead to questions of social responsibility: "As the research for this book came to an end it became clear that further studies should be undertaken, specifically of the implications for public policy of the private intelligence community's growth, especially in the matters of privacy, morality and ethics" (p. xii). Eells and Nehemkis tried to patch up this missing discussion in their book by listing 12 questions from Professor R. R. Nash (1981) about ethical business decisions:

1. Have you defined the problem accurately?
2. How would you define the problem if you stood on the other side of the fence?
3. How did this situation occur in the first place?
4. To whom and to what do you give your loyalty as a member of the corporation?
5. What is your intention in making this decision?
6. How does this intention compare with the probable results?
7. Whom could your decision or action injure?
8. Can you discuss the problem with the affected parties before you make your decision?
9. Are you confident that your position will be as valid over a long period of time as it seems now?
10. Could you disclose without qualm your decision or action to your boss, your CEO, the board of directors, your family, society as a whole?
11. What is the symbolic potential of your action if understood? If misunderstood?
12. Under what conditions would you allow exceptions to your stand?

If our list of covert operations is too focused on governments in general, this list is too focused on business decisions in general.

ECONOMIC SECURITY

Depending upon party affiliations, George Bush and Bill Clinton share credit for launching the boom in international economic intelligence. Johnson gives a nod to Bush: "A 1991 review of intelligence priorities, initiated by President Bush, led to a dramatic allocation of resources away from old Cold War concerns toward new economic targets, as the world marketplace became an ever more important battlefield for America" (Johnson, 1996, p. 147). As part of those discussions, retired Director of Central Intelligence Admiral Stansfield Turner launched a provocative proposal in foreign affairs in fall of 1991:

The preeminent threat to US national security now lies in the economic sphere. ...We must, then, redefine "national security" by assigning economic strength greater prominence. ...If economic strength should now be recognized as a vital component of national security, parallel with military power, why should America be concerned about stealing and employing economic secrets (Turner, 1991).

The larger share of the credit, though, according to Johnson (1996), should go to Clinton:

The question of economic competitiveness served as a centerpiece in the 1992 presidential campaign of Bill Clinton. On the eve of assuming the presidency, he vowed to "make the economic security of our nation a primary goal of our foreign policy." Coupled with his abiding attention to domestic economic issues, foreign economic policy became one of the president's foremost concerns during the first years of his administration. Early in office he created a National Economic Council (NEC), touted as equal in status to the National Security Council. Long a maid in waiting to defense issues, matters of trade and aid had risen high on the national security agenda. "It's the economy, stupid!' had been the mantra among Clinton's campaign strategists in 1992; now, within the government's community of national security planners, the slogan seemed to be, "It's the economy, stupid!" (pp. 146-147)

The collective wisdom of intelligence community thinktanks quickly chimed in with a collective opinion: The involvement of the US government in microeconomic intelligence was a really bad idea. In a paper presented on April 8, 1993, Randall M. Fort listed 20 reasons why it would be a bad idea. (1) The "economic threats" have always existed, are often caused by ourselves, and are probably better labeled "economic challenges." (2) Economic benefits are not black and white, but intertwined between countries, such as in the case of a Honda plant in the United States providing jobs for Americans; this idea is coded after the title of a Robert Reich article, "Who Is 'Us'?" (3) How would we decide which industries and which firms received economic intelligence? (4) Competition for economic intelligence would become a subsidy allocated on the basis of "political clout." (5) American firms are involved in alliances with non-American firms. (6) It would be difficult to protect sources and methods. (7) Productivity of intelligence assets might decline, be harmed, or dry up if the sources feel their data is being used for economic purposes. (8) Recipients of economic intelligence could leave a US firm to work for a foreign firm. (9) Retooling to provide intelligence to the private sector would be expensive. (10) Uncertain information could lead to conflicts between the US firms and the US government. (11) Economic competition with foreign governments would reduce the U.S.'s capacity to create military and diplomatic alliances. (12) US firms do not want to be associated with the US intelligence community in suppliers' and consumers' minds. (13) US firms do not consider the US intelligence community a reliable source of information. (14) Supplying intelligence to US firms would require legal changes in the enabling statutes and executive orders, in the Trade Secrets Act, in the wire fraud statutes, and in the Communication Act and Foreign Intelligence Surveillance Act. (15) Supplying economic intelligence to firms could subject the US government to civil litigation by harmed constituents. (16) Just because the French, the Israelis, the Germans, the Japanese, and the South Koreans are involved in nationally sponsored economic intelligence, that does not make it morally acceptable. (17) US sponsorship of economic intelligence would unleash more dangers for US businesspeople abroad. (18) US economic intelligence might invite economic intelligence from nations that are better at it than we are. (19) Intelligence agencies would be exposed to corruption from US firms who might benefit from preferential intelligence analyses. (20) Finally, in one of the most frequently cited arguments, US intelligence officers would not be motivated by the economic intelligence task: "Some years ago, one of our clandestine officers overseas said to me: 'You know, I'm prepared to give my life for my country, but not for a company.' That case officer was absolutely right" (Fort, p. 196, citing Robert M. Gates, Speech to the Economic Club of Detroit, April 13, 1992).

Fort summarized his arguments against US government involvement in economic intelligence by tracking the differences between DCI James Woolsey's statements in his confirmation hearings with his statements one year later:

Then-DCI James Woolsey raised eyebrows and expectations during his Senate confirmation hearing when he described economic espionage as "the hottest current topic in intelligence policy." Subsequent news stories indicate that he has reached some unenthusiastic conclusions about such an effort. One year later, he was quoted as stating that such a program would be "fraught with legal and foreign policy difficulties." Woolsey's disapproving tone is not surprising. Anyone who gets past the rhetoric about economic competitiveness and closely examines the nuts and bolts of how an economic espionage program is supposed to work cannot fail to reach the same negative conclusions (p. 196)

Despite Fort's explanation of why US microeconomic intelligence is a bad idea, the genie was already out of the bottle in 1992. The signal that the US sent was that competitive microeconomic intelligence was on the agenda. That shot heard round the world in 1992 gave other governments the motivation to ramp up their own competitive intelligence activities.

ECONOMIC INTELLIGENCE

The French, for example, asked Prefet Henri Martre to preside over a 1994 study titled "Intelligence economique et strategie des entreprises" (Economic Intelligence and Business Strategy). The report identified five trends: (1) Economic intelligence is increasingly recognized internationally as a criterion for competitiveness; (2) Economic intelligence is the raw material for the creation of a new industry of competitive intelligence firms; (3) Economic intelligence should be retained by the organization as a form of knowledge capital; (4) Economic intelligence needs to be supported by governmental units at the levels of regions, countries, and territories; (5) Economic intelligence is being defined by the Americans and others as a national security issue (Commissariat General du Plan Documentation Francaise, 1994). To respond to these five trends, the Martre report encouraged French firms, French regions, and the French state to improve their economic intelligence capabilities.

The Martre report argued that firms such as Exxon, General Electric and Boeing had used economic intelligence units since as early as 1972. In addition, the report asserted that generalized consulting firms such as McKinsey have economic intelligence capabilities, and that specialized consulting firms staffed by former intelligence officers are emerging to create a larger system of firms working together for the benefit of the US economy (p. 63).

The Martre report also argued that national cultures provided significant backdrops for the creation of intelligence systems:

It is not British Petroleum's economic intelligence tools that create their excellence in this domain, but its culture and history, which are intimately linked to the intelligence culture that the British Empire developed during its history. Economic intelligence systems created in China, Japan, the Middle East, the United States, Great Britain and Germany all have cultural roots [my translation] (pp. 64-65).

The Martre report also argued that nations created and supported economic intelligence units at two levels, defensive and offensive:

It is important to distinguish two levels of analysis. The first level is the preservation of employment and national sovereignty, and no industrial country hides the fact that it is operating this type of economic counterintelligence or industrial counterintelligence, when these types of economic intelligence attacks pass legal norms. The second level of analysis is the protection of a threatened industry. In this context, the encouragement of exports and the maintenance of economic competitiveness is as important as the protection of the national inheritance. Because of "national conscience" and "economic patriotism," economic intelligence and industrial intelligence become part of the domain of activities handled by countries' Industry Ministries, External Commerce Ministries, and economic institutes [my translation] (p. 68).

The Martre report became the foundation in France for an enthusiastic project of state-sponsored competitive intelligence programs. Admiral Lacoste (of Rainbow Warrior fame) started a DESS d'ingenierie de l'intelligence economique (a master's program in the engineering of economic intelligence) at Université de Marne-la-Vallee, east of Paris. The Université de Poitiers launched a DESS d'information et culture stratégique (a master's program in strategic information and culture). The Universite d'Aix-Marseille launched a DEA de veille technologique (a pre-doctoral degree in the surveillance of emerging technologies). The CERAM-ESC Nice business school launched a specialized master's degree in economic intelligence. A variety of regional economic intelligence initiatives were created throughout France to sensitize French executives to the importance of creating a national competitive intelligence culture.

COMPETITIVE INTELLIGENCE

Meanwhile, back in the United States, a new career path was developing around the topic of competitive intelligence. One of the best statements of the developing field is Larry Kahaner's 1996 book, *Competitive Intelligence: How to Gather, Analyze, and Use Information to Move Your Business to the Top*. Kahaner's case studies (which are rare in competitive intelligence studies) included Avon and the Marriott Corporation. Avon hired a consulting company to analyze the garbage left in trash bins on public property by Mary Kay Cosmetics, in order to find out what Mary Kay Cosmetics' strategic plans were. The collection method was legal, but Kahaner asks the question, "Yes, but is it ethical?" The two firms came to the conclusion that Avon could reassemble the shredded garbage as long as a Mary Kay Cosmetics employee was there to see what they reassembled. In the Marriott case, Marriott hired an executive recruiting firm to interview executives in the economy hotel business, which the search firm then fed back to Marriott to help them craft their strategy for entering this new market. Although Marriott did hire some of the executives interviewed, it seems that the primary rationale for the operation was intelligence collection, rather than hiring. Here again, Kahaner asks about the appearance of the operation as ethical or unethical.

Another book that helped shape the development of competitive intelligence as a career path is Leonard M. Fuld's *The New Competitor Intelligence: The Complete Resource for Finding, Analyzing, and Using Information About Your Competitors*. From years of experience trying to conduct competitive intelligence, Fuld & Company (1995) created "the ten commandments of legal and ethical intelligence gathering":

(1) Thou shalt not lie when representing thyself.
(2) Thou shalt observe thy company's legal guidelines as set forth by the Legal Department.
(3) Thou shalt not tape-record a conversation.
(4) Thou shalt not bribe.
(5) Thou shalt not plant eavesdropping devices.
(6) Thou shalt not deliberately mislead anyone in an interview.
(7) Thou shalt neither obtain from nor give to thy competitor any price information.
(8) Thou shalt not swap misinformation.
(9) Thou shalt not steal a trade secret (or steal employees away in hopes of learning a trade secret).
(10) Thou shalt not knowingly press someone for information if it may jeopardize that person's job or reputation (Fuld, 1995).

These recommendations provide a more helpful set of beginning benchmarks for the construction of social responsibility than our two previous lists, Johnson's ladder of intrusion in covert operations and Nash's questions for general business decisions.

In a preemptive move intended to protect their industry against government intervention, the Society of Competitive Intelligence Professionals (often estimated to have 5,000 members) drafted their own code of ethics:

(1) To continually strive to increase respect and recognition for the profession on local, state and national levels.
(2) To pursue his or her duties with zeal and diligence while maintaining the highest degree of professionalism and avoiding all unethical practices.
(3) To faithfully adhere to and abide by his or her company's policies, objectives, and guidelines.

(4) To comply with all applicable laws.
(5) To accurately disclose all relevant information, including the identity of the professional and his or her organization, prior to all interviews.
(6) To fully respect all requests for confidentiality of information.
(7) To promote and encourage full compliance with these ethical standards within his or her company, with third-party contractors, and within the entire profession.

This preemptive move by the competitive intelligence industry did not hold, and President Clinton signed The Economic Espionage Act on October 11, 1996. The act defines trade secrets broadly to include "all forms and types of information including financial, business, scientific, technical, economic, and engineering. It includes plans, formulas, designs, prototypes, methods, techniques, processes, procedures, computer codes, and so on" (p. 244). Penalties for stealing a trade secret include up to 10 years in prison, individual-level fines of up to $500,000, and corporate-level fines of up to $5 million. If the theft benefits a foreign entity, the penalties can rise to 15 years imprisonment and a corporate-level fine of up to $10 million.

The benchmarks that the competitive intelligence industry is generating for itself–Kahaner's case studies, Fuld & Company's ten commandments, SCIP's guidelines, and the Economic Espionage Act's sanctions–are helpful within the US context. More work needs to be done, though, on competitive intelligence activities between countries.

ECONOMIC WARFARE

One of my favorite colleagues, Patrick Lemattre, cursed with an impish sense of humor, invited me to attend one of his courses. He was hosting Christian Harbulot, who had had a hand in the Martre report, then become operational director at French military intelligence economic spin-offs DCI and Intelco, and had become the "tête pensant" or guru of the Ecole de Guerre Economique, or the School of Economic Warfare. The school opened in October 1997 under the auspices of the Ecole Superieure Libre des Sciences Commerciales Appliquees, under the leadership of General Jean Pichot-Duclos (Merchet, 1997).

Due to another course responsibility, I was not able to introduce myself to Christian Harbulot before the presentation began, so he assumed he was speaking to a room of French students and faculty members. He had transparencies showing that the Americans controlled the United Nations, the Organization for Economic Cooperation and Development, the Church of the Reverend Moon, and the Republic of Germany. He said that the first assault on France would be through Coca-Cola, McDonalds, and Disney, all of which are designed to weaken the attachment of citizens to their national cultures. He said that the second assault would be through music, movies, and television, which would be used to propagate American values around the world. The third assault, he explained, would come from General

Motors, IBM, Hewlett-Packard, Microsoft, and other American multinationals, which would then subjugate the world populations as captive employees.

How then, can France defend itself against this organized, controlled, centrally planned offensive? The explicit script was to boycott American intrusions into France: "As a Frenchman," Harbulot said, "I no longer drink Coca-Cola." The implicit script was more subtle and can be summarized in the phrase, "Tous les coups sont permis contre les americains" or "Against Americans, there are no rules—anything goes." If France and other cultures around the world feel that they are under an organized attack from an American economy, discussions of fairness, ethics, and social responsibility become irrelevant. Groupthink and a siege mentality set in (Janis, 1972), and Americans are painted as the immoral aggressors, while the French resistance can only be painted as moral and heroic.

CONCLUSION: MANUFACTURING SOCIAL RESPONSIBILITY BENCHMARKS

All of this discussion of covert operations, competitive strategy, corporate intelligence, economic security, economic intelligence, competitive intelligence, and economic warfare brings us back to the case study of the NSA eavesdropping on Thomson Electronics to shift a Brazilian defense contract away from Thomson Electronics toward Raytheon. Where does social responsibility lie in this case?

First, here's what I said at the lunch table. I said that the coordination between the economic sector and the governmental sector in the US was not at all as tight as it was in France, and my French colleagues were projecting coordinated action onto a situation where there was none. Instead, each firm was acting in its own economic self-interest, and the French were misinterpreting the cumulative effect of profit-seeking at the firm level as a grand conspiracy at the national level. I said that most Americans didn't even know where France was, so why would they spend all their time trying to overrun it economically? I argued that French firms should respond to American firms, not engineer a French societal response to a presumedly coordinated American societal attack. I also argued that it seemed that French consultants were fueling an intelligence arms race by misrepresenting the American intelligence threat. Each protest that there was no conspiracy led to new questions about how the conspiracy was structured until, thankfully, other topics emerged for discussion.

Now, though, I would not have been so eager to defend the American point of view. Instead, I see both sides of the conflict as flawed, self-serving ethical frameworks.

To the French, the Americans have moved from being an ally in a conflict between two blocs, the Soviets and the Americans, to an often-destructive singular "hyperpower." The French–as they did with the Germans in World War II–have constructed, enacted, and manufactured an ethical code that allows them enormous flexibility in defending themselves against an invasion by a hyperpower. To use a variety of means to steer the contract toward Thomson Electronics and away from

Raytheon, including the time-honored tradition of offering a secret "pot de vin," is fair, especially given the enormous advantages of the American cultural barbarians.

To the Americans, the French are just another market to conquer in a firm-by-firm quest for increased market share, increased sales, and increased profits. The stubborn French resistance frustrates the Americans, who complain that the French are exploiting a home-field advantage to skew the outcome of the competition. To use National Security Agency assets to correct an unfair influence from France, and to steer the contract toward Raytheon, is–to American eyes–a justifiable use of national intelligence resources.

How do we solve such an intractable case? We know from research on sense-making processes that human beings interpret ongoing streams of events in ways that reinforce the significance of their own identities, through intensive social discussions with people they work with, and through flawed, outdated, retrospective models (Weick, 1995). Is there any reason to believe that ethics-making is any more rational, objective, or precise than sense-making?

So, no matter how many times we attempt to rule out the chaos of the ethics of competitive intelligence, it will always come down to whether or not individuals can construct an ethical framework that allow themselves to feel good when they look in the mirror. And, in an example of how easy it is for people to feel good when they look in the mirror, 75% of American males think they are in the top 25% of athletic ability. French friends of Thomson look good in their mirrors, and American friends of Raytheon look good in their mirrors, but they are both flawed–one bribes and one eavesdrops, and the battle is only over which is the least unethical course of action.

My conclusion to the case is thus rather skeptical. Although competitive intelligence professionals are well on the road to constructing social responsibility benchmarks within homogenous cultures, the larger problem of international social responsibility benchmarks is going to take a great deal of work, given the enormous forces that encourage local-level construction of benchmarks, rather than global rational benchmarks. I suspect that the greater burden should lie with the economic "aggressors" who are having the most success, rather than the companies and countries constructing an economic "resistance." New cross-national case studies should be collected to help find the appropriate balance between nations and corporations in this question for social responsibility benchmarks in the age of competitive intelligence.

ACKNOWLEDGMENTS

This paper was financed by grants from the HEC Foundation (1994-2000) and the UNLV New Investigator Award (2000-2002).

REFERENCES

Allison, G. T. (1969). Conceptual models and the Cuban Missile Crisis. *The American Political Science Review*, 63, 689-718.

Allison, G. T. (1971). *Essence of Decision: Explaining the Cuban Missile Crisis*. Boston, MA: Little, Brown, and Co.

Allison, G. and Zelikow, P. (1999). *Essence of Decision: Explaining the Cuban Missile Crisis*. (Second ed.). New York: Addison Wesley Longman.

Besson, B. and Possin, J. C. (1997). *Du renseignement a l'intelligence strategique: Detecter les menaces et les opportunites pour l'entreprise*. Paris: Dunod.

Chandler, A. D., Jr. (1962). *Strategy and Structure: Chapters in the History of the Industrial Empire*. Cambridge, MA: MIT Press.

Cohen, M. D., March, J. G. and Olsen, J. P. (1972). A garbage can model of organizational choice. *Administrative Science Quarterly*, 17, 1-25.

Commissariat General du Plan Documentation Francaise, L. (1994). *Intelligence Economique et Strategie des Eentreprises*.

Eells, R. and Nehemkis, P. (1984). *Corporate Intelligence and Espionage: A Blueprint for Executive Decision Making*. New York: Macmillan.

Fuld, L. M. (1995). *The New Competitor Intelligence: The Complete Resource for Finding, Analyzing and Using Information About Your Competitors*. New York: John Wiley & Sons, Inc.

Gibbons, P. T. and Prescott, J. E. (1996). Parallel competitive intelligence processes in organizations. *International Journal of Technology Management*, 11(1-2), 162-178.

Janis, I. L. (1972). *Victims of Groupthink: A Psychological Study of Foreign-Policy Decisions and Fiascoes*. Boston, MA: Houghton, Mifflin.

Johnson, L. K. (1996). *Secret agencies: US Intelligence in a Hostile World*. New Haven: Yale University Press.

March, J. G. and Olsen, J. P. (1976). *Ambiguity and Choice in Organizations*. Bergen, Norway: Universitetsforlaget.

Martinet, B. and Marti, Y. M. (1995). *L'intelligence Economique: Les yeux et les oreilles de l'Entreprise*, Les Editions d'Organisation.

Merchet, J. D. (1997). La guerre economique, un art qui s'enseigne, *Liberation*. Paris.

Nash, L. L. (1981). Ethics without the sermon. *Harvard Business Review*, November-December.

Porter, M. E. (1980). *Competitive Strategy: Techniques for Analyzing Industries and Competitors*. New York: Free Press.

Simon, H. A. (1947). *Administrative Behavior: A Study of Decision-Making Processes in Administrative Organization* (First ed).

Simon, H. A. (1955). A behavioral model of rational choice. *Quarterly Journal of Economics*.

Simon, H. A. (1957a). *Administrative Behavior: A Study of Decision-Making Processes in Administrative Organization* (Second ed.).

Simon, H. A. (1957b). *Models of Man*. New York.

Simon, H. A. (1976). *Administrative Behavior: A Study of Decision-Making Processes in Administrative Organization.* (Third ed.). New York: The Free Press.

Thiètart, R. A. and Vivas, R. (1981). Strategic intelligence activity: The management of the sales force as a source of strategic information. *Strategic Management Journal*, 2(1), 15-25.

Turner, S. (1991). Intelligence for a new world order. *Foreign Affairs*, 70(4), 151-152.

Weick, K. E. (1976). Educational organizations as loosely coupled systems. *Administrative Science Quarterly*, 21, 1-19.

Weick, K. E. (1995). *Sense-making in Organizations*. Newbury Park, CA: Sage.

Chapter XIV

Strategic and Ethical Issues in Outsourcing Information Technologies

Randall C. Reid
University of Alabama, USA

Mario Pascalev
Bank of America, USA

INTRODUCTION

Outsourcing of information technology (IT) is the transfer of a company's information technology functions to external vendors. Ordinarily, such transfer is considered only with regard to its strategic and economic impact on the organization. However, as the recent practice demonstrated, cost-benefit considerations and other strategic considerations are not sufficient to analyze an outsourcing case. Important ethical concerns relating to fiduciary responsibilities, insiders' bidding for outsourcing contracts, and the like, are also pertinent to the analysis of outsourcing.

This chapter will identify major ethical problems and will propose guidelines for ethical conduct in the process of outsourcing IT. Such guidelines could have broad practical implications for the practice of outsourcing.

The chapter will analyze literature on outsourcing models and professional ethical standards. It will have the following structure. First, the benefits and models of outsourcing information technology will be discussed. Second, ethical literature in general and professional organizations' codes of ethics in particular will be considered. Third, a recent case of IT outsourcing will be presented and analyzed. The ethical standards established in the thesis will be applied to the case. Finally, generalized ethical guidelines will be suggested for outsourcing models.

LITERATURE REVIEW: OUTSOURCING MODELS

Outsourcing of information technology (IT) is the transfer of a company's information technology functions to an outside agency. The first instance of IT outsourcing was the outsourcing of payroll processing. Many big companies have or are currently engaged in outsourcing (see Table 1). For some, IT outsourcing proved to be a viable strategy; for others, it was only a big headache.

Outsourcing has become a management strategy. According to a Forbes editorial (Sept. 22, 1997), "By 2000, 75% of enterprises will employ selective IT outsourcing as a routine means to increase competitiveness or gain new resources and skills." Nam et al. (1998, pp. 104-129) prompted a number of research studies and analyses of the practice. The scholars sought a conceptual answer to the question when to outsource IT and when not. In the next section, models of IT and their anticipated outsourcing benefits will be systematically reviewed.

General Management

In the area of general management, one of the important benefits of IT outsourcing is that it frees the company to concentrate on its core business competencies, rather than dealing with something which is unfamiliar and complicated. An additional advantage is in the simplification of the general managers' agenda.

There are also disadvantages of outsourcing IT to general management. As a result of the outsourcing arrangements, management loses flexibility. Most contracts are for 5-10 years. For the duration of the contract, the company is not in a position to change its IS strategy.

Finance

In the area of finance, the most important benefit of IT outsourcing invariably cited in the literature is that the company realizes various savings. The savings are

Table 1: Prominent companies that have outsourced IT

Company	Contract Value	Duration	Vendor
Del Monte Foods	$150 million	10 years	Electronic Data Systems
Health Dimensions, Inc.	$20 million	5 years	Integrated Systems Solutions Corp.
J.P. Morgan	$20 million	5 years	BT North America, Inc.
Signetics, Inc.	$100 million	10 years	Electronic Data Systems
U.S. Dept. of Housing	$526 million	12 years	Martin Marietta Corporation and Urban Development
General Dynamics Corp.	$3 billion	10 years	Computer Sciences Corporation

Source: Cheryl Currid and Company, Computing Strategies for Reengineering Your Organization (Rocklin, CA: Prima Publishing, 1994) 135.

due to the economies of scale ensuing from the specialization and larger volume of services provided by the outsourcer. Another financial benefit is the liquification of assets. Typically, it is a part of an outsourcing contract that the vendor purchases the computer hardware of the customer. Finally, the outsourcing transforms fixed costs into variable costs. Under an outsourcing arrangement, a company could reduce its costs by reducing the level of IT activity.

It is also maintained that the outsourcing vendor holds tighter control over supplies, such as paper, toner, and the like. The whole attitude toward the consumption of IT services becomes more frugal, as the soft dollars paid for the services of the internal IT department turn to hard dollars paid to an outside party. Theoretically, it is possible that all of the cost savings realized via outsourcing IT are less than the benefits of putting one's own IT "house" in order.

Personnel

There are certain benefits from outsourcing in terms of personnel. In the present job market for IT staff, it becomes increasingly difficult to attract or to retain good talent. Outsourcing arrangements supposedly give the company access to top talent in the field at affordable costs.

Additionally, under selective outsourcing arrangements, the company could keep its own IT personnel and use it only for specific projects and IS functions where their talents are best utilized. The routine support operations could then be transferred to the outside vendor.

A definite disadvantage of IT outsourcing is the high level of anxiety and low morale resulting from the news of imminent outsourcing. The best people may leave rather than being subject to uncertainty or undesired transfer to the vendor's payroll.

Technology

In the area of technology, the most important benefit of IT outsourcing is the instant access to new technology. Outsourcing provides a quick transition to the latest technology.

There are also some dangers of outsourcing IT associated with the technological function. Importantly, the economies of scale may make the vendor unable to move quickly to new technology. The emergence of industry-specific outsourcers "could result in the spread of systems' mediocrity throughout the industry because of the lack of new ideas and product differentiation" (Grover et al., 1994, p. 100).

There are three distinctions between kinds of benefits that evolved from the above list (and will be further elaborated on below). First, some benefits in the accounting sense may not be benefits in the economic sense. The economic benefit of IT outsourcing is only the difference of the cost to provide IT services in-house while operating efficiently and the cost to purchase the IT services from a vendor while the vendor is operating efficiently. If the latter cost is higher or equal to the former, outsourcing does not make economic sense. The cost difference between providing IT in-house while working inefficiently and outsourcing these services may result in accounting savings, but not in economic savings. In fact, the same or better results could come from simply organizing the in-house IT department more efficiently. The inefficient operation of IT services imposes opportunity costs on the company.

Another distinction that can be drawn between economic benefits is ones that are legitimate and ones that are ethically or morally questionable. It may be more cost-effective to win a contract by bribing an official rather than offering the lowest bid. Nevertheless, such conduct is unacceptable. A third useful distinction suggested by the earlier discussion is that between strategic and nonstrategic benefits of outsourcing IT. This distinction responds to the objection raised before that some benefits of outsourcing IT are not commensurate.

Strategic Discrepancy Model

Theng et al. (1994, 75-103), in an article titled "Strategy-Theoretic Discrepancy Model," argue that the decision to outsource information technology is based purely on strategic considerations (as opposed to accounting for various benefits). In practice, only the technological factors listed earlier are taken into account. They are evaluated in terms of their adequacy to the purposes of the organization. Teng et al. put forth three concepts. First, information technology is considered more generally as the capacity to manage information for strategic advantage. Further, strategy is defined as the match of internal organizational resources and the environmental opportunities and risks in view of the goals of the organization. Lastly, the authors propose that outsourcing will take place when there is a perceived gap between internal IT resources and the requirements of the environment. These concepts will be presented and discussed in turn.

First, Teng et al. propose a generalized view of information technology, shifting emphasis from technology and systems to information. They propose that IT management shifts from "a focus on technology to a focus on better information utilization and management, that leads to performance improvements and competitive breakthrough." Thus, IT is no longer simply one asset among the assets. It is information, a key asset, and indispensable for a firm's performance.

Other authors also support the strategic discrepancy model. After giving the received list of benefits and costs of IT outsourcing, McFarlan and Nolan also argue that the core of the outsourcing decision is in the strategic relevance of IT to a company at a particular time (McFarlan & Nolan, 1995, p. 15). Even though it is not as analytically rigorous as Teng et al., McFarlan and Nolan's paper has the advantage of offering a good practical decision-making tool. Current strategic relevance of IT to a company is plotted against the future importance of information resource management. The result is a "strategic grid" that could be used as a decision-making tool. (See Figure 1.)

As can be observed in Figure 1, four different strategic orientations are possible depending on present and future reliance on IT with their respective presumptions concerning outsourcing.

Figure 1: Strategic grid for information resource management

Factory-uninterrupted service-oriented information resource management *Outsourcing Presumption:* Yes, unless company is huge and well-managed Reasons to consider outsourcing: • Possibilities of economies of scale for small and midsize firms. • Higher quality service and backup. • Management focus facilitated. • Fiber-optic and extended channel technologies facilitate international IT solutions.	**Strategic information resource management** *Outsourcing presumption:* No Reasons to consider outsourcing: • Rescue an out-of-control internal IT unit. • Tap source of cash. • Facilitate flexibility. • Facilitate management of divestiture.
Support-oriented information resource management *Outsourcing Presumption:* Yes Reasons to consider outsourcing: • Access to higher IT professionalism. • Possibility of laying off is of low priority and problematic. • Access to current IT. • Risk of inappropriate IT architectures reduced.	**Turnaround information resource management** *Outsourcing presumption:* No Reasons to consider outsourcing: • Internal IT unit not capable in required technologies. • Internal IT unit not capable in required project management skills.

HIGH (top left) — Current Dependence on Information

LOW   Importance of IT for Competitive Advantage   HIGH

Source: F. Warren McFarlan and Richard L. Nolan, "How to Manage an IT Outsourcing Alliance" (Palvia and Parzinger, 1995, p. 16).

LITERATURE REVIEW: ETHICAL LITERATURE

Classical Approach to Ethics

Since ancient times, people have striven to come up with a way to tell right from wrong in a nonarbitrary way. The classical approach to this determination is to find principles founded in nature or ones that are self-evident and deduce rules for evaluation of conduct using correct reasoning (logic). As a result of this approach, a huge body of literature has arisen. Most influential streams in normative ethics today are the consequentialist (utilitarianism) and deontological (Kantian) ethics. Also prominent today are virtue ethics, feminist ethics of care, ethical egoism and contractarianism.

Utilitarianism maintains that we should judge the ethical merit of an action by the consequences it produces. Particularly, an action is good to the extent to which it tends to promote the greater happiness for the greater number of people. An action is bad to the extent to which it produces the opposite of happiness. The most important utilitarians are Jeremy Bentham and John Stuart Mill (Mill, 1979). Utilitarianism has a great intuitive appeal. It is predominant in contemporary health-care debate, allocation of scarce medical resources, organ transplants and the like. The notion of quality-adjusted life years is an elaboration on utilitarian ideas.

Kantian ethics maintains that an action is good to the extent to which it is done out of pure goodwill (i.e., done entirely out of good intentions). The most famous representative of this vein is the German Immanuel Kant. He believed that all rules of conduct should be tested against the so-called categorical imperative. Everybody should desire that a rule such as "Thou shalt not kill!" becomes a universal rule, without creating a logical contradiction.

It is unfortunate that ethical theories have adopted principles that contradict each other at a very fundamental level. It seems that we are left with little to do besides either disregarding the conclusions of ethical theories (anything goes), or stop worrying about fundamental principles and just focus on practical rules of ethical evaluation.

Rawls' Decision Procedure for Ethics

American philosopher John Rawls suggests a way of thinking about ethical evaluation which entirely sidesteps the issue about the first principles. Rawls asks: "Does there exist a reasonable decision procedure which is sufficiently strong, at least in some cases, to determine the manner in which competing interests should be adjudicated, and in instances of conflict, one interest given preference over another. ... " (Rawls, 1957, p. 177). The focus is shifted from foundational issues such as whether objective moral values exist, whether moral judgments are based on emotions, or whether autonomy or pursuit of happiness is the defining characteristic of human nature. The focus now is on the issue of whether a reasonable procedure for validating moral rules is available.

Rawls contends that such a decision procedure for ethics is available. "Competent moral judges" should be able to adjudicate in cases of conflicting interest and come up with valid ethical rules. The competency of these judges is defined as follows: The judges could be any people who know about the world what an average intelligent person would know. They are reasonable (i.e., they reason logically and are aware of their intellectual and moral predilections and take them into account when they consider particular cases). The moral judges are compassionate to the moral interests which are represented in the particular cases (Rawls, 1957, pp. 178-182).

The judgment rendered by the competent judges also is subject to a number of requirements. The judges should be immune from all foreseeable consequences of the judgment. The judgment adjudicates over actual conflicts of interest, as opposed to hypothetical cases. Further, the judgments are stable (i.e., at other times and places the competent judges would have arrived at the same conclusions about the same cases). Finally, the judgments should be intuitive rather than determined with a conscious reference to ethical principles.

The ingenious decision procedure for ethics proposed by Rawls is a very useful normative decision-making tool. The battleground of controversy about first principles, the nature of moral judgments, and the like is skillfully removed from the more pragmatic discussion of what is the right or wrong thing to do in a particular case. Rawls' procedure supplies professional ethics with a conceptual tool for adjudication in cases of conflicts of interest and for justification of moral rules.

Professional ethics goes through the throws of emancipation from academic philosophical ethics with its overwhelming conceptual heritage. The form it usually takes is paying lip service to one of the classical theories and moving on to reference of generally accepted social and moral values. The reason that professional ethicists would like to refer to classical theories is the need for validation of the generally accepted rules. The importance of the Rawlsian decision procedure is that it provides justification for the ethical rules based simply on the appropriateness of the procedure and not on the foundational justification of principles.

One important implication of the adoption of the Rawlsian decision procedure is the support it grants to the codes of professional ethics. Given that the rules in professional codes of ethics are subject to the decision procedure (i.e., their authors are intelligent, reasonable, and compassionate, and the judgments are impartial, stable, and intuitive), then these codes could be considered collections of valid ethical rules.

Testing the codes of professional ethics for the appropriateness of the decision procedure used for their creation is a major undertaking. Such a testing is clearly beyond the scope of the present inquiry. In order to simplify the task, it will be assumed that if distinct peer groups accept a rule independently, then it approximates a valid rule according to the decision procedure. This will leave us with somewhat tentative results, but one will be able to outline some important implications for the outsourcing model.

Outsourcing IT and Ethics

Potential Conflicts of Interest in the Context of Outsourcing IT

The types of potential conflicts of interest in the context of outsourcing include the interest of the following agencies: corporation customer (artificial person), corporation vendor (artificial person), agents of the customer, agents of the vendor, employees of customer, and general public. Potential conflicts of interest could arise between agents of the customer and their principal--the corporation customer (duties of loyalty and fiduciary duties), the agents of the vendor and their principal (duties of loyalty), customer and vendor (obligation to fulfill promises, loyalty to customer), and corporation customer and its employees (promises).

Professional Organizations' Codes of Ethics and Standards of Conduct

Although there is more than one way to present an ethical argument, the way proposed by John Rawls in *A Theory of Justice* has particular merit for its intuitive appeal. Ethical justification, according to Rawls, is an argument addressed to those who disagree with us or to ourselves when we are of two minds. To justify a moral conception to someone is to give him a proof of its principles from premises that we both accept. There are two elements in this method. The first element is the existence of mutually recognized starting points, that is, some consensus. The second element is the use of logical proof, or establishing logical relations between propositions. The appeal of this way of ethical justification is that it does not require subscribing to grand theories. It merely requires some agreement among reasonable persons.

Earlier, in the discussion of the decision procedure for ethics, it was determined that we could treat the codes of professional ethics as an approximation of valid ethical rules as long as these rules are arrived at independently by distinct professional communities. This framework will be used to research the professional codes of ethics for rules guiding the cases of conflicts of interest pertaining to outsourcing IT. If and when such rules are identified, they will be applied using deductive reasoning to analyze a particular outsourcing case.

There is a general consensus concerning agent-principal relations, loyalty and fiduciary duties in the DPMA's Code of Ethics, the Draft-Software Engineering Code of Ethics, the ACM's Code of Ethics, the IPG Society Code of Ethics, and the European Informatics Skills Structure Code of Professional Conduct. Particularly, these codes of professional ethics agree that an agent should refrain from "misrep-resenting and withholding information" from his or her employer (http://courses.cs.vt.edu~cs3604/lib/WorldCodes/DPMA.Standards.html). He or she must "avoid or disclose any conflict of interest, which might influence his/her actions or judgment." He or she must "have no financial interest, direct or indirect, in any materials, equipment, hardware, or commercial software used by his/her employer ... unless he informs his/her employer in advance of the nature of the interest." An agent should refrain from using "resources of... employer for personal gain." He or she should "avoid conflicts of interest." The Draft Software Engineering Code of Ethics also speaks on the principal-agent conflict of interest. The IT professional must "promote no interest adverse to their employer's without the employer" (http://computer.org/standards/sesc/Ethics/Code.html) [4, 4.09].

With regards to the general societal interests, the agent should not take advantage of the lack of information... on the part of others for personal gain. The IT specialist shall not give opinions or make statements on professional program-ming projects that are inspired or paid by private interests. In the same vain, the professional shall act to correct or report any situation which could cause losses, whether humanly injurious or financially damaging. He or she should not promote their own interest at the expense of the profession, client or employer (Ibid. 6.04). The latter rule references the harm to society by such activities as insiders' trading.

The general consensus which we discover in the various reviewed codes of ethics suggests that members of the IT profession independently arrive at a core set of shared rules of conduct. Although only an approximation of the decision procedure for ethics, these rules pass the Rawlsian test. Therefore, it is established that there exists a set of rules of ethics against which to evaluate moral conduct in the IT field. Particularly, it is established that the codes of professional ethics of the relevant peer organizations such as DPMA and ACM contain rules condemning breaches of loyalty and fiduciary duties, lying, theft and conspiracy to cheat society out of fair competition. In the following section, a recent case of outsourcing IT will be presented and its implication for the ethics of outsourcing IT will be discussed.

A CASE OF OUTSOURCING INFORMATION TECHNOLOGIES

In this section, a recent fraud case of outsourcing will be discussed. Special consideration will be given to the ethical issues emerging in the case. Three top executives of a company producing a component for the automobile industry, namely the CEO, the executive vicepresident of technology and the executive vicepresident of operations, induced the director of management information systems to create a company to which the IT functions were outsourced. The profits were allegedly funneled back to consulting companies headed by each of these individuals.

The ethical merits of the case are considered from the perspective of widely shared ethical beliefs. The conditions for ethical justification are applied to the case. First, this is the presence of agreement on at least some basic principles and, second, this is the acceptance of the logic rules of derivation. The actions of the executives violate beliefs about right and wrong which are widely accepted by the computer and information technology profession. Ultimately, these actions violate basic moral standards of the society. At least four elements of the executives' behavior appear to be unethical. The ethical violations include withholding material information from the employer, disregarding and harming the interest of the employer for one's own gain, misrepresenting the facts regarding future savings, unfair competitive practices based on insider information, and imposing undue hardships on the employees of the Company without appropriate justification.

The Company is an automobile manufacturing supplies firm, a subsidiary of an international parent company. In the beginning of 1990s, the Company experienced problems with excessive administrative overhead costs, including increased information technology costs. The parent company chairman repeatedly called for cost cutting. All functional areas were scrutinized for savings possibilities. The IT department, which had a reputation for lagging behind schedule and cost overruns, was particularly vulnerable.

In the early '90s, the IT staff consists of 40 application developers and 40 people associated with support and operations. The information systems were being run on an IBM mainframe computer. There were some microcomputers located at the plants that were used primarily for operations control. The software used was either written internally or bought off-shelf and customized. The expertise of the IT staff was primarily in COBOL and similar languages.

As the computer industry was moving away from mainframe computing towards server/client and UNIX environments, the Company's systems would require major revamping. Both systems and IT staff skills were becoming obsolete. The top management considered outsourcing of the IT function in order to solve the looming problems. It is a legitimate possibility that outsourcing was the best way for the Company to go. The problem is therefore not with the outsourcing decision per se. Rather it is with the motives of the decision makers and the ways they used to achieve it.

Three executives of the Company, its president and two executive vice-presidents, induced the director of management information systems to create a firm that will be referred to as IT Vendor, to which the Company outsourced its information technology (IT) functions for a period of 10 years. The outsourced functions include all mainframe processing services, personal computers and technical support. The new firm would supposedly reduce the projected IT costs of the Company from 72.4 to 52.8 million.

The particulars of the outsourcing agreement include that the Vendor was to maintain the same level of service, however, all orders would be fulfilled in time. The IT department was to be reduced to five managers, serving as liaisons with the Company. The Vendor would hire some of the IT personnel. A third party would operate the data center.

The CEO and the two vice presidents accepted the proposal without seeking alternative bids for the job. The agreement was signed without publicity and was approved by the board of directors. Seventy-five people were immediately fired. Things improved in some ways, for instance, some projects were completed faster. Backlog of projects still existed because of the cuts. Also, the managing of the communication between the Company and the Vendor was hard for the five remaining managers. Three of them left their jobs by the end of the year. The costs steadily overran the projections. Finally, the outsourcing contract was terminated as part of legal action against the top executives. Besides the outsourcing deal, there were two other alleged fraud schemes including the sale of natural gas wells and leasing agreements.

Application of Ethical Standards to the Case

There is nothing morally controversial in outsourcing of IT per se. Outsourcing is based on prudential considerations of cost-effectiveness, access to expertise and technology, and competitiveness. The decision about outsourcing of IT depends on the particular circumstances of a firm, the type of industry, the importance of control and security of data, and the like. The ethical issues do not relate to the practice itself. Rather they relate to the way the practice is conveyed. Five types of ethical violations have been identified in the actions of the former executives. These are harming the interest of the employer in order to further one's own interest, withholding information crucial for decision making, misrepresenting the facts (lying) regarding future savings, unfair competitive practices based on insider information, and imposing undue hardships on the employees of the Company without sound economic program. The actions of the former executives violated the standards of ethical behavior generally accepted in the society and in the ethical theory.

Putting personal interest higher than the interest of the employer: The Company, supposedly because of the influence of the group, did not solicit alternate bids. The presence of more than one bidder would have revealed the costs of providing the service better.

The proposal did not offer access to new computer or managerial talent, as the new firm hired some of current management and most of the technical personnel. The new firm didn't offer access to new technology or expertise. Technically, the only two relevant outcomes were the transfer of ownership and control and the reorganization of existing resources. The former benefits only the executives and constitutes outflows for the Company. The latter might benefit the Company.

If we assume that the proposal sincerely advertised cost reductions through reorganization, these could not come from better-trained employees or the use of the advanced technology and expertise of an existing outsourcing firm. None of these could have been provided under the agreement. Savings could be expected only from areas such as business reorganization (improved managerial practices or layoffs). These means, however, were available to the management even before the outsourcing agreement. Avoiding a conflict of interest would require that the management pursued the reorganization within the Company, without claiming transfers to them.

Disloyalty: If the managers were sincere about reduction of costs, then they knew the reasons for high costs already. It was disloyal to withhold knowledge and information material for the performance of the firm. If, to the contrary, the managers did not believe that these means will really work, then they engaged in outright fraud. Of course, the managers might have both defrauded the Company and withheld potentially important information.

Misrepresentations of facts: Further developing the reasoning in above, we have to understand that the managers misrepresented facts when they suggested the amount of savings from the outsourcing deal. The deal looked attractive only because the current situation was poorly handled. It is not clear how much things would improve if the Company made a serious effort to reduce costs and improve the organization of its IT division from within. In any case, it would have been better that the current situation of mismanagement. The managers hid the issue of the baseline of comparison and presented the potential of self-improvement of the organization as a benefit which the new company contributes.

Obstructing fair competition: By using inside information to make an attractive offer to the Company, the managers deprived the companies providing IT outsourcing services of a fair chance to offer their bids and to reduce the Company's (and societal) costs. A bid like this is similar in nature to inside trading. It prevents fair competition, creates market imperfections, and increases societal costs.

Harming employees without redeeming reasons: The process of outsourcing involved layoffs, relationships of fear, and resentment among the affected employees. Causing emotional distress is only acceptable if it is dictated by offsetting reason. If I interpret the case correctly, and the major consideration was the personal gratification of the executives, then the suffering of the employees was unjustified.

Conclusions from the Case

Based on widely shared ethical beliefs, the actions of three top executives in outsourcing the IT department were morally wrong. There are at least four elements of their behavior to be unethical. The ethical violations include withholding material information from the employer, creating a conflict of interest, misrepresenting the future payoffs of the outsourcing agreement, unfair competitive practices based on insider information, and imposing undue hardships on displaced employees of the Company without justification.

The case study demonstrated that cost-benefit considerations are not sufficient to analyze an outsourcing case. Important ethical concerns relating to fiduciary responsibilities, insider bidding for outsourcing contracts, and the like are also pertinent to the analysis of outsourcing.

Seeking higher profits is a legitimate business goal. However, ends do not justify the means. Higher profits do not warrant ethically or morally questionable means. Under the pretense of seeking the benefits of IT outsourcing for their company corrupt agents may engage in fraud or breach of duties of loyalty. Establishing procedures of openness, solicitation of multiple bids, and the like will prevent companies from slipping into ethical controversies, costly lawsuits, and loss of face and reputation.

IMPLICATIONS OF THE STUDY FOR OUTSOURCING MODELS

The analysis of the outsourcing case demonstrated that ethics is an important consideration in an outsourcing decision. The practice of outsourcing sets the stage for a number of potential ethical conflicts, importantly, breach of trust and loyalty and breach of fiduciary duties. These could take place between the principal and its agents at the outsourcing customer, between the principal and its agents at the vendor, between customer and vendor, and between employer and employees. Agents could enter self-dealing schemes to the detriment of their company, or a company could use outsourcing to get rid of long-term commitments (i.e., retirement benefits) to employees. There may be other types of ethical conflicts, but they are not prominent in the present case.

The most important conclusion from the present analysis is that when a company considers outsourcing, it should take into consideration potential ethical conflicts. Perhaps, it is enough to say that acts that are ethically wrong should not be done. Still, allowing unethical behavior on the part of the company or its agents does some very real harm. These include, on the company level, dwindling of the morale of the employees, resignations of important employees who would not like to be a part of the disgraced company, loss of respect for the management of the company, and distrust of the mission and objectives of the company. On a societal scale, there could be costly lawsuits and loss of the goodwill of the public, as well as loss of trust by business partners. Most importantly, there will be misallocation of economic resources.

It is suggested that the models for evaluation of outsourcing decisions should include the ethics factor into their consideration. The reader recalls that the strategic discrepancy model is preferable to the list of benefits model in that it identifies the key strategic impact of an outsourcing decision for a company, rather than considering factors of varied degrees of relevance. The strategic interaction model was preferred to the strategic discrepancy model in its inclusion in the analysis of the interaction with the vendor. It is important to understand that the goal of this chapter is not to determine the best model for evaluating outsourcing decisions. It is not necessary to accept the strategic interaction model in order to accept the points about the need for ethical concern in outsourcing. The conclusions of the analysis are available for the adherents of all three models. Briefly, each of the models will be improved if it includes ethical analysis of the particular decision.

List of Benefits and Ethics

According to the logic of this model, the absence of ethical concerns will be listed as a benefit of a particular outsourcing deal. The potential and actual ethical concerns will be listed as disadvantages of the outsourcing deal. Loss of the goodwill of the community will be considered as a disadvantage in the area of general management. The dwindling of morale, resignations, and detriment of leadership are disadvantages in the area of human resources management. The model warns against these but, as stated before, it leaves it open whether an instance of unethical behavior has more weight in the mind of a manager than some petty savings.

Strategic Discrepancy and Ethics

This model would make even more adequate use of the ethical analysis. It recognizes that some factors are greatly more important than others for the company, as they affect its strategic goal. The decision to adhere to the professional code of ethics is a strategic decision. Internally, it affects the human resources of the company. If the company is loyal to its employees and the agents are loyal to their principal, that keeps the morale high and protects the authority of the management. Externally, the decision affects the overall public perception of the company and

Figure 2: Ethical issues on the strategic grid

HIGH

Factory-uninterrupted service-oriented information resource management	Strategic information resource management
Outsourcing Presumption: Yes, unless company is huge and well-managed	*Outsourcing presumption:* No
Considerations in outsourcing: • Possibilities of economies of scale for small and midsize firms. • Higher quality service and backup. • Management focus facilitated. • Fiber-optic and extended channel technologies facilitate international IT solutions. • Vendor's vagaries.	Considerations in outsourcing: • Rescue an out-of-control internal IT unit. • Tap source of cash. • Facilitate flexibility. • Facilitate management of divestiture. • Embezzlement. • Vendor's disloyalty. • Company's disloyalty to employees.
Support-oriented information resource management	Turnaround information resource management
Outsourcing Presumption: Yes	*Outsourcing presumption:* No
Considerations in outsourcing: • Access to higher IT professionalism. • Possibility of laying off is of low priority and problematic. • Access to current IT. • Risk of inappropriate IT architectures reduced. • Vendor's vagaries.	Considerations in outsourcing: • Internal IT unit not capable in required technologies. • Internal IT unit not capable in required project management skills. • Embezzlement. • Vendor's disloyalty.

Current Dependence on Information (left axis, HIGH to LOW)

LOW   Importance of IT for Competitive Advantage   HIGH

creates goodwill. Insider trading and obstruction of fair competition are activities that would generally antagonize the public and will produce a negative reaction (legal action, regulation, or simply a negative image). Including ethical issues to be considered in each strategic quadrant could enhance McFarlan and Nolan's strategic grid presentation (see Figure 2).

Strategic Interaction and Ethics

The final model also would benefit from the inclusion of ethical considerations. Everything said about the previous model applies here. The decision to adhere to ethical standards is a strategic one. It influences the internal management of resources, as well as environmental factors. The model is represented graphically as a two-dimensional grid which maps the extent of involvement by vendors against the strategic impact of an IS function. Then the functions are projected on vertically,

Figure 3: Ethical dimension in the interaction between a customer and a vendor

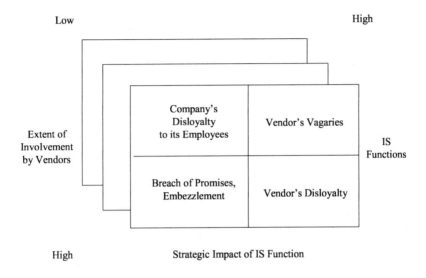

forming a third dimension. The ethical analysis could appropriately be depicted on one of the functional cards (see Figure 3).

The diagram suggests that we could classify ethical conflicts in the context of outsourcing according to the level of involvement of the vendor and the strategic role of IT technology. When the vendor's involvement is low, the potential for ethical damage is within the company-employees relationships. The anticipated ethical issues stemming from the vendor will be limited to vagaries, lack of commitment, and the like. As the involvement of the vendor increases, considerations such as embezzlement become more prominent. When the vendor's involvement is high and the IT function is strategic for the company, there exists a potential for vendor's disloyalty, such as betraying secrets of the company.

At a more conceptual level, first, the diagram brings home the idea that ethical conflicts are a strategic concern for a company involved in outsourcing. The higher the roles of the IT function, the bigger the impact of ethical conflicts. Second, the diagram emphasizes the interactive nature of outsourcing and the related source of ethical conflict. Ethical conflict could be internal for the company, or it could be embedded in the interaction between the company and the vendor.

CONCLUSION

Outsourcing of IT is the transfer of a company's information technology functions to external vendors. Such transfer is typically evaluated with regard to its strategic and economic impact on a company. However, as the analysis of a recent case demonstrated, ethical concerns relating to fiduciary responsibilities, insider bidding for outsourcing contracts, and similar ethical conflicts are also pertinent to the analysis of outsourcing.

The analysis identified major ethical problems and suggested a systematic way of evaluating ethical conduct in the process of outsourcing IT in the context of a company's strategy. The ethical considerations were incorporated in the most influential models of outsourcing: the list of benefits model, strategic discrepancy model, and strategic interaction model. The models were developed as to include a classification of ethical conflicts with regards to the level of the vendor's involvement and the strategic importance of the IT function for the company. Hopefully, this study will enhance the way companies look at the decision to outsource information technologies and provide practical guidelines for outsourcing IT.

REFERENCES

Grover, V., Cheong, M. J. and Teng, J. T. C. (1994). A descriptive study on outsourcing of information systems functions. *Information and Management*, 27, 32-44.

Kant, I. (1993). *Grounding for the Metaphysics of Morals*. Translated by James W. Ellington. 3rd ed. Indianapolis: Hackett.

McFarlan, F. W. and Nolan, R. L (1995). *Sloan Management Review*, 36(2), 9-23.

Mill, J. S. (1979). *Utilitarianism*. (George Sher, Ed.). Indianapolis, IN: Hackett.

Forbes. (1997). Outsourcing to the rescue. *Forbes*, September, 1(1), 22, 25-26.

Palvia, P. and Parzinger, M. (1995). Information systems outsourcing in financial institutions. In Khosrowpour, M. (Ed.), *Managing Information Technology Investments with Outsourcing*, 129-154. Hershey, PA: Idea Group Publishing.

Theng, J. T. C., Cheong, M. J. and Grover, V. (1994). Starategy-theoretic discrepancy model. *Decision Sciences*, 25(1), 75- 103.

Nam, K., Chaundhury, A., Rajagopalan, S. and Rao, H. R. (1998). Dimensions of outsourcing: A transaction cost framework. *Managing Information Technology*, 104-129.

Rawls, J. (1957). Outline of a decision procedure for ethics. *Philosophical Review*, 66, 177.

Chapter XV

Social Responsibility in IS/IT Project Management

Joseph T. Gilbert
University of Nevada, Las Vegas, USA

Project managers obviously have a responsibility to manage their projects. In this chapter we explore the question of social responsibility of project managers. We take it as given for purposes of this chapter that the project involves information systems and/or information technology. Social responsibility implies something beyond technical responsibility (the project, when completed, is technically efficient and reliable and meets the project specifications).

In this chapter we will use the stakeholder approach, which is common in discussions of business ethics and the role of business in society (Donaldson & Preston, 1995; Evan & Freeman, 1983) to identify various groups to which project managers have social responsibility. We will discuss the difference between legal responsibility and moral or ethical responsibility. We will use a rights and duties approach to apply principles from business ethics to the problem of identifying project manager responsibilities. After this general discussion, we will identify five specific groups to whom IS/IT project managers have responsibilities. For each group, we will identify the project manager role or roles which connect to the rights of the group and discuss the duties which those rights impose on project managers. In concluding the chapter, we will briefly consider how the duties or responsibilities of project managers can be viewed in a positive light as opportunities which most employees and many managers do not have.

THE STAKEHOLDER APPROACH

The stakeholder approach (Freeman, 1984, 1995) is often used for determining the responsibilities of a corporation, but it can also be used to analyze the responsibilities of a project manager. Stakeholders are defined as "any group or individual who can affect or is affected by the achievement of the organization's objectives" (Freeman, 1984, 46). Thus, for a corporation, stakeholders include employees, customers, regulators, suppliers, lenders, and other groups. The notion of stakeholders was introduced to widen the view of corporate responsibility beyond that to the owners or stockholders (Jones, 1995). There is some evidence that corporations with greater social awareness also have better financial performance (Barney & Hansen 1994; Berman, Wicks, Kotha & Jones, 1999). Applying the approach of identifying a project's stakeholders, we can begin to identify the individuals or groups to whom a project manager owes responsibility.

Perhaps the two most obvious groups to whom the project manager owes responsibility are, first, the employer who has commissioned the project and, second, the employees who work on it. If the project manager is an employee of the organization for which the project is being done, then the project manager owes the same responsibilities or duties that are owed in general by employees to their employers, but additionally owes specific duties as a project manager. If the project manager is a consultant or other outsider who is directing the project under some sort of contractual arrangement, then the duties owed to the management of the company for which the project is being completed (the project sponsor) are somewhat different from those of an employee to an employer. In this case, the project manager also has duties to his or her employer (unless the manager is in the position of a self-employed consultant). Whatever the project manager's employment status, he or she also has duties or responsibilities to those working on the project under his or her direction.

A third group of stakeholders comprises those who will subsequently have to maintain and improve the code involved in the project. Needless to say, this could involve programmers working on the code years from the time of the project. While less visible than other stakeholders, this group is also important.

The fourth group of stakeholders involves the financial supporters of the project sponsor. In a corporation, these will be the stockholders of the company. For a public agency, taxpayers are the ultimate financial supporters. In either case, someone has invested or paid money with an expectation of results.

The fifth group of stakeholders, users of the completed project, might include employees of the company for which the project is done, customers of that company, and workers at other companies which have interfaces with the completed project (for example, projects involving B2B Internet usage have wide user involvement). If the project is being undertaken for a public sector organization, such as a school district or police department, segments of the general public might be users in this case–parents of students, employers of school graduates, victims of criminal activities.

RIGHTS AND DUTIES: A PHILOSOPHICAL ANALYSIS

What this introduction suggests is that project managers have responsibilities which extend far beyond delivering to their boss a completed project on time and at or under budget. Where might such responsibilities arise? In philosophy, ethics deals with such topics as morally right and wrong actions (DeGeorge, 1995). One of the principal ways in which ethics approaches questions of morality is a consideration of rights and duties. This approach includes legal rights and duties, but also goes beyond these.

While the legal and the moral often coincide, they do not always do so. In the United States at the present time, most jurisdictions have no legal prohibitions against adultery, yet most people consider adultery immoral, at least for their spouses. There are three basic sources of moral rights. Some we have by reason of being human: an example is the right to life. No human society condones sheer random killing. What constitutes a sufficient reason to take a human life may vary from society to society, but the need for a strong reason to do so in all societies points to an underlying human right to life. Some rights come from citizenship or membership in a society. These are often discussed as legal rights. Americans have rights to free speech and assembly that are greater than those granted in many other societies. Finally, some rights come from position. Police officers have the right to detain individuals, and financial officers have the right to disburse company funds. The philosophical analysis of the sources of rights is beyond the scope of this chapter.

Business ethics is a field of study which applies general ethical theories to business settings. This sets it apart both from general ethics (how should humans act?) and from other specific fields such as medical ethics or legal ethics. The study of specific rights and duties in business situations is grounded in the broader ethical theory of rights and duties.[1] For a right to have meaning, someone must have a duty. If I have a right to privacy, you have a duty to leave me alone. As we explore the issues of social responsibilities of IS/IT project managers, we will treat responsibilities and duties as interchangeable. By combining the concepts of stakeholders and rights and duties, we have the basic tools needed for our analysis.

THE ROLE OF PROJECT MANAGERS

One further idea needs to be introduced at this point. Project managers are, as their title states, managers. We need to explore briefly what the job of the manager is, as opposed to that of programmer or analyst or other technical jobs.[2] While a project manager without technical IS/IT skills is unlikely to succeed, the job of the project manager is to oversee and coordinate the work of others (Freeman & Soete, 1997, see especially, 197-265; Tushman & Moore, 1988). If any one person is responsible for delivering a well-done project on time and at or under budget, it is the project manager. Clearly, on projects of any significant size or scope, he or she cannot do all the work alone. On small projects, where the project team is small and the tasks of oversight and coordination are minimal, the project manager may well be an active participant in the technical work. However, on projects where oversight and coordination constitute a full-time job, the project manager's task is not to do analysis or to write and test code. It is to oversee the work of those who do. While this fact may appear obvious, many project managers, especially those relatively new to the task, are more comfortable with technical work and revert to it especially when the project appears to be falling behind in time or quality of output.

The responsibilities of programmers and analysts are different from those of project managers. In order to intelligently analyze the social responsibilities of project managers, we must be clear on what their task is and what responsibilities or duties it entails (Katz, 1997). Managers are responsible for the work of those they manage. They are also responsible for the interface of their work group with stakeholders–those who affect or are affected by their work group. This work group can vary from two or three subordinates to the many employees of a large organization. For purposes of our discussion in this chapter, we will assume that the project manager is no more than one level of supervision removed from the actual workers: that is, he or she either oversees workers or oversees the direct supervisors of workers.

FIVE AREAS OF PROJECT MANAGER RESPONSIBILITY

The first set of duties or responsibilities of project managers comprises those owed to their clients and/or organizational superiors. These are clearly social in the sense that they affect both the larger organization of which the project team is a part and the client (if it is not the same organization) who is paying for and depending on the completion of the project. Representative of such duties are financial and time management of the project, accurate reporting, and quality control.

Financial and time management are related but not identical. It is possible to stay within the budget and fail to complete the project on time, and it is possible to greatly overspend the budget and thus complete the project on time. It is, of course, also possible and not unusual to overspend the budget and also be late with project completion. For the project manager, financial management requires at least a rudimentary knowledge of accounting. In large organizations, the project manager's role in this area may simply be to review accounting reports prepared as a matter of course by others in the organization. In a smaller organization or in a consulting situation, the project manager may have to be considerably more involved in the gathering and reporting of financial data relevant to the project. While the gathering and reporting of cost data may well be beyond the expertise of a project manager, provisions to have it done competently must be made by someone. Project managers have a duty (because project sponsors have a right to know) to report the financial status of a project.

Time management is obviously a critical element of successful project management. Projects not completed on time typically run over budget, but they may also be of less use to the project sponsor because of issues external to the project. A new voting system must be ready before election day. The computer support system for a new financial product must be ready before the product is introduced to the sales force and the public. The stakeholders here include the project sponsor, but might also include voters, salespeople and potential customers. The consequences of late projects are sometimes much more severe than those of projects delivered on time but over budget. One or another worker's lack of progress may hinder the on-time completion of the project. It is the project manager's responsibility to know whether the project is proceeding on an acceptable time line and to inform the sponsor and make agreed-upon changes either to the project or to the time line if it is not.

In addition to financial and time management, project managers also have a responsibility to provide accurate reporting of progress to their own managers and to project sponsors. We said earlier that the project manager is responsible for delivering a completed project on time and at or under budget. He or she is also responsible for reporting progress on such goals. While there are sophisticated tools available for project scheduling and time management, it is ultimately the duty of the project manager to provide accurate reporting. This duty arises from the right of the project manager's superiors and the project sponsor to know where the project stands before the completion date. The project manager is best situated both to have and to report this knowledge, hence the duty falls on him or her.

It goes without saying that in order to report accurately the project manager must know accurately. It is a well-documented fact that subordinates tend not to deliver bad news to their superiors, at least not in undiluted form. It is also a well-known fact that many superiors discourage the reporting of bad news by subordinates by (metaphorically) killing messengers who bring bad news. The fraternity of messengers is close-knit. Once a manager has reacted badly to the delivery of bad news by one subordinate, other subordinates are much less apt to repeat such delivery. Hence, a project manager who has a duty to report accurate information also has a duty to act in such a way that truthful reporting by subordinates is encouraged rather than discouraged.

Does a project manager have a duty to report bad news regarding either cost or timeliness if not specifically asked? Just as subordinates prefer not to deliver unwelcome news to project managers, those same project managers are often inclined not to deliver such news to their organizational superiors or to project sponsors. There may be no need (and hence no obligation) to report a 2-day delay in a 6-month project, or a $5,000 overrun on a million dollar project. However, the rights and duties approach says that if a stakeholder has a right to know, then someone has a duty to report. Both organizational superiors and project sponsors have a right to know if a project is running over in cost or late in time. Therefore, given the human tendency to hope that things will fix themselves before discovered, the project manager at a minimum has a duty to seriously and honestly review the issue of reporting any overruns of time or money.

A third responsibility or duty that project managers owe to their organizational superiors and project sponsors, as well as to other stakeholders, is quality control. A project completed on time and under budget, but with poor quality, cannot be judged a success. Project sponsors pay to have projects done in order to accomplish goals of their organizations. In businesses, projects are intended to aid, in one way or another, the provision of goods or services to customers at a profit. In private organizations, projects are also intended to forward one or more organizational goals: the teaching of students in a school district, treatment of patients in a hospital, or service of patrons in a library district.

Part of quality control is technical. In an IS/IT project, there may be more than one way to complete a project so that it works as intended, but there are many ways to complete it in such a manner that it does not fully deliver the intended results. While technicians on the project team may have more detailed technical knowledge than the project manager, it is ultimately the project manager who is responsible for seeing that the completed project meets appropriate quality standards. Testing, debugging, and other means are used to find and fix problems. The project manager can also influence quality by the tone that he sets for the project. If there is frequent and repeated emphasis on speed, quality may well suffer unless it also receives its fair share of emphasis. If the project manager implements regular reviews and follows through on quality problems found while the project is progressing, the final product is more apt to meet quality standards. The work of the project manager in this regard is all the more important because users often do not have access to the work product while the project is in progress. If the project manager is not attentive to quality while the project is under way, finding and fixing errors when it is complete becomes the only alternative, and it is a costly one.

A second set of duties or responsibilities of the project manager is made up of those owed to the project team. We now consider three of these duties: those of resource provider, coordinator, and evaluator. This is by no means an exhaustive list. Rather, it is meant to be representative of this set of responsibilities of project managers. Are these social responsibilities? To the extent that these are responsibilities involving people, rather than technical or financial goals, they are social.

One of the roles of a project manager is that of resource provider for the project team. A team of people, even if technically skilled and highly motivated, cannot deliver the desired result (a project completed on time and at or under budget) without resources. Clearly, it is not efficient or effective to let each project team member fend for herself in acquiring the physical resources needed to accomplish their work. While the larger organizational structure will sometimes provide for the necessary resources, it is not uncommon to have a project team attempting to work without sufficient space or equipment. Further, if members of the team need information resources, they can sometimes efficiently attain these on their own, but it is sometimes either necessary or more expedient for the project manager to attain them.

The second responsibility of the project manager to the project group is to coordinate their activities, both internally and with other relevant groups or individuals. A clear division of labor is one of the most basic principles of organization theory. It is at least cumbersome and time-consuming for a group of workers who are peers to work out an optimal division of labor. Hence, this task is one that normally falls to the project manager. If he or she is directly overseeing the workers on the project team, then coordination is the project manager's personal responsibility. If there are supervisors between the project manager and the workers, the task of coordination for the project manager is done through these supervisors, with the manager coordinating the work between or among sections. Again, while this responsibility may seem too obvious to need discussion, more than one project has foundered because of failures of coordination.

A third responsibility of the project manager to the team members is that of evaluation. This can take several forms. If the team is permanent or quasi-permanent, then the organization will normally have performance evaluation procedures in place. If the team is more or less temporary, there may be no formal evaluation procedures. Evaluation serves at least two purposes. One is to assure the timeliness and quality of the project. The second is to provide the workers with feedback on their work and information for guidance in their quest for salary increases, bonuses and promotions. For project managers who are personally more comfortable with technical matters than with interpersonal dealings, this can be a difficult (and hence often neglected) part of their job. If it is neglected, projects are less likely to succeed, and the long-term contributions of project team members are apt to be suboptimal.

The third (and often forgotten) group of stakeholders for project managers is comprised of those who will subsequently maintain or improve the programs that are involved in the completed project. Many a programmer or analyst has cursed the lack of adequate documentation of programs that he or she was trying to correct or upgrade. Idiosyncratic code, inadequately documented, can be very costly to an organization. How much of the money spent on Y2K fixes could have been put to better use if previous projects had been adequately documented? This may be the ultimate example of social costs resulting from inadequate project management.

The responsibility or duty to write and document code that can be subsequently understood and maintained by others rests ultimately with individual programmers. However, project managers are responsible for the joint product of individual project team members and for setting and enforcing standards for the work done by those team members. If project managers do not take due care in this regard, it is unlikely that anyone else will.

The fourth group of stakeholders to whom the project manager has responsibilities or duties consists of the financial supporters of the organization for which the project manager works. In private corporations, this group consists of investors. Those who own stock in the company and those who have loaned it money (banks and bondholders) have a clear interest in the company's profitable performance. If the organization is a public entity such as a school district or police department, its financial supporters are ultimately the taxpayers. While these groups may seem far removed from the concerns of a project manager, in fact they do have rights which impose duties on project managers.

We said earlier that the reason for undertaking IS/IT projects is to help an organization to better perform its mission. For-profit corporations have a mission of earning a profit. This can be done by selling airplane rides or providing banking services or selling groceries. Public agencies have a mission of providing some service to one or more segments of the public. This can involve educating children or administering welfare payments or repairing streets. In both the private and the public organization, the tasks cannot be adequately accomplished, and hence the organizational missions cannot be fulfilled, without information processing. Information processing cannot continue to provide adequate mission support to organizations unless it is periodically improved and expanded through IS/IT projects. While it is certainly not the only contributor to organizational success, the project team does have a causal link to such success. One needs only to think of specific failed projects to see the results on organizational performance.

The responsibility or duty that project managers owe to the financial supporters of their organizations involves many of the same things discussed under duties to employees, employers, and sponsoring organizations. This duty involves delivering completed projects of appropriate quality on time and at or under budget. Why raise the issue of responsibilities to financial supporters at all if it involves the same activities and results as other duties of the project manager? Project managers often become so caught up in the details of their work that they lose sight of the larger picture of which they are a part. The reality is that the success of very large and complex organizations depends to some extent on individual managers at relatively low levels within those organizations. It is important in practical terms for project managers and their project teams to understand how much depends on their work. It is also important for those who manage large organizations and those who depend on them for airplane rides or new highways to understand that the results of these organizations depend on real people with specific jobs and not on some nameless, faceless "they" (as in "they never get it right!").

A fifth set of responsibilities for project managers involves their duties to users of their project. The users, whether they are customers of for-profit organizations or the clients of public agencies, want completed projects to work for them, whether this means easier online shopping or more efficient school bus scheduling for their children or simpler registration for their graduate courses at the university. As with the previous set of responsibilities, we discuss these not because they require different or additional actions on the part of project managers but because they indicate how many people depend in one way or another on successfully completed projects.

In a society as complex as the one we live in, we all depend on many people in different roles to make our lives better in some way. The users of IS/IT projects do not know, as a general rule, who develops these projects, yet, to the extent that the projects succeed or fail, the lives of the users are made a little bit better or worse. This does constitute a responsibility for project managers.

THE SOCIAL IMPACTS OF PROJECT MANAGEMENT: AN OPPORTUNITY

We have now reviewed five different sets of stakeholders who have rights in some way that impose duties on project managers. By using stakeholder analysis, a common tool in business ethics, we have identified more responsibilities or duties of project managers than might otherwise have appeared. The subject of this chapter is the social responsibility of IS/IT project managers. We have seen that responsibilities and duties can be discussed interchangeably. The ethical analysis of rights and duties shows that a right is meaningless unless someone has a corresponding duty. The duties or responsibilities of project managers arise from the rights of various groups that have a stake in the outcome of the project. The sum of these duties equates to the social responsibility of project managers. Some of these responsibilities are detailed and immediate. An example is the duty of project managers to their subordinates working on the project. Other responsibilities of project managers are more remote. An example of such responsibilities can be found in the duties owed to those who will later maintain and update the programs and systems which the project team produces. In total, project managers have an impressive array of duties and responsibilities.

The reality and validity of these duties and responsibilities can be seen from considering the consequences of successful and unsuccessful projects. Much of the applied innovation which has produced such values as increased productivity and improved communication comes about because of successful projects. Unsuccessful projects typically do not yield such benefits. Rather, they result in wasted money and frustrated project team members, users, sponsors and others. The difference between successful and unsuccessful projects often turns on the efforts and skills of project managers. Certainly projects have succeeded in spite of poor project management and failed despite heroic efforts by project managers. Nonetheless, there is a clear link between good project management and good projects.

The social responsibilities of project managers have been analyzed in terms of duties to various stakeholders or constituencies. In conclusion, we will briefly view these duties or responsibilities from a different perspective. Project managers have many opportunities to provide benefits to individuals and groups. Because of the positions that they hold, their work and its results can have real and significant impacts on a variety of people, for good or for ill. The opportunity to provide meaningful benefits to others through one's work is not a universal one. Project managers have this opportunity to a greater degree than many other workers, including other managers. Technical considerations are properly involved in the work of the project manager, but people considerations are as well. As indicated above, the work of the project manager involves people. He or she leads the project team, interfaces with organizational supervisors and often with project sponsors, and produces through the project team results which improve the functioning of organizations and the lives of individuals. This is no small responsibility, but it can also be a matter for legitimate pride and satisfaction.

ENDNOTES

1 For readers interested in pursuing some of the basic issues of ethics and in particular of business ethics, the following sources will prove useful. Full citations are included in the bibliography. Boatright, J.R.: *Ethics and the Conduct of Business*, 3rd ed. (2000); De George, R.T.: *Business Ethics*, 4th ed. (1995); Dienhart, J.W.: *Business, Institutions, and Ethics* (2000); LaFollette, H. (Ed.): *The Blackwell Guide to Ethical Theory* (2000); Singer, P. (Ed.): *A Companion to Ethics* (1993); White, T.: *Business Ethics: A Philosophical Reader*, (1993).

2 For readers unfamiliar with the literature on management and organization theory, the following brief list provides a starting place for exploring some of the major ideas and writers on this topic. While not the most current available publications, many of these sources are considered classics and are still widely read. Full citations are included in the bibliography below. On management: Drucker, P.F.: *Managing For Results* (1964), *Management: Tasks, Responsibilities, Practices* (1973), *Management Challenges for the 21st Century* (1999). On leadership: Bennis, W. & Nanus, B.: *Leaders: The Strategies for Taking Charge* (1985); Gardner, J.W.: *On Leadership* (1990). On organizations: Ott, J.S. (Ed.) *Classic Readings in Organizational Behavior*, 2nd ed. (1996); Wilson, J.Q.: *Bureaucracy: What Government Agencies Do and Why They Do It* (1989). On Organizational Culture: Kotter, J.P. & Heskett, J.L.: *Corporate Culture and Performance* (1992); Schein, E.H.: *Organizational Culture and Leadership*, 2nd ed. (1985).

REFERENCES

Barney, J. B. and Hansen, M. H. (1994). Trustworthiness as a source of competitive advantage. *Strategic Management Journal*, 15, 175-190.

Bennis, W. and Nanus, B. (1985). Leaders: The strategies for taking charge. New York: Harper & Row.

Berman, S. L., Wicks, A. C., Kotha, S. and Jones, T. M. (1999). Does stakeholder orientation matter? The relationship between stakeholder management models and firm financial performance. *Academy of Management Journal*, 42, 488-506.

Boatright, J. R. (2000). *Ethics and the Conduct of Business*, (3rd ed.). Upper Saddle River, NJ: Prentice Hall.

DeGeorge, R. T. (1995). *Business Ethics*, (4th ed.). Englewood Cliffs, NJ: Prentice Hall.

Dienhart, J. W. (2000). *Business, Institutions, and Ethics*. New York: Oxford University Press.

Donaldson, T. and Preston, L. (1995). The stakeholder theory of the corporation: Concepts, evidence and implications. *Academy of Management Review*, 20, 65-91.

Drucker, P. F. (1964). *Managing for Results*. New York: Harper & Row.

Drucker, P. F. (1973). *Management: Tasks, Responsibilities*, Practices. New York: Harper & Row.

Drucker, P. F. (1999). Management Challenges for the 21st Century. New York: HarperCollins.

Evan, W. and Freeman, R. E. (1983). A stakeholder theory of the modern corporation: Kantian capitalism. In Beauchamp, T. and Bowie, N. (Eds.), *Ethical Theory in Business*, 75-93. Englewood Cliffs, NJ: Prentice-Hall.

Freeman, C. and Soete, L. (1997). *The Economics of Industrial Innovation*, (3rd ed.). Cambridge, MA: MIT Press.

Freeman, R. E. (1984). *Strategic Management: A Stakeholder Approach*. Englewood Cliffs NJ: PrenticeHall.

Freeman, R. E. (1995). Stakeholder thinking: The state of the art. In Nasi, J. (Ed.), *Understanding Stakeholder Thinking*, 35-46. Helsinki: LSR.

Gardner, J. W. (1990). *On Leadership*. New York: The Free Press.

Jones, T. M. (1995). Instrumental stakeholder theory: A synthesis of ethics and economics. *Academy of Management Review*, 20, 404-437.

Katz, R. (Ed.). (1997). *The Human Side of Managing Technological Innovation*. New York: Oxford University Press.

Kotter, J. P. and Heskett, J. L. (1992). *Corporate Culture & Performance*. New York: Free Press.

LaFollette, H. (Ed.). (2000). *The Blackwell Guide to Ethical Theory*. Malden, MA: Blackwell.

Ott, J. S. (Ed.). (1996). *Classic Readings in Organizational Behavior*, (2nd ed.). Belmont CA: Wadsworth.

Schein, E. H. (1985). *Organizational Culture & Leadership*. San Francisco: Jossey-Bass.

Singer, P. (Ed.). (1993). A companion to ethics. Oxford, UK: Blackwell.

Tushman, M. L. and Moore, W.L. (Eds.). (1988). *Readings in the Management of Innovation*, (2nd ed.). New York: Harper Business.

White, T. (1993). *Business Ethics: A Philosophical Reader*. New York: Macmillan.

Wilson, J. Q. (1989). *Bureaucracy: What Government Agencies Do and Why They Do It*. New York: Basic Books.

Chapter XVI

Self-Employed and Small-Business Computer Users: Challenges and Directions for Progress

Phil Carter
Auckland University of Technology, New Zealand

INTRODUCTION

The new convergence of computing, communications, and media are enriching people's lives in delightful and diverse ways. Increasing numbers of self-employed people and small businesses are taking up the new applications and opportunities to assist them in their work even though the computer is not the main focus of their business. However, these users face many challenges and difficulties. Most are naive to the use of computers and world of IT and they generally differ from computer users within larger organizations because they face IT on their own with the limited resources they can organize and pay for.

The main aim of this chapter is to describe interventions and perspectives that help self-employed and small-business computer users to use computers to further their life and work purposes. There are also important and useful messages for computer companies, system designers and developers, and computer sales and support people. But the main orientation here is on the users and what they can do to help themselves given the current situation they face and the probability that from their point of view, system usability, information security, and support will not fundamentally change in the near future.

The first section of this chapter looks at why we need to address this problem and suggests how we might do this. The second section presents data from several long-term, in-depth studies done with individuals that illustrates the situation. Interventions that were tried in these studies are also presented. These are discussed in the section following and directions for progress and recommendations are proposed.

BACKGROUND

Self-employed and small-business computer users are often new to the world of computers and IT. They face many challenges, most of them on their own. They have to make decisions about whether to invest in IT or not. They have to decide what hardware and software to buy. They have to decide what to learn and how to learn it. And when things go wrong, they have to either work out how to fix the problem or identify those who could solve it. The more they use and benefit from IT, the more vulnerable they can become.

The situation presents a number of important and obvious messages for computer companies, system designers and developers, and computer sales and support people. More effort is required to make systems as usable as possible. Giving power and control to the end user and aiming for security need to be priorities. Comprehensive support is essential and needs to include a number of approaches such as clear on-screen help facilities and help desks.

However, the end user can not wait for an ideal world to eventuate. If there were no new developments, then usability, security, and support would improve. However, computer designers and developers surge excitedly ahead developing new applications and devices. Complexity increases (Norman, 1997) and it becomes hard to imagine usability, security, and support suddenly improving (Druffel, 1997). From the users' perspective then, what can be realistically done with immediate benefits? One approach is to look at what users can do to help themselves which is the main focus of this chapter. However, whatever the approach, clarity around what occurs when people use or think about computer systems will be beneficial (computer behaviour).

Studies of Computer Behaviour

There have been different approaches to the study of human behaviour with computers. Survey instruments have been popular. These typically ask respondents to rate the degree of fit of statements such as, "I enjoy computer work" and "I'll need computers for my future work" (Gardner, Discenza & Dukes, 1993; Woodrow, 1991). These studies often make the assumption that the computer is one "discrete" thing to which there is one clear attitude. However, computers are no longer monolithic systems. There are many different applications, such as word processors, email and browser applications, accounting packages, and multimedia applications that users can have quite different experiences of and attitudes toward.

User satisfaction instruments provide greater discrimination by asking questions on specific systems or applications. For example, "Is the system accurate?" and "Is the system easy to use?" (Doll & Torkzadeh, 1988). However, these instruments can introduce ambiguity, create interference in measurement of task and interface satisfaction, and result in a tremendous amount of detail being lost (Zmud et al., 1994). Even an instrument that breaks down questioning into many specific areas of usability such as in the Questionnaire for User Interface Satisfaction, generalizations must be made. For example, one of the 12 parts relates to the screen and within that there are 14 questions such as "Amount of information that can be displayed on the screen," to which the respondent gives a degree of fit on a 9-point scale from inadequate to adequate. If the amount of information that can be displayed varies in different parts of the system, then valuable information is lost in a generalization that may not mean much.

Perhaps the "overuse of general measurement instruments accounts for much of the inconsistency that pervades the IS literature" (Zmud et al., 1994). For example, studies that have used such instruments to look for correlations between computer anxiety and variables such as gender, experience, and age are inconsistent. Several studies found gender differences in computer anxiety but several found none (see Maurer, 1994, for a summary). Lack of experience has been associated with anxiety (Miller & Varma, 1994) and even suggested as a causal factor (Charlton & Birkett, 1995). Yet, high-level anxiety has been found to remain for some students after training (McInerney, McInerney & Sinclair, 1994) and computer anxiety has even been found to increase with experience- "Each additional computer experience strengthens their negative affective reactions and promotes further computer avoidance" (Rosen & Maguire, 1990, p. 187).

Studies on age differences have found age highly significant to anxiety (Torkzadeh & Angulo, 1992) while others have found little effect (Maurer, 1994; Rosen & Maguire, 1990). The limited ability of the survey research design to provide for contextual complexity typically leaves researchers making guesses as to why. For example, Dyck and Smither (1994) found older adults (>55 years) less computer anxious and more positive to computers than young adults (<30 years). They hypothesized that the types of use influenced this: the older adults used the computer for work and recreation and the younger adults used them in university courses.

When Miller and Varma (1994) found older school children had more negative attitudes, they guessed that computers were perceived as getting more difficult and the older children were less likely to engage in activities that were perceived as having negative achievement risks; older children were expected to engage in more sophisticated computer experience; and there was more book learning later so computers became more foreign. However, Krendl and Broihier (1992) found fourth to tenth graders' preference for and perception of learning value declines (even with the introduction of sophisticated, challenging and visually stimulating software) and perceived difficulty remains the same (move from games to word processing). They introduced the ideas that older students were more sceptical and there were novelty effects.

The results of the above studies suggests important variables and dimensions are being missed and complex phenomena are being unsuccessfully broken down into separate variables with the loss of significant interrelationships. At best, such survey orientated studies can only demonstrate correlational effects and would struggle to establish causal effects, although researchers sometimes claim such effects.

Astute observation and careful description of behaviour within the context that it occurs will assist in progressing the study of computer behaviour. Usability testing of the types outlined by Nielsen (1993) provide finer levels of detail and discrimination than attitudinal and user satisfaction instruments. But even here, the usability laboratories can not have some of the situational factors that can impact on usability, for example, phone interruptions and office noise. More importantly, the focus tends to be on the usability of the interface, and other motivational and attitudinal factors are not realized.

Approaches that integrate fine-grain examination within the context of occurrence offer promise. Interpretative field studies benefit by frequently relating detailed study of parts of the whole back to the whole to ascertain significance and maintain perspective (Klein & Myers, 1999). Open investigative studies of antecedents to user satisfaction and performance with computers also show promise to obtain the astute observation and careful description that is needed (Collins & Caputi, 1999).

Pathological Orientation

The pathological focus of much research has been a serious limitation to progress. There is a proliferation of terms such as computer anxiety and computerphobia. There is a predisposition in the "West" to "problems" and their solving. For example, Western medicine is founded on an allopathic focus on identifying disease and then treating the disease. Other traditions focus on identifying health and strengthening that. Within information systems development, even methodologies that take a relatively more systemic and open approach, such as soft systems methodology and multiview, define the first stage as problem definition (Avison & Fitzgerald, 1995).

This problem orientation could also help explain why we have a tendency to bring in wide ranging changes hiding behind a "robust" methodology, rather than building incrementally through valuing tradition with its learned appreciation of quality of materials and workmanship (Introna & Whitley, 1997). How can we appreciate these qualities if we begin with and focus on problems? Appreciating things that go well, that are of value, enjoyment, and quality, also help, raise the human spirit.

If one believes that computer anxiety plays a role in a significant underutilization of computer resources (Torkzadeh & Angulo, 1992), then a pathological focus may seem reasonable. However, there are dangers. One danger is that such terms as anxiety can connate bad, negative, and unuseful, which is how most researchers appear to have viewed it. This may not always be accurate as context and the subjective view of the person may dictate otherwise. For example, anxiety can be used as a positive motivator (Collins & Caputi, 1999). Also a worker may be justifiably anxious about a pending computer system because of possible loss of control or even job loss. From his perspective, this anxiety may be well placed.

Another danger of a pathological focus is that the positive is robbed of attention. Careful consideration and appreciation of what is positive and building on that is an alternative and potentially more useful strategy. Instead, health and progress are viewed as a double negative; i.e., "let's attack the pathology," or "What computer anxiety reduction techniques will work?" (Maurer, 1994). For example, Greene, Kincade and Hays (1994) found cognitive appraisal (perceived benefit and/or challenge of a computer interaction) had a strong relationship with anxiety. They concluded that by influencing antecedents to these appraisals computer anxiety could be reduced. From this they suggested "introductory material should be presented to show that computers are tools to be used, not machines to replace or control workers" (p. 337). While it might have been true in their case, assuming that computerization is always beneficial is naive and simplistic. But at least these studies make an effort to stimulate and effect desirable change, which is rare.

CASE STUDIES

This section presents a study done with several individuals and some of the dynamics of computer use that were revealed. Several interventions aiming for desirable change in behaviour are also described.

Method

The study was done with several individuals. These people responded enthusiastically to the idea of looking at their behaviour with computers with the intent of making some desirable change. Several sessions were conducted with each participant over an extended period of months. Approximately a year later, participants were followed up to see how they were doing with computers. The participants are similar in that they are using computer systems largely on their own. The small number of participants means that they can not represent a cross section of this type of user. However, it is hoped that by detailed study many of the common dynamics and forces that impact on the situation may be revealed.

Participants were encouraged to tell their stories concerning computer use. This method assists the projection and presentation of reality as it is seen and experienced. The full range of elements, personalities, and forces that impact on an individual's behaviour with the computer can be revealed in their proper perspective, significance, complexity, and context. An individual's approaches to, attributions about, and perceptions of the technology can be appreciated (Krendl & Broihier, 1992).

The approach of the study drew on two traditions: action methods and action research (AR). Characteristics of these two traditions and their connections are given in Table 1.

There is not space in this chapter to give a detailed description of action methods or AR so the interested reader is directed to the references given at the footer of Table 1. However, one important part of the method not outlined in the table is the ability to take part of a process and examine it in detail while still retaining the systemic context. This ability to iterate from part to whole is an important ability central to some research methods (Klein & Myers, 1999). For example, the fundamental principle of the hermeneutic circle is:

> The movement of understanding is constantly from the whole to the part and back to the whole. Our task is to extend in concentric circles the unity of the understood meaning. The harmony of all the details with the whole is the criterion of correct understanding. The failure to achieve this harmony means that understanding has failed. (Gadamer, 1976, 117).

Data from the study is used to present several dynamics of computer use and some interventions that were successfully used. Events, stories, or quotes from the participants are indicated in the upcoming text by a different typeface.

Table 1: Action research and action methods

Action Research*	Action Methods**
critical; evaluative	investigative; focus on discriminating analysis and informed body-mind cognition
participatory; collaborative	devised as a group method; focuses on encounter and interaction
empowering; emancipatory	expands psychological and social functioning; focuses on creativity and spontaneity
active	involves dramatic techniques, interventions, and participants taking initiative
systematic; cyclic	practice informed by theory; involves phases of production, investigation, and intervention
reflective	use of sharing and mirror techniques; theory informed by practice

* Summarized from Melrose (2001), Reason and Bradbury (2001) and Zuber-Skerritt (1996)

** Summarized from Clayton (1992, 1993, 1994) and Moreno (1946, 1953)

Some Dynamics Revealed

A common dynamic for participants was the existence of both being attracted and excited by the new tools and also being repulsed and frightened. A typical example of this is Jean.

Jean has a rush of excitement as she realizes she has made contact with a like-minded person in Afghanistan on the email list group. It feels strange, like stepping into another dimension, but she welcomes having her habitual perceptions and beliefs challenged. She wants to be a bolder surfer of the Web and someone who utilizes and commands computer tools in her work as an organizational consultant.

But, one day as Jean is preparing for an important meeting where she will use the computer, letters start appearing randomly on the screen. She tries all she knows and can't fix it. It feels to her as if the computer is possessed. Later, she finds it extremely difficult to communicate with the fix-it people and feels like she has to become robotic like them. She feels overwhelmed, helpless, and alienated: "There's just too much for one person to know. What have I got myself into? The computer is erratic, I don't trust it, I can't get it fixed easily. And what about viruses, hackers, security, and the neutrality of information?"

Jean's story was similar with the other case studies and supported the hypothesis that self-employed and small-business users largely face IT on their own. Even users who were very positive about what the computer could do for them experienced being vulnerable and dependent on others.

The following extracts also reveal the limitations of some current research methods and the need for research to be finer grained and more discriminating. The following story indicates clearly that a person can have different attitudes toward different applications, in this case, word processing and digital art tools.

Angela is an artist who uses manual tools to create visual and tactile artworks. Recently, she has been frequently urged by her contemporaries to try digital imaging. However, she finds the computer an extremely poor tool for her artwork. She finds using the computer doesn't engage her body and mind like using her manual tools do. She finds artwork created on the computer lacks real depth, whereas she can create real depth with her tools. One colleague accuses her of living in the dark ages. She feels bullied and is becoming extremely tired of that. However, she is open to computers. She loves using it for word processing. She finds it assists her in organizing her thoughts and loves the security of being able to easily back her work up.

Angela would not be able to express the reality of her situation using the typical type of survey instrument because it is making the assumption that the computer is one "discrete" thing to which she has one clear attitude. Computers are no longer monolithic systems.

The application of a typical computer attitude survey to the next person would also not be very useful. It would reveal a largely negative attitude, but it would not reveal the primary reason for that which has little to do with the computer.

Noleen bought a computer to assist her with the onerous task of writing and to assist communication with colleagues using email. But things seem to constantly crash and do mysterious things. In response she finds herself getting very angry. She simply does not have the time or the interest to work them out. Her experiences with computers just seem to reinforce her perception as a person who is hopeless around mechanical things. On top of that, the computer just seems to exasperate the feeling of isolation she experiences when writing.

In the absence of consideration of her attitude to the task she is using the computer for, writing and self-efficacy concerning mechanical things, the survey would not tell us much. And it would not be useful in guiding interventions to assist her. When the full systemic situation of different users is revealed and appreciated, then interventions that work more with causes and underlying dynamics rather than symptoms can be seen. For example, with Noleen, work could be done with her attitude and behaviour around writing.

Health-Focused Interventions

Some of the interventions that were found to be useful are presented in this section. The interventions share a core focus on building on what is already healthy rather than focus on what is wrong and pathological.

Building the Witness

The initial interview with Noleen revealed that when she encountered computer difficulties, she lost her cool and had little problem-solving capabilities. There was a question of whether Noleen had problem-solving capabilities in any area of her life. In response to this, she recounted the building of a garden path, the difficulties it had presented her, and what she had done.

> The path had not been straightforward to make. She thought it would be, but when she first laid the stones, they wobbled and the sides of the path were not secure enough. But she was determined to do a good job and knew it would take time and care. She was confident about what needed to be done, she had people to assist her who she was happy to guide, and she was looking forward to doing it.

She noticed that most of the effective functioning that assisted her to do a good job with her path were absent when she encountered computer difficulties: She didn't involve those who might assist, she wasn't confident of what to do, she didn't accept it would take time and, importantly, she didn't really value or look forward to doing it. She was also able to appreciate that she did have problem-solving capabilities. She was also able to recognize and compliment herself for some new functioning that she had been developing within herself, being compassionate with herself.

These insights for Noleen were dependent on her ability to witness her behaviour. Witnessing is an ability to observe your own behaviour within its context of occurrence without any sort of morality or judgement of right and wrong and without any overwhelming emotional disturbance. However, it is not total detachment and noninvolvement, as it is important for the person to remain connected with him- or herself. The awareness is a key prerequisite for desirable behaviour change (Reekie, 1992). Untangled from crowding and confused thoughts and feelings, a person has an opportunity to see things as they are and have space to engage a different response.

Developing Progressive Functioning

The appreciation of an event where Noleen successfully problem solved gave her an opportunity to appreciate a difficult job done well and build her experience and confidence as a competent, resourceful person. This was a progressive movement from the inferior position she had traditionally taken in this area when comparing herself to her father and brother. When she experienced disappointment about her inability to take hold of technology she said she would like to be more like her father and brother; they would work it out, they were the clever ones.

Follow-up about a year later suggested that Noleen had built on her progressive functioning as a competent and resourceful person. She had changed the self-defacing and inferior position she took in this type of situation to her father and brother without having to directly focus on these relationships. Notice also that she has benefited from emerging from isolation concerning the computer and engaging with others who may assist her work with computers.

"I've come a long way. About half the way I want to go. Churned out a research assignment." She acknowledges computers are modern day and women use them. She has disconnected from the notion that the computer is a man thing that is complicated and will blind her with science. She has only had one lesson, but benefited, especially from the modelling of an attitude of experimentation to find things out on the computer. She has greater awareness of her functioning in situations where things go wrong and now her response is more adult, not like a tantruming child. She accepts patience and tolerance are timesaving in the long run. Writing is still a mixed bag for her.

There appears to be good effect in the developing of existing progressive functioning rather than focusing on pathology. "The most workable plan in most instances is to place the primary and greatest emphasis on those roles which are progressive and therefore functional" (Clayton, 1992, 61). Focusing on her perceived incompetence when compared with her father and brother could have reinforced unuseful self-conceptualizations if not done carefully.

Another broad strategy that can assist is the "transference of skills," where skills and functioning in one area of life are transferred to another; for example, the transferring of problem-solving skills in an area of life where they are solid, for example, gardening or sport, to an area where they are weak, such as with computer problems. Noleen took the first step towards doing this by being aware of her problem-solving skills under different breakdown or problem situations.

Orientating on Life and Work Purposes

Orientation on life and work purposes can assist in many of the problem areas of computer behaviour and the IT world. For example, it can make people less susceptible to computer sales sharks and technical evangelists. People can have a strong and emotional response to such provocation and feel they have to reject the technology that is being pushed as well as the aggressor. In such a battle of wills, life purposes and what and where IT might assist are lost. Attempting to change or get rid of the sales sharks or evangelists is wasted effort. They will not go away. It is better to make people stronger so that the aggressors are ineffective or irrelevant and then people can make more sober and objective decisions about IT use.

Consider Angela's response to a contemporary urging her to use new computer-based digital tools for her art:

"But you're working with archaic implements," a contemporary exclaims. "There's these amazing new digital tools. You're mad to deny your potential and the possibilities by not using them."

"Yeah, yeah," she replies, feeling bullied and determined not to be. "They're not relevant to me. I'm not attracted to the tool."

"Oh, you're such a purist. You haven't even seen what they can do. Look at this." He proudly shows her his screen.

"Sorry, it doesn't do a thing for me," she responds and then feels awful when she notices he looks so disappointed. "There's nothing tactile here; I need to feel something for it to be relevant for me," she tries to explain. "You only have the illusion of depth here; I can create real depth with my hand tools."

She wishes she wouldn't get into this comparison thing, but she feels bullied and negated. She's tired of the ongoing debate and the self-justifications. But they're getting too big for their boots; they need put in their place.

Angela was able to realize that her rejection of digital tools was being influenced by her strong response to this individual who she experienced as condescending and manipulative and needing "put in place." She found herself responding in like manner, a kind of combative snob who was isolated. Exploration of her life and work purpose to be an artist revealed there was a more progressive expression of this functioning.

He left his treasured tools for his granddaughter, the wild one. She loves the look, the smell, and the feel of them. Manipulating them with her hands, her body and mind are engaged and connected and she materializes visual and tactile artworks. Concretizations of her soul. Others also experience a religious or sublime quality in her work. They find there are many layers to move around in.

"There's a play between absence and presence in a lot of my work," she explains. "Isn't it interesting that that which is abundant is not appreciated until it is scarce."

Angela values being scarce or being an odd one out, on the edge, a maverick. This is archetypal of the artist on the frontier of human consciousness and creativity. This is also reflected in her artwork when she plays with the differing values of scarcity and abundance. This desire can manifest itself both in a healthy and progressive way and one that is more pathological and fragmenting. As the self-affirming maverick described above, she values who she is independent of others' opinions. She is much more able to examine and evaluate what computers have to offer her and her work. If she acts as combative snob and isolate to get her sense of self-worth or identity, she will be less likely to be connected with reality and other people and less able to examine what computers offer.

The increased ability to discriminate and stronger connection with her life purposes appear to have paid off in her attitude and analysis of the computer when she described the situation a year later.

Angela doesn't feel bullied anymore and she remains open to the computer and what it might offer. She realizes computers are a "vehicle" and "good things are happening" and kids nowadays need to become proficient. Meeting someone who collects computers as valued objects in themselves was a revelation. She would even love to use the new Mac (she loves being able to see inside it), but there is only so much she can do, and gardening and her home have priority. Interestingly, there is now another person in her life who is wildly enthusiastic about computers and wants to get her to use them. He has a sense of humour and uses seduction. She enjoys this.

Having a clear connection with life purposes can also facilitate and encourage people to embrace and use technology. Jean, for example, is very anxious and conflicted about using the computer. She often feels like sleeping beauty waiting to be rescued. In these states, she is very tentative and restrictive in her computer use. However, when she focuses on the thing she values the most, the connecting with like-minded individuals, and she realizes the Internet can facilitate this in new ways, she is much more able to take hold of the technology and be a bold Web surfer. The anxiety and tentative behaviour is overwhelmed by the passion of her purpose.

So connection with life and work purposes can assist people in taking technology and moulding it to their purposes rather than being controlled by fear of it. Without a clear sense of what is wanted and valued, it is easier for someone to be fearful of something that threatens to take them somewhere they don't really want to go. For example, in group situations, if individuals are not committed to connecting with others, then there tends to be more self-absorption and concerns about safety and exposure (Clayton, 1994). Connection with life and work purposes fosters focus on adventure, discovery and doing, rather than focus on threat and self-preservation. From this orientation, people can also better judge if the technology can assist them. Without a clear connection with life and work purposes there is likely to be more conflict about use of IT.

But, many people are not achieving strong connection or commitment to their life and work purposes. We are faced with many family, societal, and cultural expectations and norms that may conflict with our own personal aspirations and sensibilities. Somehow we need to find space to experience the particular orientation or desire, the feeling or caring for, the thing which fills us with vitality and a feeling of meaning. The following story demonstrates how David has gained enormously from aligning computers with his purpose of being a potent professional and how the commitment to his purpose has fostered the motivation he has needed to overcome the various difficulties he has faced with computer use.

Being diagnosed as dyslexic at the age of 50 was a profound event for David. Finally, he had confirmation from an authority that he wasn't a slow dimwit but an intelligent person who has difficulties sequencing and processing certain types of visual information such as words. It marked the time from when he fully embraced himself and made a firm commitment to becoming a potent professional and getting recognition from others of that. He assembled a range of computing tools to assist him in doing this. With tenacity and sustained effort, he has made huge progress in this area. It was very difficult to learn to use the computer because instructions were written down which were hard for David to access due to his dyslexia.

Now instead of his client files being a mass of unorganized pieces of paper, they are centrally organized. Reading from the screen is vastly easier for David. He selects and highlights a paragraph and uses the cursor to follow the words. With paper he easily becomes disorientated. He has a messaging system which handles phone, email, and fax messages and this is integrated in with his scheduling diary system. From this diary he can open and edit client files. A voice recognition system enables him to dictate and use verbal commands to operate the machine. Initially he had difficulty using it, as he expected more feedback like what he gets from normal conversation. Once he realized this, he was more able to let go of the expectation. In the process of adapting to the machine he has learnt more about the way he processes new information and his memory. His confidence has continued to grow and he is going to produce written evidence of his work in order to get the formal recognition he deserves. He is excited about using an email list group to connect with his global community of contemporaries and establish connections for his worldwide trip. He even used email in cyber cafes during a recent trip to Africa.

DISCUSSION

This section begins with implications and recommendations for the IT world. There are then messages for self-employed and small-business computer users, most of which are relevant to any computer user.

Implications for the IT World

The necessity to see behaviour with computers (computer behaviour) in a systemic way has long been proposed, but little practised. The boundary of all that impacts on the human-computer relationship still needs to be expanded (Jackson, 1997). Computer behaviour involves people's actions, perceptions, feelings, attitudes, beliefs, and thoughts; and it is set within a dynamic context where all environmental factors can impact on the behaviour. Open explorative studies of what is occurring are needed for the astute observation and careful description so essential for the initial efforts of a robust and successful scientific inquiry.

Information systems (IS) has responded to previous challenges by reaching for expertise from other disciplines such as cognitive psychology for usability and interfaces, organizational theory and sociology for impact of IT, and philosophy for ethics (Spaul, 1997). Now, expertise and experience in psychotherapy could also be employed to greater appreciate the factors that impact on computer behaviour and to assist in the devising of interventions. The different empathetic abilities of the psychotherapist could be added to expand the current functioning of system developers when interacting with end users, which currently tend to be more like a prosecuting lawyer or police interrogator (Ackroyd & Hughes, 1992). Empathetic connection is the core of psychotherapy (Bohart & Greenberg, 1997), where psychotherapy is the science and art of assisting people in realizing their potentials, becoming emancipated, and leading satisfying and progressive lives. Researchers and educators who wish to understand and assist people using computers will greatly benefit from entering into people's lives in an empathetic way, appreciating their experience and the things and events that provide meaning and vitality. It is through the actual experience of something that we intuitively apprehend its essence; we feel, enjoy, and understand it as reality (Reason, 1994). Empathetic connection does not mean that one colludes with or is involved in some sort of emotional entanglement, nor does it mean that analytical efforts are suspended.

The case studies mentioned in this chapter suggest that the appreciation of seemingly unrelated aspects of people's lives such as grandfathers and garden paths can be significant and useful for work with computer behaviour, especially if beneficial change is entertained. If IS is to realize its principal goal of assisting people in leading emancipated and creative lives in close relationship with IT (Jackson, 1997), then combining interventions with investigation is essential. The principles of action research provide a good structure that can be successfully applied in the IT arena (Klein & Myers, 1999). More importantly, a focus on building areas of already progressive functioning is essential. The case studies have suggested some ways this can be done and the following section will discuss these and formulate a perspective that offers us progressive change.

There are also important and obvious messages for computer companies, system designers and developers, and computer sales and support people. A common dynamic of all the case studies is the dependency and vulnerability of the end users. Giving power and control to the end user and aiming for security need to be priorities. However, the continuing development of IT and increasing complexity mean this will be difficult to achieve (Norman, 1997). Increasing the range and quality of support are things that can be achieved (Druffel, 1997). A range of approaches are needed from improving on-screen help facilities to providing help desks and support personnel who can relate with the end users. However, end users can also greatly benefit from having a more accurate picture of the world of IT so that their expectations and goals can be realistic (this is discussed in the following section).

Making systems as usable as possible is also an obvious and already important goal for system developers. In human-computer interface design there is movement to make technology more transparent to the task (Norman, 1990) and to engage the body more. Currently, using computers requires amounts of competencies unrelated to the task the technology is applied to, such as learning the operating system, finding out where to get help and learning the jargon. Jean wonders what she has let herself in for, Noleen has a mysterious machine, and David has to put in a Herculean effort to make sense of manuals and online help.

The current computer interface tends to engage the hands, eyes, and brain which is different from the fuller engagement that can occur with more manual tools such as those used by Angela. However, if we appreciate and value the design and functionality of everyday things (Norman, 1990) and get clever, we could have a whole new approach of putting the computer into things that already work well, rather than putting things into the current keyboard, mouse, screen interface. We can see the beginnings of this with cell phones with email messaging abilities, digital white boards that combine the functionality of white boards with the power of the computer, and e-ink.

The importance of involving the body with the tool is illustrated by Brian Eno's (1999) "horribly unmusical experience" of working with an advanced recording studio. He was "struck by the insidious, computer-driven tendency to take things out of the domain of muscular activity and put them into the domain of mental activity" (p. 176). He found when muscular activity was rendered useless, the creative process was frustrated. He believes the instruments and tools that endure have limited options that can allow them to be used intuitively and that ultimately we crave intimacy with our tools. Desired technologies have "personality," which is something you can have a relationship with. "Which is why people return to pencils, violins, and the same three guitare chords" (p. 176). The indication here is that IT need not be invisible; that if it is combined with the manual tools that engage the mind-body, then other possibilities open up. "It is not just that we are influenced by our tools and machines, but that by using them we are able to rediscover the environment and ourselves" (Rybczynski, 1983, p. 225). Technology is a manifestation of ourselves as we discover our possibilities.

Implications for End Users

The usefulness of looking at all factors that impact on computer behaviour has already been illustrated. As have strategies focusing on building health, such as building the witness, developing progressive functioning, and orientating on life and work purposes. The case studies also revealed that the underlying value when the computer was being used was not the computer. This is discussed in the following section. It is also important for end users to gain a bigger picture on the nature of uncertainty and place of IT in our identity and for being creative. These are also discussed.

IT Is Not the Value

For computer companies, application developers, and computer salespeople, computers are their primary orientation. It is probably appropriate then for them to primarily focus on computers and understandable if they believe IT is the value. For the rest of us, IT is *not* the value. When Jean connects with a like-minded person in Afghanistan, the essential value is not the email system, but the human-to-human connection. When one participant in the case study was creative with his computer's multimedia application, it was his creative process with the visual images and how they impact upon him as a human being that was the essential value. The computer is an important and inseparable part of the process that has a significant impact, but it is not the essential value.

When innovations become solutions looking for problems and invention the mother of necessity, we can become distracted from our purposes and invest money on "must-have" innovations and new versions of software and expend valuable time and energy setting them up and learning how to use them. On a larger scale, IT projects fail to fulfil the exaggerated promises of their proponents. Even methods to assist systems development can distract-"methodologies developed in the methodism mindset reveal their limitations by becoming the visible focus of attention rather than the invisible tools for completing the task at hand" (Introna & Whitley, 1997).

The overinflated opinion of the capabilities of computer-based systems is evidenced by the magical properties users can project onto them. Most of the time, this only creates frustration and disappointment for the user. However, misplaced trust has also resulted in extensive wildlife deaths, long-term environmental damage, and loss of human life (Neumann, 1995).

Insecurity Is Not New

It was perceived that in the early days of computing many people were attracted to computers because they were safer and more predictable than interacting with humans. Ironically, now users experience the computer as unsafe, uncontrollable, and unpredictable. Jean and Noleen reveal the intense frustration many people feel when the computer fails or does something they don't understand. The complexity of computers and the difficulty of knowing what is wrong when something goes wrong mean it is easy for people to feel overwhelmed and not in control.

> One of the greatest human fears is losing control. ...We need to learn where and when control goals, desires, and strategies are reflexive, limiting, and potentially destructive and to channel them in life-affirming and health-promoting ways. The quality of people's lives, the lives of those around them, and ultimately the well-being of the planet may, in large part, be determined by where and how people, as individuals and as a species, seek to gain and maintain a sense of control. (Shapiro, Schwartz & Astin, 1996, p. 1224).

Discrimination is needed to know when control goals, desires, and strategies are reflexive, limiting, and potentially destructive; and abilities are needed to channel them in life-affirming and health-promoting ways. This is no simple matter with computer systems. No guarantee can be given on security of information. It is therefore important that users acknowledge this vulnerability, have realistic expectations, and have some risk management. "No amount of technology will protect a user who does not take the necessary precautions to use the technology properly" (Druffel, 1997, p. 207). Jean worked out that the computer was not a key element in her work. Yet, in a time of performance with clients, she was committed to using the computer unnecessarily and was not prepared when it suffered problems.

It is also useful and appropriate to reflect on our insecurity and our efforts to lessen or control it from a broader perspective. It is erroneous to believe that anxiety and insecurity are a product of the new age and reliance on technology (Coyne, 1998). They have been our companions since the very beginning. Being born into the certainty that our bodies will age and decay and we will die could be considered a rough deal. Our development and use of technology is an understandable response in order to assert our influence and control over such a universe.

Ironically, while delivering more control in some respects, technical innovations and interventions increase the rate of change and complexity and ability to control in other respects. "One thing seems clear about the technology of the future: it will get more complex" (Norman, 1997, p. 106). And it is folly to believe "that through applying the methods of science and technology to every aspect of the human condition ... the world will become tidy, organized. ...It is ludicrous to think we can control uncertainty" (Angell, 1997, p. 366-367).

It is essential we find new warm-ups to states of unknowing and unpredictability. These are particularly highlighted in situations of breakdown. We have breakdowns on the way somewhere in the car, in relationships, and in computer systems, and many of us have unuseful scripts (beliefs and behaviour) around breakdowns: "This shouldn't happen," "its my fault," "its your fault," or "I'm hopeless, I'll never be able to make it right." The case studies showed that techniques such as application of the witness and orientation on life and work purposes can assist in these areas. However, a fundamental change requires more.

The alchemist is a fine role model (Angell, 1997). The alchemist understands change and that all things are crouched in a desire to transform and expand. Like the joker, jester, and clown, the alchemist has the ability to stay connected and use the sabotages of outrageous fortune and turn them to creative, aesthetic, and humorous ends. The Buddhists have consolidated lifetimes of observation and consideration into some simple truths. A central one is that the source of human suffering is attachment, the desire to attach to some imagining that is no longer founded in reality or the inability to be in touch with the constantly changing moment.

Evolving With IT

Staying open and relaxed to the emerging moment is no trivial task. It would appear that human beings mainly operate out of fear and insecurity and have been for some time, maybe since the very beginning. Many reasons are given for this. Myths such as the Garden of Eden suggest our ability to be self-aware and cognizant resulted in alienation. Others say we lack courage (Trungpa, 1984). Another view is that we have lost sense of our inherent facility to be masters of creation. There is a good argument that we have accepted messages that together diminish the centrality and importance of the human being and have resulted in low levels of self-esteem and dignity. This is reflected in our urgency to self-promote, fragile bubbles of self-importance, and ineffectual strivings for control (Shapiro, Schwartz & Astin, 1996). They are not signs of the quiet surety that emanates from self-esteem and dignity.

Copernicus showed that the earth is not the center of the universe, but moves around the sun; it is just a speck in infinite space, ruled by specific physical laws like the rest of the world; with Copernicus' theory the supreme position of Man in the cosmos was gone. Darwin showed that Man as a species is a part of a biological evolution, the descendent of a human-like ape; with this the idea of Man as a special creation was gone. Marx showed that human history itself is determined by mass movements, economic classes of men; the single man, isolated from the mass, is powerless. Mendel showed that the conception of the individual soma is determined by genes, Freud showed that the individual psyche of Man does not follow his will but is a product of unconscious drives. (Moreno, 1983, p. 11).

Now we are warned that "the future doesn't need us" and we may not survive our new technologies of genetic engineering, human-like robots, and self-replicating nanotechnologies (Joy, 2000). Paradoxically, our amazing achievements with technology should strengthen our fragile self-esteem. Perhaps they are. Certainly, overtly or covertly, many of us are wanting and willing new advancements in technology to work. This is evidenced by the blind faith that resources high-tech projects that were always destined to be little more than hyperware (Neumann, 1995).

Some see the technology as the evil. This can range from a gut feel that anything "natural" is better than anything "man-made" to spiritual causes that assert our linguistic conceptualizations and symbol making, which are at the very core of technology, create a barrier to our natural, unseparated state. They argue for a disengagement from our thoughts and feelings as they are illusionary.

Joy's (2000) response appears sensible and reasonable: "The only realistic alternative I see is relinquishment: to limit development of the technologies that are too dangerous, by limiting our pursuit of certain kinds of knowledge" (p. 254). However, it is unlikely that this pathological focus will elicit willing participation or succour the human spirit. If one accepts the argument that we are low in dignity and self-esteem, then we need building. To apply the main principle of this chapter, we need to promote health rather than fight pathology.

The heart of our health suggested in the case studies is the ability to create and be creative. Humanity and the universe are open systems that have an innate propensity and urging towards creativity and expansion of experience and consciousness (Clayton, 1994; Moreno, 1977). Whether this previous statement is accurate or not cannot be answered in finality because one must step outside of a system in order to make any conclusion on it (Hofstadter, 1979) and we cannot step outside of either ourselves or the universe. The limits of self-referencing can be demonstrated by answering the next sentence. This statement is incorrect. Nevertheless, new insights from science increasingly support the view of an open and creative universe:

Thus an inherent spontaneity in the life of nature has once again been recognized by science, after a denial lasting over 300 years. The future is not fully determined in advance; it is open. Insofar as it can be modelled mathematically, it has to be modelled in terms of chaotic dynamics. And this chaos, openness, spontaneity and freedom of nature provide the matrix for evolutionary creativity. ... Indeterminism, spontaneity and creativity have re-emerged throughout the natural world. Immanent purposes or ends are now modelled in terms of attractors. ... For the modern conception of nature gives an even stronger sense of her spontaneous life and creativity than the stable, repetitive world of Greek, medieval and Renaissance philosophy. All nature is evolutionary. The cosmos is like a great developing organism, and evolutionary creativity is inherent in nature herself. (Sheldrake, 1990, p. 71, 75).

Fundamentally, we need to strongly connect with and build our inherent ability to be spontaneous and to create. A good starting point would be the healing of the artificial split between our identity as technical beings and our identity as sacred and spiritual beings. This split between technology and spirituality has strengthened at various times through history. For example, the Protestant reformists of the 17th century were on a holy crusade to enforce the belief that God was the only sacred being in creation and that the world was essentially an inanimate place over which "man" had dominion. They set about to destroy sacred places and things and break the intimate connections people had with nature and its forces. This fitted well with the scientists of the day, who sought to understand the laws the universe operated under, and rationalists, who wanted a sensible, human and civilized society (Saul, 1993). They rejected a world at the mercy of mysterious forces and lives dictated by the whims of superstitions.

It is understandable then that some see technology and spirituality as opposing and that technology is something foreign. However, these views are not accurate. New communication and computing technologies are an extension of symbol making and manipulation (language) and logic and reasoning (Coyne, 1999). If we accept language and logic are part of who we are, then IT is of us, an extension of ourselves; technology is not foreign. Technology need not be the enemy of spirituality; they are not mutually exclusive. Science and sacredness, technology and spirituality can support and enhance each other and may be the only way either will progress (Sheldrake, 1990).

We will also need to awaken to our abilities to be spontaneous and creative and have a love affair with creating not just the acts of creation. This can be assisted by cultivating a wakefulness and openness to the here-and-now reality bathed in a warmth and sympathy for ourselves, others, and the world we live in (Clayton, 1994; Moreno, 1953). Somehow we need to find the courage to connect with our environment and act. Seeing the here-and-now moment as fundamentally our only place of experience and attaching great significance to it will help:

The ordinary events of our daily lives carry within them a seed that can grow into something of great significance. ... Do we know what will emerge in the course of the ordinary events of our life. Can we afford to wipe another person off ... any moment may be explored leading to enrichment of our lives ... something important can be learned in any situation. (Clayton, 2000, p. 8).

Pace (2000) is a good example of how flow, the deep involvement in an enjoyable activity (Csikszentmihalyi, 1997), can be used to understand user experiences on the Web and to provide guidelines on development. The experience of flow is one of concentrated engagement with the here-and-now moment, where action and awareness are integrated and self-consciousness is diminished or non-existent. Perhaps one could say there is a synthesis of the Eastern tradition of being in the moment with the Western tradition of creating and becoming.

Flow can also be augmented by and/or result in the realization that there is a lot in the world that has a warm and generous acceptance of us, even though we may also realize there are predatory forces. We may also link with the creative source that gave rise to our being and awaken our human dignity as powerful beings. Respect and sensitivity for the world we live in will naturally arise from this increased dignity and self-esteem, and thereby our need to control creativity or nature should diminish. We can then have a relationship with nature that is based on nurture, respect, and cooperation (Sheldrake, 1990, p. 23) and so we will avoid self-destruction or the enslavement predicted by Bill Joy without having to relinquish anything: "Humanity stands at the cross-roads of great decisions: before it lies the Path of Power, through control of the forces of nature-a path leading to enslavement and self-destruction-and the Path of Enlightenment, through the control of the forces within us-leading to liberation and self-realization" (Govinda, 1969, p. 13).

CONCLUSION

Entering into self-employed and small-business people's lives who are using computers reveals that there are complex webs of interrelating factors that impact on their behaviour with computers. Physical, psychological, social, and spiritual aspects of being human can all impact on a user's behaviour with the computer. This work has shown that the boundary of all that impacts on the human-computer relationship still needs to be expanded (Jackson, 1997). Even seemingly unrelated aspects of people's lives such as grandfathers and garden paths can be significant and useful. Open explorative studies of what is occurring are needed for the astute observation and careful description so essential for the initial efforts of a robust and successful scientific inquiry. The predominant use of survey instruments seems premature and of limited usefulness.

There are also important and obvious messages for computer companies, system designers and developers, and computer sales and support people. Giving power and control to the end user and aiming for security need to be priorities. However, the continuing development of IT and increasing complexity means this will be difficult to achieve. End users will benefit from being aware of this and having realistic expectations. But there is an area where a lot more effort would be useful: support for the user.

To achieve the aim of IS to assist people in leading emancipated and creative lives in partnership with IT, research needs also to focus on effecting desirable change. Researchers need to broaden their mission as truth seekers and theorists to also being active agents of progressive change. This can be achieved through building already existing progressive behaviour rather than focusing on the pathology, such as computer anxiety. This appears to require a paradigm shift.

The case studies also revealed that IT does not do the very meaningful things in our lives. The value of email is the communication. Intimacy with others is something we must do; technology can not do it for us. Recognizing that IT is not the value is important for assisting people in using IT to further their life and work purposes rather than being driven by IT, and in having realistic expectations of what IT can do. Recognition that insecurity has been around before computer systems and that it will continue is also useful for users so that they can develop attitudes and strategies that will work.

However, rather than being continually overwhelmed by the complex computer and its world, the participants in the study showed great resilience, resourcefulness, and integrity. They were willing to get familiar with computers and to have them as allies in their life journeys. If there was danger the computer would subvert their life, then it was given up and put aside.

The computing industry can take some heart from this. Users are robust and they are willing to take initiatives to help themselves. The loosely organized computerization movement of technical evangelists and aggressive salespeople does not dominate (Kling & Iacono, 1988). The warning that "humanity is now subservient to the technological structures of its own making" (Angell, 1997, p. 365) appears to be too grim. To fear that the machine will coerce and subvert all decent human values is to underestimate our resilience and ability to discern and to lack faith in our resourcefulness and irrepressive creativity.

By connecting with our innate creative abilities, we do not need to see technology as foreign to us, but as something that will help us evolve. In the process, we may strengthen our dignity and ability to appreciate and be attuned to the world we live in and thereby in an easy and voluntary way use our technical abilities to benefit ourselves and the world. We may develop a new warm-up to the uncertainties of life. Progress can be made to make IT more humane, to conceptualize and frame IT from a Heideggerian perspective, where it exists in relationship and context, grounded in the ever-present and emerging moment, and integrated and associated with care, feeling, and openness.

REFERENCES

Ackroyd, S. and Hughes, J. A. (1992). *Data Collection in Context*, (2nd ed.). London: Longman.

Angell, I. O. (1997). Welcome to the "Brave New World." In Mingers, J. and Stowell, F. (Eds.), *Information Systems: An Emerging Discipline*, 363-384. London: McGraw-Hill.

Avison, D. E. and Fitzgerald, G. (1995). *Information Systems Development:*

Methodologies, Techniques and Tools, (2nd ed.). London: McGraw-Hill.

Bohart, A. C. and Greenberg, L. S. (Eds.). (1997). *Empathy Reconsidered: New Directions in Psychotherapy*. Washington, DC: American Psychological Association.

Charlton, J. P. and Birkett, P. E. (1995). The development and validation of the computer apathy and anxiety scale. *Journal of Educational Computing Research*, 13(1), 41-59.

Clayton, G. M. (1992). *Enhancing Life and Relationships: A Role Training Manual*. Caulfield, Victoria, Australia: ICA Press.

Clayton, G. M. (1993). *Living Pictures of the Self: Applications of Role Theory in Professional Practice and Daily Life*. Caulfield, Victoria, Australia: ICA Press.

Clayton, G. M. (1994). *Effective Group Leadership*. Caulfield, Victoria, Australia: ICA Press.

Clayton, M. (2000). Annual report of the board of examiners. *ANZPA Bulletin*, March, 20, 8-10.

Collins, C. and Caputi, P. (1999). Broadening our horizons with qualitative methodologies: Investigating antecedents of end user satisfaction and performance. Paper presented at the *OZCHI '99 Interfaces for the Global Community*.

Coyne, R. (1998). Cyberspace and Heidegger's pragmatics. *Information Technology & People*, 11(4), 338-350.

Coyne, R. (1999). *Technoromanticism*. London: MIT Press.

Csikszentmihalyi, M. (1997). *Finding Flow: The Psychology of Engagement with Everyday Life*. New York: Basic Books.

Doll, W. J. and Torkzadeh, G. (1988). The measurement of end user computing satisfaction. *MIS Quarterly*, June, 259-274.

Druffel, L. (1997). Information warfare. In Denning, P. J. and Metcalfe, R. M. (Eds.), *Beyond Calculation: The Next Fifty Years of Computing*. Copernicus.

Dyck, J. L. and Smither, J. A. (1994). Age differences in computer anxiety: The role of computer experience, gender and education. *Journal of Education Computing Research*.

Eno, B. (1999). The revenge of the intuitive: Turn off the options, and turn up the intimacy. *Wired*, January, 176.

Gadamer, H. G. (1976). The historicity of understanding. In Connerton, P. (Ed.). *Critical Sociology, Selected Readings*, 117-133. Harmondsworth, UK: Penguin Books.

Gardner, D. G., Discenza, R. and Dukes, R. L. (1993). The measurement of computer attitudes: An empirical comparison of available scales. *Journal of Educational Computing Research*, 9(4), 487-507.

Govinda, L. A. (1969). *Foundations of Tibetan Mysticism*. Maine: Samuel Weiser.

Greene, B. A., Kincade, K. M. and Hays, T. A. (1994). A research-based modification of a computer program for reading instruction. *Journal of Educational Computing Research*, 10(4), 341-348.

Hofstadter, D. S. (1979). *Godel, Escher, Bach: An Eternal Golden Braid*. London:

Penguin Books.

Introna, L. D. and Whitley, E. A. (1997). Against method-ism: Exploring the limits of method. *Information Technology & People*, 10(1), 31-45.

Jackson, M. C. (1997). Critical systems thinking and Information Systems research. In Mingers, J. and Stowell, F. (Eds.), *Information Systems: An Emerging Discipline*, 201-238. London: McGraw-Hill.

Joy, B. (2000). Why the future doesn't need us. *Wired*, April, 238-262.

Klein, H. K. and Myers, M. D. (1999). A set of principles for conducting and evaluating interpretative field studies in information systems. *MIS Quarterly*, 23(1), 67-94.

Kling, R. and Iacono, S. (1988). The mobilization of support for computerization: The role of computerization movements. *Social Problems*, 35(3), 226-243.

Krendl, K. A. and Broihier, M. (1992). Student responses to computers: A longitudinal study. *Journal of Educational Computing Research*, 8(2), 215-227.

Maurer, M. M. (1994). Computer anxiety correlates and what they tell us: A literature review. *Computers in Human Behavior*, 10(3), 369-376.

McInerney, V., McInerney, D. M. and Sinclair, K. E. (1994). Student teachers, computer anxiety and computer experience. *Journal of Educational Computing Research*, 11(1), 27-50.

Melrose, M. (2001). Maximizing the rigour of action research: Why would you want to? How could you? *Field Methods*, 13(2), 160-180.

Miller, F. and Varma, N. (1994). The effects of psychosocial factors on Indian children's attitudes towards computers. *Journal of Educational Computing Research*, 10(3), 223-238.

Moreno, J. L. (1946). *Psychodrama: First Volume*, (4th ed.). New York: Beacon House.

Moreno, J. L. (1953). *Who Shall Survive?* (First Student Edition ed.). Roanoke, Virginia, Australia: Royal.

Moreno, J. L. (1983). *The Theatre of Spontaneity*. Pennsylvania: Beacon House.

Neumann, P. G. (1995). *Computer-Related Risks*. New York: ACM Press.

Nielsen, J. (1993). *Usability Engineering*. Boston: Academic Press.

Norman, D. A. (1990). *The Design of Everyday Things*. Currency/Doubleday.

Norman, D. A. (1997). Why it's good that computers don't work like the brain. In Denning, P. J. and Metcalfe, R. M. (Eds.), *Beyond Calculation: The Next Fifty Years of Computing*. Copernicus.

Pace, S. (2000). Understanding the flow experiences of web users. *OZCHI 2000: Interfacing Reality in the New Millennium*. Conference Companion. Macquarie University, NSW, Australia.

Reason, P. (1994). Three approaches to participative inquiry. In Denzin, N. K. and Lincoln, Y. S. (Eds.), *Handbook of Qualitative Research*, 324-339. Thousand Oaks: Sage.

Reason, P. and Bradbury, H. (Eds.) (2001). *Handbook of Action Research:*

Participatory Inquiry and Practice. London: Sage.

Reekie, D. (1992). Watch yourself: Becoming effective in personal relations through psychodrama. *Unpublished Psychodrama Thesis*.

Rosen, L. D. and Maguire, P. (1990). Myths and realities of computerphobia: A meta-analysis. *Anxiety Research*, 3, 175-191.

Rybczynski, W. (1983). *Taming the Tiger: The Struggle to Control Technology*. New York: Penguin Books.

Saul, J. R. (1993). *Voltaire's Bastards: The Dictatorship of Reason in the West*. Vintage Books.

Shapiro, D. H., Schwartz, C. E. and Astin, J. A. (1996). Controlling ourselves, controlling our world. *American Psychologist*, December, 51(12), 1213-1224.

Sheldrake, R. (1990). *The Rebirth of Nature: The Greening of Science and God*. London: Century.

Spaul, M. (1997). Discipline and critique: The case of information systems. In Mingers, J. and Stowell, F. (Eds.), *Information Systems: An Emerging Discipline*, 63-96. London: McGraw-Hill.

Torkzadeh, G. and Angulo, I. E. (1992). The concept and correlates of computer anxiety. *Behaviour & Information Technology*, 11(2), 99-108.

Trungpa, C. (1984). *Shambhala: The Sacred Path of the Warrior*. Boston: Shambhala.

Woodrow, J. E. J. (1991). A comparison of four computer attitude scales. *Journal of Educational Computer Research*, 7(2), 165-187.

Zmud, R. W., Sampson, J. P., Reardon, R. C., Lenz, J. G. and Bird, T. A. (1994). Confounding effects of construct overlap: An example from IS user satisfaction theory. *Information Technology & People*, 7(2), 29-45.

Zuber-Skerritt, O. (1996). *New Directions in Action Research*. London: Falmer Press.

Chapter XVII

On the Role of Human Morality in Information System Security: From the Problems of Descriptivism to Non-descriptive Foundations

Mikko T. Siponen
University of Oulu, Finland

INTRODUCTION

The relevance of security solutions and procedures depends on the motivation of the users to comply with the security solutions/procedures provided. Many studies indicate that users fail to comply with information security policies and guidelines (e.g., Goodhue & Straub, 1989; Parker, 1998; Perry, 1985). It is widely argued (e.g., Loch & Carr, 1991; Anderson, 1993; Parker, 1998; Vardi & Wiener, 1996; Neumann, 1999) that a remarkable portion of security breaches are carried out by organizations' own employees. Several proposals have been made to tackle this human problem, the solutions range from 1) increasing the users' motivation (e.g., McLean, 1992; Perry, 1985; Siponen, 2000; Thomson & von Solms, 1998), 2) using ethics (e.g., Kowalski, 1990; Leiwo & Heikkuri, 1998a, 1998b), 3) organizational/professional codes of ethics (e.g., Harrington, 1996; Straub & Widom, 1984; Parker, 1998), to 4) using different deterrents (e.g., Straub, 1990). With respect to the second issue–Can human morality function as a means of ensuring information security?–the existing works can be divided into two categories. The first category covers expressions concerning the use of human morality including Kowalski (1990), Baskerville (1995), Siponen (2000) and Dhillon and Backhouse (2000):

- "Security administrators are realizing that ethics can function as the common language for all different groups within the computer community" (Kowalski, 1990).
- "Proper user conduct can effectively prevent [security] violations" (Baskerville, 1995, p. 246).

The second claims that the use of ethics is useless or, at best, extremely restricted (Leiwo & Heikkuri, 1998a, 1998b).

This chapter argues, following the scholars of the first category, that human morality has a role as a means for ensuring security. But to achieve this goal solid theoretical foundations, on which a concrete guidance can be based, are needed. The existing proposals (e.g., Kowalski, 1990; Baskerville, 1995; Dhillon & Backhouse, 2000) do not suggest any theoretical foundation nor concrete means for using ethics as a means of ensuring security. The aim of this paper is to propose a framework for the use of ethics in this respect. To achieve this aim, a critique of the relevance of ethics must be considered. The use of human morality as a means of ensuring security has been criticized by Leiwo and Heikkuri (1998a, 1998b) on the grounds of cultural relativism (and hacker ethics/hacking culture). If cultural relativism is valid as an ethical doctrine, the use of human morality as a means of protection is very questionable. It would only be possible in certain "security" cultures, i.e., cultures in which security norms have been established–if at all. However, the objection of Leiwo and Heikkuri (1998a, 1998b) is argued to be questionable. We feel that cultural relativism has detrimental effects on our well-being and security. Things might be better if the weaknesses of cultural relativism were recognized. This paper adopts the conceptual analysis in terms of Järvinen (1997, 2000) as the research approach. An early version of this paper was presented at an international conference on information security (IFIP TC11, Beijing, China, 2000).

The chapter is organized as follows. In the second section, the possible ethical theoretical frameworks are discussed. In the third section, the objections to the use of ethics as a means of protection based on cultural relativism (descriptivism) are explored. In the fourth section, an alternative approach based on non-descriptivism is suggested. The fifth section discusses the implications and limitations of this study. The sixth section summarises the key issues of the chapter including future research questions.

THEORETICAL FRAMEWORKS

Ethical Theories

The philosophical ethical theories can be classified into two categories, descriptivism and non-descriptivism (Hare, 1997). In this chapter, descriptive theories refer to ethical doctrines that attempt to draw a morally or action-guiding conclusion purely from a set of factual premises, such as prevailing cultural habits. In other words, the separation between descriptivism and non-descriptivism can be retraced to Hume's thesis that moral norms (what we ought to do) cannot be drawn from a set of factual matters. Those theories arguing that factual matters imply moral norms are called descriptivism, as opposed to non-descriptivism (see Figure 1). This simplistic division is chosen for a practical reason; it is perhaps the simplest classification and therefore helps us to understand the different theoretical possibilities available and their one fundamental difference.

We have left out religion-based ethical theories (e.g., Christian ethics) from the categorization. The reader is advised to look at Outga (1972) for more religion-based ethical theories and the question of desriptivism versus non-descriptivism ("is/ought"-problem). We believe Siponen (2001), Siponen and Vartiainen (2001), as many others have already proposed (e.g., Hare, 1981, 1997; Taylor, 1975), that descriptive theories such as cultural relativism and intuitionism are inadmissible as moral qualifiers. Instead of attempting to find what is morally right and wrong, descriptive theories, at best, pay lip service to prevailing cultural moral notions (cultural relativism) or individuals' intuitions (intuitionism). In the worst possible scenario, descriptive theories may be used as an excuse to indulge in morally questionable behaviour (e.g., Nazism or hacking), as shall be seen in Section 3. In Section 4, it is proposed that we should look to non-descriptivism to provide solutions. In this study, the term moral means what people regard as right and wrong–how we should act in the final analysis. Ethics refers to moral philosophy, i.e., ethical theories discerning what is morally right and wrong.

Overriding Thesis

In order for human morality to be useful in security procedures, it is necessary that we should have an intrinsic sense of moral responsibility, in other words, a sense of duty forcing us to follow our moral concerns: to find out what is morally right. If all people were totally amoral (i.e., did not care what is morally right) or if theories

Figure 1: Depicts the division and some ethical theories

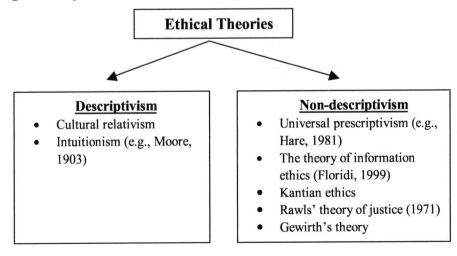

such as cultural relativism were considered as valid moral qualifiers (as proposed by Leiwo & Heikkuri, 1998a, 1998b), human morality could not function as a means of ensuring security. We need to examine whether there is such a thing as "moral responsibility"? And, if there is, how strongly does it guide our behaviour? These two questions (and the relevance of human morality for security) can be retraced to the validity of the overriding thesis suggested by R.M. Hare (1963). Hare claims that moral concern overrides all other nonmoral concerns (overriding thesis). In other words, given that one regards unauthorized copying of software as morally wrong (moral concern), one should not copy software even if one would receive financial gain (nonmoral concern). Ladd (1982, 1989) has suggested a similar view: Our moral responsibility (what is morally right) overrides other forms of responsibilities. Smith (1984) even argues that it is more understandable to act for moral reasons than for nonmoral ones. This latter view has been criticised by Dancy (1994) on the grounds that moral, or justified, reasons do not imply motivation per se (Dancy argues that one may see nonmoral reasons as understandable as well). If Hare's overriding thesis is valid, appealing to human morality is crucial for ensuring security.

ANALYSIS OF THE EXISTING DESCRIPTIVE APPROACH AND ITS WEAKNESSES

Theoretical Underpinnings

Leiwo and Heikkuri (1998a, 1998b) argue that human morality cannot serve as a means of protection against security violations–particularly in a global environment (e.g., the Internet)–because of cultural relativism. They argue that moral values are subjective in the sense that they cannot be transferred from one place or moral system to another (Leiwo & Heikkuri, 1998b, p. 275). In other words, the morality of an action depends on culture: What is morally right in one culture may be morally wrong in another culture. This argument also involves ethical descriptivism, since they indicate that moral judgement has a truth value (e.g., true/false): "the truth values of ethical value systems ..." (Leiwo & Heikkuri, 1998b, p. 275).

Leiwo & Heikkuri further engage in cognitivism, which is mainly an epistemological claim stating that values can be known to be true. In the case of cultural relativism, exploring the moral values of cultures is argued to validate this cognitivistic claim (values can be known to be true). Because it is regarded as a sociological fact that morality (what people do/consider as right and wrong) depends on culture, relativists claim that what every culture does is equally right or true. The reasoning of Leiwo and Heikkuri is similar to this. They argue that cultural relativism is valid and moral views differ with respect to information security. The culture of hackers and hacker ethics was provided as a proof (Leiwo and Heikkuri,

1998b, p. 275). Since "hacker ethics" by hacker "Knightmare" (see more Fiery, 1994) and cultural relativism were provided by Leiwo & Heikkuri as an example to indicate the inadequacy of human morality as a means of ensuring security, we next examine these concepts in more detail.

Weaknesses of the Descriptive Approach

Is-Ought Dualism

The approach of Leiwo and Heikkuri does not take into account the factual/ normative dualism first recognised by David Hume. This dualism is also known as Hume's law or the thesis "no ought from an is." We share Popper's view that Hume's law is "perhaps the simplest and most important point in ethics" (Popper, 1948). "No ought from is" means that factual premises alone, i.e., "is" cannot imply norms, i.e., "ought" statements. So, for example, what people/culture regard as morally right ("is") does not provide the answer to what one morally ought to do ("ought"). Leiwo and Heikkuri (1998a, 1998b) fall into this ("is" implies "ought") fallacy by first observing "is" matters: hacker ethics/culture. From this they deduce that, due to relativism (what every culture does is right), the actions of hackers (or hacker ethics) are right per se, therefore they are implying an ought from an is.

Although there are attempts to prove the invalidity of Hume's thesis "no ought from an is," including Searle (1964), Gewirth (1974) and MacIntyre (1981), they do not serve as persuasive objections especially when addressing cultural relativism. For example, Searle's attempt to break Hume's law is widely criticised as being a game which can only be played if the players accept the rules of the game provided by Searle (Hare, 1964a). It may serve as an indication that it is possible to persuade someone to form an "ought" (or moral) judgement by giving "is" matters without "ought" matters. But does this prove that this kind of treatment would be desirable? The most difficult problem with Searle's argument is that "the rules of the game" are based on persuasion, and the rules do not provide any restrictions regarding the contents of the strategy agreed upon, which means that the game is, for instance, open to lying. The main objection to this is, if lying is acceptable, we are throwing ethics and morals out of the window. Gewirth's idea (of equality) is closely connected to the universality thesis, which serves as a basis for his ethical theory/ sociopolitical theory (e.g., see Gewirth, 1978) and therefore, even if accepted, does not help cultural relativists. Moreover, Kohlberg's thesis is the opposite of cultural relativism as it accentuates Kantian universality thesis ("act only on maxims which you want to be universal laws") as the highest state of moral development.

Is-Ought Dualism and a Practical Example

The weakness behind the thesis of Leiwo and Heikkuri (1998a, 1998b) can also be considered by using a more down-to-earth example. An employee is working in a company involved in a top-secret project. The employee joins an association that has its own moral code and the company accepts their employee's joining this association because the company considers the activities of the association harmless. Later, the members of the association start to take an interest in philosophy and find out that their background has been forgotten and is rather different to the one they assumed was correct. They are advocates of cultural relativism and so they perform a "who are we really/what are our moral values" perusal (e.g., provided by Sandel, 1982). This is a way to reflect "is" matters, i.e., how things were/are, and to allow this to determine how things should ultimately be. As a result of this, they find a new moral code that better reflects their original background and they are positive that this is their real moral code. This new code allows hacking, the result being that the employee is now encouraged to break into his company's system (or otherwise allow the association access to top-secret information). If the company and the employee acknowledge cultural relativism as a valid moral qualifier, they have no (moral) right to either prevent such actions or take any stand with respect to these actions, otherwise they have interfered with the other culture.[1] Thus, as mentioned, any (moral) involvement with the other culture is not acceptable according to cultural relativism. The company in our example therefore cannot take any moral stand concerning some other culture (the association in our example). This is not a very convincing justification.

Hacker Ethics and Cultural Relativism

Knightmare states, "hacking is something that I am going to do regardless of how I feel about its morality" (Fiery, 1994, p. 162). It is difficult to see how such a view can have connections to the domain of moral discourse (or real hacker ethics). However, such evasions of moral reflection can be justified given that cultural relativism is regarded as a valid moral qualifier. Knightmare could insist that hackers form a culture and due to cultural relativism, we should allow them to do whatever they do. This illustrates another weakness of culture relativism (and hacker ethics, as well). Cultural relativism and Knightmare's version of hacker ethics do not truly attempt to discover what is morally right and wrong. Rather they avoid moral scrutiny and uphold dogmatism.

Hegel: Cultural Relativism and Hacker Ethics

Leiwo and Heikkuri (1998a, 1998b) also validate cultural relativism and hacker ethics on the basis of Hegel. This totally relativistic view is not shared by Hegel.[2] Hegel recognises the problems associated with cultural relativism. Cultural relativism holds that all beliefs/belief systems are equally true. Hegel does not share this view. Hegel sees that moral conflicts should be solved in such a way that one's freedom and above all the coherence of the state (i.e., government/country) are ensured (Sabine, 1963, p. 655). Hence, if one follows Hegel's doctrine when considering if it is acceptable to allow hacking, one needs to ponder which alternative ensures the coherence of the state. Note that hacker ethics contain the rule "Mistrust authority–promote decentralization" (Fiery, 1994). This implies that governments should be mistrusted. Therefore, hacker ethics are in conflict with Hegel's doctrine. Hacker ethics also state "All information should be free." To let all information be free does not maintain the coherence of state (government) and is therefore wrong from the Hegelian viewpoint. Hence, Hegel's moral theory does not allow hacking in a general sense.

Self-Refutation

The theory of cultural relativism involves a contradiction (explicitly the reductio ad absurdum). It does not make any logical sense to claim that all moral judgements are relative, while maintaining that moral relativism itself is absolutely true (being non-relative). If all moral beliefs are relative, as relativists claim, absolutely true theories are an impossibility (Hare, 1986; Niiniluoto, 1991). This would also apply to cultural relativism.[3]

NON-DESCRIPTIVE USE OF ETHICS

The central task of moral philosophy is to determine what kinds of actions are right or wrong (Warburton, 1996; Hare, 1981). Descriptivistic theories such as cultural relativism fail to accomplish this mission: for example, cultural relativism does not explore what is morally right or wrong, but rather emphasizes what the moral habits of cultures are. It is argued that non-descriptivism offers more solid ground. Non-descriptive theories to discern what is truly morally right, what we ought to do, instead of appealing to our intuitions or cultural conceptions.

We see that many information security activities have strong moral dimensions. Information security protects against actions such as hacking or computer viruses, which may raise serious moral concerns. People who are victims of such activities (e.g., hacking or destructive viruses) are likely to express strong moral disapproval of the people responsible for such activities. However, without such personal experiences (Gattiker & Kelley, 1999), critical moral thinking or ethical education, etc., some users might feel neutral about such activities. In fact, computer ethics literature agrees that the ordinary computer user is often incapable of extending their moral reflection in cases where computers are involved. Several reasons to explain this problem are proposed. Moor (1985) explains this phenomena by the conceptual muddle and policy vacuum, i.e., the existing policies, such as legislation, do not cover computer ethics issues. Conger (et al., 1994) and Rubin (1994) argue that there is moral distance; e.g., the Internet creates a distance between users, and this distance decreases our moral sensitivity. Severson (1997) believes that people are in moral crisis. Siponen (2001) and Siponen and Vartiainen (2001) postulated that such users are conventionalists, i.e., they are pretty much incapable of engaging in critical moral thinking, but their acts reflect the prevailing moral views. As computer ethics issues are new and the existing prevailing moral conventions do not yet cover computing issues, conventionalists are unable to react to computer ethics issues. According to Dunlop & Kling (1992) and Rogerson (1996), computer users are under the spell of computers, forgetting the negative consequences of their usage. One may also argue, on the basis of Floridi (1999) and Gorniak (1996), that the existing ethical theories are inadequate to address computer ethics issues.

It is believed that some of these problems–such as moral crisis (Severson, 1997), moral distance (Rubin, 1994), conventional moral notions (Siponen, 2001; Siponen & Vartiainen, 2001) and the "spell" of computers (Dunlop & Kling, 1992; Rogerson, 1996) may be tackled with proper education. This effort may help in securing an organization's information systems, as well. However, in order that appealing to human morality would be useful for information security, the following conditions need to be met. An organization's business activities must be able to stand up to moral scrutiny and the organization's activities must not include double standards of morality. If the employees of the organization regard the organization's activities as improper, it is unlikely that they will respond to educational efforts. Organizations must display proper (moral) respect for their employees. If employers disrespect their employees, employees may have a reserved or negative attitude concerning such educational efforts. Organizations should facilitate an open climate for communication. Open environments for discourse as described by Habermas (1984, 1987) should be created. The immorality of acting against security policy can, with the help of ethical theories, be effectively argued. If an organization's employees are convinced that it is morally praiseworthy to follow the organization's security policy/procedures, they may be more willing to follow the policies/guidelines (consider the overriding thesis in Section 2). Equally, if an employer/educator is able to awaken employees' moral disapproval regarding acting against security policies/guidelines, it may be presumed that the employees will be more willing to follow security policies/guidelines (again consider the overriding thesis in Section 2).

In addition to the aforementioned prerequisites for using ethical education in organizations, the following guidelines for using ethics to persuade the listener can be used:

- Justify the principles (e.g., veil of ignorance/universality thesis as described below): State that the chosen principle is the best possible for the situation.
- Apply this principle and justify the results (justify the claim that the situation is morally acceptable and favourable).

These principles also facilitate the requirements of free will and autonomy. In other words, the problem of indoctrination might be avoided if the reasons for choosing certain ethical theories are justified. Indoctrination should be avoided since it halts autonomy–free will and autonomy are prerequisites for ethical decision-making (cf. Hare, 1964b, 1975).

Example of the Use of the "Veil of Ignorance"

Let us consider whether hacking is allowed, i.e., whether is it morally acceptable to obtain unauthorized access to information systems. This action is considered in the light of a simplified version of Rawls' theory of justice, which is affiliated with the universality principle proposed by Confucias (Singer, 1991), Kant, Hare (1963, 1981), Christian ethics (the Golden Rule), and Gewirth (1978). The limitations of the "veil of ignorance" are discussed in Kukathas and Pettit (1990) and Pogge (1989). The limits of universality theses are discussed generally in Siponen (2001), Siponen and Vartiainen (2001), and Hare's version of universalizability of moral judgement in Seanor and Fotion (1988).

Rawls (1971) proposes that the principles of justice–herein: should we allow hacking or not–should be selected under an imagined ignorance of our own role in the world (called a "veil of ignorance"). Under the veil of ignorance we are ignorant of our status, age, gender and the like. In doing this, the veil of ignorance strives to achieve impartiality since we are choosing principles that are equal for all; irrespective of our differences in terms of age, status, gender, colour of skin, cultural background–and systems, etc. This action prevents us from tailoring our moral principles to suit our role and disregarding the principles of the occupants of other roles (Hare, 1981; Rawls, 1972). Furthermore, the mentioned qualifiers (e.g., age, sex, reference to particular information systems) are ruled out since they are likely to be morally irrelevant to the choice of principles of justice (Rawls, 1971; Hare, 1963, 1981, 1989; Siponen, 2001). It just does not make any sense to claim that e.g., gender or ethnical background is relevant to the question of who is allowed to break into information systems.

So, in the case of hacking, given that the application of the veil of ignorance is desired, we need to imagine a situation in which we are unaware of our social status, age, sex, profession, etc. From behind this veil of ignorance we would need to ask ourselves whether we accept that hacking is allowed for *everyone*–i.e., anyone can break into any information systems at any time. This means that if we engage in hacking, we have to allow everyone else the same "right," even at the risk of them breaking into our systems. We submit that most of us, under the veil of ignorance, would not find hacking acceptable in a general sense. The reason being that if hacking is morally acceptable, there are no such things as company business secrets and individuals' privacy. Therefore "private" information such as medical information, social security numbers and financial information would be freely available for all to inspect. The result of which is most people feel more comfortable living in a society where hacking is not acceptable.

DISCUSSION, LIMITATIONS OF THE STUDY AND FUTURE RESEARCH QUESTIONS

The existing views on the relevance of ethics and human morality as a means of protection can be divided into two categories. First ethics and human morality can be used as a means of ensuring security and, second, the use of ethics is, at best, highly restricted, if not impossible. The underlying theories and justification for the two views differ. Proponents of the first view have not offered any theoretical background to justify their claims. In turn, the second view (the use of ethics is restricted to certain "security cultures") is based on cultural relativism (and hacker ethics) and can be classified as descriptivism. This paper explored the theoretical foundations of using human morality, criticised the descriptive view and proposed a non-descriptive approach for using human morality as a means of protection. Conceptual analysis was chosen as the research approach. This is a relevant choice since there is a lack of a solid ethical framework in current literature, and there is a need for a critical analysis of the existing descriptive view. Therefore, firm conceptual/theoretical foundations are needed as a first step, and conceptual analysis is the proper way to build such foundations.

Implications for Research and Practice

As for researchers and practitioners, this paper has clarified the point that human morality has a role in terms of security within organizations. This study also demonstrated that the argument against the relevance of human morality as a means of protection, on the basis of cultural relativism and hacker ethics, was fallacious. The study also clarified the limits of human morality (see Limits of the Findings). Furthermore this study has suggested several future research questions (see below). Moreover, with regard to practitioners, this paper has offered practical guidance on how ethics can be used as a means of ensuring security. It should be noted that the use of human morality at the fullest extent calls for educational skills and knowledge on moral philosophy. The application of ethical theories at an organizational level is not an impossibility. The question and challenge is where the educational and research/development efforts at universities and in organizations should be invested. Is an organization's security only a technical matter? Or has it strong social dimension, as is increasingly recognised by scholars?

Limitations of the Findings

The use of ethics as a means of ensuring security has a few limitations, however. First and foremost, it should be noted that the use of ethics is not a panacea. There is evil in the world (e.g., Warburton, 1996). This means that there are likely to be people who want to behave egoistically or maliciously, regardless of the moral status of such behaviour. Secondly, human morality can be used as a means of indoctrination. This may have short-term positive consequences from an organizational viewpoint. However this may turn against the organization in the long run. Moreover, intentional indoctrination is not morally acceptable since employee autonomy and free will are violated. Thirdly, moral philosophy would be useful for security only when an organization's security or business actions can withstand moral scrutiny. An organization's security or business activities are not per se morally right. For example, organisations may use information hiding (steganography) to carry out morally questionable activities. Fourthly, the use of ethics requires knowledge of ethical theories and persuasive discussion skills. Fifthly, without skillful education, the problem of indoctrination may come into play: A charismatic educator may ignorantly indoctrinate the employees. Sixthly, even if we want to behave morally right the fact remains that our decisions are deemed to be subjective. For example, it is possible, at least in theory, that after an application of the same ethical theory (e.g., the universality thesis) people would end up with differing views (philosophers are debating whether this is the case or not; see, e.g., Seanor & Fotion, 1988; Hare, 1999). The likelihood of the fourth problem may increase when we want to respect autonomy in moral matters, i.e., avoid indoctrination. Finally, we hold with R.M. Hare that, "Nobody can hope to write the last word on a philosophical subject; the most he can do is to advance the discussion of it by making at least some things clearer" (Hare, 1981).

Future Research Questions

There are a few research questions that future research should address. First, given that practitioners could use human morality as a means of ensuring security, studies that show how different ethical theories (non-descriptive) can be used for this purpose should be conducted. Secondly, empirical investigations are needed to explore whether computer users perceive morality as overriding over other non-moral (such as financial) concerns (cf. Hare's overriding thesis in Section 2). Finally, further studies are needed to investigate what are effective persuasion strategies in ethical discussion (whilst at the same time avoiding indoctrination) and what are their effects. The possible research approaches would be conceptual analysis and empirical (theory testing/theory creating) research.

CONCLUSIONS

There is no doubt that the user has a significant role to play in building information security in organizations. Therefore, it is no wonder that the relevance of ethics as a means of ensuring security has been debated in information security literature. However, the current literature lacks solid theoretical foundations. Firm foundations are important to justify whether human morality has a role as a means of protection. It is necessary to examine the question of applicability and how to appeal to human morality as a means of protection. To build this foundation, we look to the wisdom of ethical theories. To increase our understanding of the fundamental differences between ethical theories, the theories were classified into two categories, descriptivism and non-descriptivism. It was shown that the question of whether ethics and human morality have any relevance can be retraced to Hare's overriding thesis (moral overrides all other concerns). The descriptive claim that ethics cannot serve as a means of ensuring security, based on cultural relativism, was considered. It was shown that this descriptive view–that ethics is of little use in securing organizations–encompasses several problems. To avoid these problems, an alternative non-descriptive approach was proposed and an example of its use was given. Four prerequisites and a two-step persuasion guideline for using ethics as a means of ensuring security were put forth. Moreover, limits of the use of human morality were considered. Finally, several future research questions were suggested.

ACKNOWLEDGEMENTS

I am grateful to Mr. Pekka Abrahamsson, Prof. Juhani Iivari, Prof. Marius Janson, Prof. Jussipekka Leiwo and Dr. Kari Väyrynen for their comments on the earlier version of this paper. I would also like to thank the anonymous reviewers of this special issue for their comments.

ENDNOTES

1 One may raise an objection towards my use of the word "culture" by stating that an association, in this example, is not a culture, but it exists within a culture. If tribes or hackers are considered to be "cultures" then associations should be accorded the same treatment. At any rate, further considerations concerning whether an association is a culture or not are irrelevant for this example. The example given can be safely modified so that the association is not a culture, but is within a culture, and the values of this culture are exactly the values of the association (and the company is outside of this culture).

2 Hegel can perhaps be seen to be a kind of "relativist" as, in his view, we must recognise the fact that we all have a history. Because of this, Hegel believes that we cannot share the same categorical imperatives, as put forth by Kant, for instance. This may violate Hume's law provided that the different histories are regarded as "is" matters from which an "ought" conclusion is inferred.

3 Similar reductio ad absurdum fallacies, with respect to cultural relativism, have been formulated. Hare (1986), for example, has pointed out another such fallacy he claims that the existence of such fallacies raises objections to all descriptive views, given that they lead to cultural relativism. The association example provided earlier illustrates another contradiction. The association accepts hacking while the company does not, and the "culture" of the company is just a short distance away from "the culture" of the association. Hence, there seems to be a contradiction in saying that the exact same action in all respects (e.g., hacking) is acceptable (by the association) and not acceptable (by the company). This idea also conflicts with the supervenience relation, e.g., see (Hare, 1952, 1984; Kim, 1984, 1991), as it is inconsistent to claim that the same action can be simultaneously both wrong and right, depending on the culture.

REFERENCES

Anderson, T. E. (1993). Management guidelines for PC security. *Proceedings of the 1992 ACM/SIGAPP Symposium on Applied Computing (vol. II): Technological Challenges of the 1990's*. Kansas City, USA.

Baskerville, R. (1995). The second-order security dilemma. In Orlikowski, W., Walsham, G., Jones, M. and DeGross, J. (Eds.), *Information Technology and Changes in Organizational Work*, 239-249. London: Chapman & Hall.

Conger, S., Loch, K. D. and Helft, B. L. (1994). Information technology and ethics: An exploratory factor analysis. *Ethics in the Computer Age Conference Proceedings*, Gatlinburg, Tennessee, November 11-13.

Dancy, J. (1994). Why there is really no such things as the theory of motivation. *Proceedings of the Aristotelian Society*.

Dhillon, G. and Backhouse, J. (2000). Information system security management in the new millennium. *Communications of the ACM*, 43(7), 125-128.

Dunlop, C. and Kling, R. (Eds.). (1992). Social relationships in electronic commerce–Introduction. In *Computerization and Controversy–Value Conflicts and Social change*, 322-329. New York: Academic Press.

Fiery, D. (1994). Secrets of a super hacker. *Loompanics Unlimited*. Washington, DC: Port Townsend.

Floridi, L. (1999). Information ethics: On the philosophical foundation of computer ethics. *Ethics and Information Technology*, 1(1), 37-56.

Gattiker, U. E. and Kelly, H. (1999). Morality and computers: Attitudes and differences in moral judgements. *Information Systems Research*, 10(3), 233-254.

Gewirth, A. (1973-1974). The "is/ought" problem resolved. *Proceedings and Addresses of the APA*, 47, 34-61.

Gewirth, A. (1978). *Reason and Morality*. Chicago, IL: The University of Chicago Press.

Gewirth, A.. (1982). *Human Rights: Essays on Justification and Applications*. Chicago, IL: The University of Chicago Press.

Gewirth, A. (1996). *The Community of Rights*. Chicago, IL: The University of Chicago Press.

Goodhue, D. L. and Straub, D. W. (1989). Security concerns of system users: A proposed study of user perceptions of the adequacy of security measures. *Proceedings of the 21nd Hawaii International Conference on System Science (HICSS)*.

Gorniak, K. (1996). The computer revolution and the problem of global ethics. *Science and Engineering Ethics*, 2(2).

Habermas, J. (1984). *The Theory of Communicative Action–Reason and the Rationalisation of Society,* I, Boston, MA: Beacon Press.

Habermas, J. (1987). *The Theory of Communicative Action–The Critique of Functionalist Reason*, Vol II, Beacon Press, Boston, MA.

Hare, R. M. (1952). *The Language of Morals*. Oxford, UK: Oxford University Press.

Hare, R. M. (1963). *Freedom and Reason*. Oxford, UK: Oxford University Press.

Hare, R. M. (1964a). *The Promising Game*. Revue Internationale de philosophie 70.

Hare, R. M. (1964b). Adolescents into adults. In Hollins, T. C. B. (Ed.), *Aims in Education*. Manchester.

Hare, R. M.. (1975). Autonomy as an educational idea. In Brown, S. C. (Ed.), *Philosophers Discuss Education*. Macmillan.

Hare, R. M. (1976). Some confusions about subjectivity. In Bricke, J. (Ed.), *Freedom and Morality*. Kansas University Press.

Hare, R. M. (1981). *Moral Thinking: Its Levels, Methods and Point*. Oxford, UK: Oxford University Press.

Hare, R. M. (Ed.). (1984). Supervienience. *Proceedings of Aristotelian Society*, suppl. 58. Reprinted In (1989), *Essays in Ethical Theory*. Oxford, UK: Clarendon Press.

Hare, R. M. (1986). A reduction ad absurdum of descriptivism.Shanker, S. (Ed.), *Philosophy in Britan Today*. London, UK: Croom Helm.

Hare, R. M. (Ed.). (1989). Principles. In *Essays in Ethical Theory*, 48-65. Oxford< UK: Oxford University Press.

Hare, R. M. (Ed.). (1997). A taxonomy of ethical theories. In *Sorting out Ethics*. Oxford, UK: Oxford University Press.

Hare, R. M. (1999). *Objective Prescriptions and Other Essays*. Oxford, UK: Oxford University Press.

Harrington, S. J. (1996). The effect of codes of ethics and personal denial of responsibility on computer abuse judgements and intentions. *MIS Quartely*, September, 20(3).

Järvinen, P. (1997). The new classification of research approaches. Zemanek, H. (Ed.), *The IFIP Pink Summary–36 years of IFIP*, Laxenburg, IFIP.

Kant, I. (1993). *The Moral Law: Groundwork of the Metaphysic of Morals*, Routledg, London.

Kim, J. (Ed.). (1984). Concepts of supervenience. *Philosophy and Phenomenological Research*, 45, 153-176. Reprinted in (1993), *Supervenience and Mind*. Cambridge University Press.

Kim, J. (Ed.). (1991). Supervenience as a philosophical concept. *Metaphilosophy*, 21, 1-27. Reprinted in (1993), *Supervenience and Mind*. Cambridge University Press.

Kowalski, S. (1990). Computer ethics and computer abuse: A longitudinal study of Swedish University students. *IFIP TC11 6th International Conference on Information Systems Security*.

Kukathas, C. and Pettit, P. (1990). *Rawls–A Theory of Justice and its Critics*. California: Stanford University Press.

Ladd, J. (1982). Collective and individual moral responsibility in engineering: Some questions. *IEEE Technology and Society Magazine*, 1(2), 3-10.

Ladd, J. (1989). Computers and moral responsibility: A framework for an ethical analysis. In Gould, C. (Ed.), *The Information Web: ethical and Social Implications of Computer Networking*, 207-227.

Leiwo, J. and Heikkuri, S. (1998a). An analysis of ethics as foundation of information security in distributed systems. *Proceedings of the 31st Hawaiian International Conference on System Sciences (HICSS-31)*.

Leiwo, J. and Heikkuri, S. (1998b). A group-enhanced ISSI model for secure interconnection of information systems. *Proceedings of the IFIP TC11, 14th International Conference on Information Security (IFIP/Sec'98)*.

Loch, K. D. and Carr, H. H. (1991). Threats to information system security: An organizational perspective. In *Proceedings of the Twenty-Fourth Annual Hawaii International Conference on System Sciences (HICSS)*.

MacIntyre, A. (1981), After virtue. *A Study in Moral Theory*. London, UK.

Mackie J. L. (1981). *Ethics, Inventing Right and Wrong*. London: Penguin Group

Mautner, T. (Ed.), (1996). *A Dictionary of Philosophy*. Oxford, UK: Blackwell.

McLean, K. (1992). Information security awareness–selling the cause. *Proceedings of the IFIP TC11 (Sec '92)*.

Moore, G. E. (1903). *Principia Ethicia*. UK: Cambridge.

Neumann, P. G. (1999). Inside risks: risks of insiders. *Communications of the ACM*, 42(12), 160.

Niiniluoto, I. (1991). What's wrong with relativism. *Science Studies*, 4(2), 17-24.

Outga, G. (1972). *Agape: An Ethical Analysis*. Yale University Press.

Parker, D. B. (1998). *Fighting Computer Crime–A New Framework for Protecting Information*. USA: Wiley Computer Publishing.

Perry, W. E. (1985). *Management Strategies for Computer Security*. Boston, MA: Butterworth Publisher.

Pogge, T. W. (1989). *Realizing Rawls*. Cornell University Press.

Popper, K. (1948). What can Logic do for Philosophy? *Aristotelian Society, Supplementary*, 22.

Rawls, J. A. (1972). *A Theory of Justice*. Oxford, UK: Oxford University Press.

Rogerson, S. (1996). The ethics of computing: The first and second generation. *The Business Ethics Network News*, 6.

Rubin, R. (1994). Moral distancing and the use of information technologies: the seven temptations. *Proceedings of Ethics in the Computer Age Conference*, Gatlinburg, Tennessee, November 11-13.

Sabine, G. H. (1963). *A Gistory of Political Theory*. Third edition. London, UK.

Sandel, M. (1982). *Liberalism and the Limits of Justice*. UK: Cambridge University Press.

Seanor, D. and Fotion, N. (Eds.). (1988). The levels, method and points. In *Hare and Critics–Essays on Moral Thinking*, 3-8. Oxford, UK: Oxford University Press.

Searle, J. (1964). *How to Derive "Ought" From "Is."* Ph. Rev. 73.

Severson, R. J. (1997). *The Principles of Information Ethics*. Armonk (N.Y.) M. E. Sharpe cop. USA.

Singer, P. (1991). *A Companion to Ethics*. UK: Blackwell.

Siponen, M. T. (2000). A conceptual foundation for organizational information security awareness. *Information Management & Computer Security*. 8(1), 31-41.

Siponen, M. T. (2001). The relevance of software rights: An anthology of the divergence of sociopolitical doctrines. *AI & Society*, 15(1-2), 128-148.

Siponen, M. T. and Vartiainen, T. (2001). End-user ethics teaching: Issues and a solution based on universalization. *Proceedings of the 34th Hawaii International Conference on Systems Sciences*.

Smart, N. (1986). Relativism in ethics. In Macquarrie, J. and Childress, J. (Eds.), *A New Dictionary of Christian Ethics*. London, UK: SCM Press LTD.

Smith, M. (1984). *The Moral Problem*. Oxford, UK: Blackwell.

Straub, D. W. (1990). Effective IS security: An empirical study. *Information System Research*, June, 1(2), 255- 277.

Straub, D. W. and Nance, W. D. (1990). Discovering and disciplining computer abuse in organization: A field study. *MIS Quartely*, March, 14(1).

Straub, D. W. and Widom, C. P. (1984). Deviancy by bits and bytes. In Finch, J. H and Dougall, E. G. (Eds.), *Computer Security: A Global Challenge, Proceedings of the Second IFIP International Conference on Computer Security (IFIP/Sec '84)*.

Taylor, P. W. (1975). *Principles of Ethics–An Introduction*. Encino, CA: Dickenson Publishing.

Thomas, R. K. and Sandhu R. S. (1994). Conceptual foundations for a model of task-based authorizations. *Proceedings of the 7th IEEE Computer Security Foundations Workshop*.

Thomson, M. E. and von Solms, R. (1998). Information security awareness: Educating our users effectively. *Information Management & Computer Security*, 6(4), 167-173.

Warburton, N. (1996). *Philosophy: The Basics*. Second Edition. Cornwall, UK: T J Press Ltd Padstow.

Vardi, Y. and Wiener, Y. (1996). Misbehavior in organizations: A motivational framework. *Organization Science*, March-April, 7(2), 151-165.

Chapter XVIII

Aspects of a Viable Social Responsibility Program in the Information Age

Gurpreet S. Dhillon
University of Nevada, Las Vegas, USA

Various chapters in this book have addressed a broad range of social responsibility issues. In many ways, each chapter has identified a category of social responsibility concerns which if ignored are going to result in some ethical strain. In the paragraphs below, based on an understanding of potential ethical strains, key elements of a viable social responsibility program are identified and described

SOCIALLY RESPONSIBLE INDIVIDUAL PRACTICE

As has been noted elsewhere (Dhillon & Moores, 2001) and in this book (Chapter 6), even law and regulatory frameworks call upon individuals to engage in some sort of "self-regulation." However, prior to expecting individuals to self-regulate, it is not only important to make them aware of the various issues, but also to train and motivate them to consider various social responsibility issues.

In a recent paper, Dhillon (2001), while discussing violations of safeguards by trusted personnel, notes that had individuals within Barings Bank been aware and well trained to be socially responsible, the demise of the 223-year-old merchant bank could have been prevented. Since various groups of individuals within the bank lacked the ability to recognize patterns related to abuse of position and circumvention of organizational and technological controls, they failed to recognize any mis-dealings on part of Nicholas Leeson, the accused.

In a similar vein, if an average user of technology is not made aware of the manner in which various Internet businesses infringe the right to individual privacy, they would not be able to even recognize if any transgression has taken place. Such an issue is more important today than ever before (see Chapter 6), since concrete laws either do not exist or are still in the process of being defined.

ETHICAL SYSTEMS DEVELOPMENT

Given that majority of IT implementations within organizations result in failure or inappropriate use, there is a need to consider the ethical aspects of the systems development process. Consider the recent Nevada Department of Motor Vehicle's (DMV) systems development fiasco. The goal was to implement one-stop shopping for driver's licenses and registration, Internet and telephone transactions, registration at smog check stations, and of course the reduction of abnormally long waiting times. This was to be achieved using a $35 million computer system that was, unfortunately, not implemented skillfully, full of bugs and slower than expected; it certainly did not help the backlog that the DMV was struggling with initially. One and a half years later, lines are finally shorter and clients are less unhappy, for they are seeing some results and improvements. Still, the project is not totally complete, employee morale is low and turnover high, the public bothered, and the new system at the branch level is not much easier, and not any quicker, than the old.

At the heart of the DMV's problem with the computer system is not so much a technological issue, but a sheer lack of ethical standards and inadequate social responsibility. Clearly a lack of good management and poor planning and design undermined the good intentions. The political (and contractual) constraints on time and staffing, as well as other problems that come with being a state agency, set the stage for a "mission impossible." Still, the legislature believed two consultants were up to the task, and for enough money they took it on. These are ethical and social responsibility IT project management issues as identified by Gilbert (2002) in Chapter 15 of this book.

There are several issues that contributed to the poor implementation, untimely completion, and unsatisfactory result of the DMV computer system. Among these are poor project management, the confusing role of two consultants, non-replaced downtime of existing employees for training, and other human resource matters. As has been argued elsewhere (e.g., see Wood-Harper et al., 1996; Rahanu et al., 1996), such issues could have been rectified by focusing on project management and systems development ethics. Clearly the system analysts had a social responsibility to elicit the right requirements, systems developers the responsibility to design a system to fit the needs of the current environment, and project managers the responsibility to meet stakeholder expectations.

ESTABLISHING RESPONSIBILITIES

The call to establish responsibility structures can best be described by considering the context of the Therac-25, a computerized radiation therapy machine briefly mentioned in chapter 1. This machine had been built after the Therac-6 and the Therac-20 models, originally developed in the early 1970s. The Therac-25 was considered more compact, more versatile and possibly more user-friendly than the previous two models. The Therac-25 had some software that was reused from the Therac-6 and Therac-20 but it eliminated the use of some of the hardware previously used. Because the Therac-25 took advantage of the computer's abilities to control and monitor the hardware, it was decided not to duplicate all the safety mechanisms and interlocks that the previous models used. The manufacturer, perhaps to cut the expenses, removed the hardware interlocks and backups, thus putting more faith on software. There were 11 Therac-25's installed in the US and Canada in 1985. Between 1985 and 1987, six accidents involving massive overdoses to patients occurred. In 1987 the Therac-25 was recalled so that not only the software could be corrected but also the machines could be redesigned to include hardware safeguards against software errors. During this recall, it was discovered that related problems existed in the Therac-20 software.

This case calls forth numerous questions about responsibility and liability related to modern technology. More specifically, given the medical use of the technology in this case, questions of professional standards and ethical codes are raised. It seems all too often, as with this case, consumers (or patients) find themselves nowadays in a state of "buyer beware." But as the patient or the consumer, is this really your responsibility? It is completely unreasonable to expect that individuals in need of radiation therapy would have in-depth knowledge (or bear the time and cost to obtain it) regarding all the medication and equipment that will be inflicted upon them. Clearly in the Therac case the specialist upon which the patients (and the public at large) were relying did not live up to their responsibilities. The manufacturer was clearly negligent in relation to this treatment equipment, from the original design stage through the much overdue safety renovations. The manufacturer mistakenly believed that taking pieces from various proven machines would create a likewise successful new machine. This was a serious flaw in system design. More importantly, though, the priorities in system quality were poorly arranged with simplicity of use threatening safety. There is a level of social responsibility that companies are entrusted with as we proceed into an era of all-consuming technology. The manufacturer would have been far better off to meet those responsibilities proactively rather than reactively. As a manufacturer, however, the company is not held to any professional ethics like doctors themselves.

Another question that arises is to ask where the governmental agencies should step in? Although it is true the Therac-25 was saving many lives in the same period in which it took three and irreparably damaged others. The manufacturer, however, being previously negligent in their responsibilities, should not have been instructed (and entrusted) to notify the users. The FDA should have taken the notification actions itself. While the two exchanged meaningless correspondence about what the users should be told, more patients were harmed. The FDA's likewise reactive approach also leaves a lot to be desired. The agency should be far more proactive in regulating the initial release of equipment, rather than ambulance chasing later to find enough faults for recall or required renovations.

In this case the middlemen, the technicians, are not without some responsibility. Taking a carefree and resigned approach, as they did, to using machinery of this magnitude was erroneous on their part. Machines should never have been told to proceed as many as five times after malfunctioning, or patients segregated from the technician in such a manner that they could not be seen or heard. The continued use through the day of malfunctioning equipment is troubling at best.

It is therefore important to understand and establish adequate responsibility structures. It may be prudent to delineate the roles when, say, a new technology is introduced or a change is made in the functionality. Not only is it important to identify high-level stakeholders, so as to influence current and future policy initiatives, but also to establish stakeholders at an operational level, so as to have identifiable incumbents where the buck would stop. Such individuals would obviously have to be empowered. In the Therac case, had the technicians been empowered to make a decision not to use the machines, a number of tragedies could have been prevented. Another important issue related to empowerment is that of training, which would enable individuals to recognize that a problem exists in the first place.

INSTITUTING TRAINING PROGRAMS

Besides a lack of planning, inadequate training is perhaps an important reason for failure of IT implementations (e.g., see Martocchio, 1992). Any organization is socially obliged and is responsible for training end users to manage technology. As is evident from a number of case studies, lack of training has a knock-on effect on customer service, employee morale and increased incidents of crime and fraud.

In the Nevada DMV case discussed above, besides other reasons, inability of the organization to institute well-thought-through training programs resulted in an organization failing to capitalize on the technology. Since a DMV system services the needs of a large proportion of the population, one could argue that the organization failed to uphold its social responsibility. Similar instances of lack of training and inability of the employees and end users to understand and appreciate corporate change initiatives can be found in IT implementations at the Oregon DMV, Californian DMV, the 1992 London Ambulance IT implementation fiasco, to name a few.

What can easily be taken from the above studies and conclusions is that organizations need to take the time to really get to know their employees. Rapid technological change is going to continue into the next decade and unprepared reactive response to that change is not going to be good enough. Organizations need to begin to prepare themselves now by restructuring the human resources and training and development departments of their businesses. The goal behind this restructuring should be to create highly skilled, motivated, self-assured and socially responsible groups of individuals who will be prepared for change when it comes about. Organizations will need to begin to address and improve the issue of low self-efficacy through ongoing training courses tailored to the knowledge and confidence levels of these associates. These courses should be designed to address the individual areas of concern and increase their self-efficacy prior to the need for new technology training by slowly introducing computer functions at an individual pace. Training should not solely be focused on technological aspects, but psychological issues of low self-efficacy should be concentrated on as well. Therefore, motivational training should be a large portion of this undertaking. As Smith-Jentsch et al. (1996) note "Pre-training motivation is expected to prepare trainees to learn by heightening their attention and increasing their receptivity to new ideas."

Corporations can no longer afford to let their own employees hinder them from continued growth. Therefore, organizations that can recognize now the need to escort their associates into the future by preparing them ahead of time for inevitable technological changes will be the ones that would be more successful, more ethical and responsible.

END USERS NEED A LESSON IN ETHICS

Clearly end users need a lesson in ethics. This is because business corporations and governments alike have increasingly become dependent on IT. However, we are constantly reminded of spectacular intrusions into supposedly secure computer installations for a variety of illicit purposes, including theft, fraud and sabotage. Such is the concern that international bodies such as the Organization for Economic Cooperation and Development, the International Chamber of Commerce, and the Council of Europe, among others, have focused on the question. In the UK the Department of Trade and Industry has also launched several initiatives to address the issue.

While it is clear that business organizations and society at large are directly affected because of their dependence on computers, it is difficult to find reliable figures for monetary loss and to assess the extent of impact. The 1994 UK Audit Commission survey revealed that in the previous three years the total value of cases reported went up by 183%. Figures coming from the US suggest anything up to yearly damages of $2billion could be involved, although something in the region of $145million-$730million seems more realistic.

What may be trivial in its self-evidence but profound in its truth is that prevention of computer-related abuse is more effective than treatment. At a societal level, the diffusion of ideas about ethical use of computers as part of the cultural infrastructure could reduce the burden placed on the shoulders of IT managers. Many large organizations are engaging in awareness campaigns that seek to increase understanding of and sensitivity towards misuse/abuse of computers among the broad base of their employees, rather than merely concentrate on those with responsibility for computer systems. There are initiatives being developed seeking to educate youngsters in ethical use of technology as they learn about computers.

Ultimately the need is to have both a higher level of awareness among the workforce generally about the costs and benefits of good ethical practices and a framework of computer law and enforcement to provide necessary support where the more informal system of checks and balances fails.

CONCLUSION

Clearly there is a need to understand various aspects of ethical strains and potential social responsibility concerns. Such issues gain significance when the task at hand is of either managing a new technology or introducing innovative technologies into business settings. Mars (1982), for instance, notes that "There is only a blurred line between enterpreneuriality and flair on the one hand and sharp practice and fraud on the other." This is indeed an outcome of the ambitious attitude of the society towards many fiddles. Mills (1956) portrayed business as operating in a "subculture of structural immoralities." Moreover Croall (1992) feels that the "blurred line" gives ample scope for the offenders to argue that their activities fall on the right side of the line.

Today, management fears computer fraud more than any other kind of fraud. Evidence coming from across the globe indicates that computer related crime afflicts practically all nations, even those we might consider unlikely. For the organizations, the pressing question is how to control this new affliction. One of the cornerstones of control and management of computer crime is a social responsibility framework and ethical principles to adequately protect and manage diverse systems. However control can be implemented at two levels. At a macro-level by enacting relevant laws and at a micro-level by adopting better management practices.

Various readings in this book have focused on these two aspects of managing in the information age. Research presented in this collection of papers has also set the tone for setting a future research agenda that will hone in on social responsibility issues in the information age.

REFERENCES

Croall, H. (1992). *White Collar Crime*. Milton Keynes, UK: Open University Press.

Dhillon, G. (2001). Violation of safeguards by trusted personnel and understanding related information security concerns. *Computers & Security*, 20(2).

Dhillon, G. and Moores, T. (2001). Internet privacy: interpreting key issues. *Information Resources Management Journal*, 14(4).

Gilbert, J. (2002). Social responsibility in IS/IT project management. In Dhillon, G.

(Ed.). *Social Responsibility in the Information Age: Issues and Controversies*. Hershey, PA: Idea Group Publishing.

Mars, G. (1982). *Cheats at Work: An Anthropology of Workplace Crime*. London: George Allen & Unwin.

Martocchio, J. J. (1992). Microcomputer usage as an opportunity: The influence of context in employee training. *Personnel Psychology*, 45, 529.

Mills, C. W. (1956). The power elite. Oxford: Oxford University Press.

Rahanu, H., Davies, J. and Rogerson, S. (1996). Ethical analysis of software failure cases. Paper presented at the *3rd International Conference on Values and Social Responsibilities of Computer Science (ETHICOMP96)*, Madrid, Spain, November.

Smith-Jentsch, K. A., Jentsch, F. G., Payne, S. C. and Salas, E. (1996). Can pretraining experience explain individual differences in learning? *Journal of Applied Psychology*, 81(1).

Wood-Harper, A. T., Corder, S., Wood, J. R. G. and Watson, H. (1996). How we profess: The ethical systems analyst. *Communications of the ACM*, 39(3), 69-77.

About the Authors

Gurpreet S. Dhillon, BSc (Hons), MBA, MSc (Econ), PhD (MIS) is a MIS professor at the University of Nevada, Las Vegas. Previously he has been on the faculties of Cranfield School of Management (UK) and City University of Hong Kong. He is a graduate of the London School of Economics (University of London). His research interests lie at the interface of strategic management and IS/IT use. The application domain of his research has covered information security, computer crime and fraud. His research has been widely published in numerous journals including *Communications of the ACM, Computers & Security, Information Systems Journal, European Journal of Information Systems, International Journal of Information Management, Journal of End User Computing, International Journal of Public Sector Management, Topics in Health Information Management*, among others. He is the author of the books *Managing Information System Security* (Macmillan, 1997) and *Information Security Management: Global Challenges in the New Millennium* (Idea Group, 2001). He also serves as vice president, publications, for the Information Resources Management Association and North American regional editor of *International Journal of Information Management.*

***

Janice M. Burn is foundation professor and head of the School of Management Information Systems at Edith Cowan University in Perth, Western Australia and director of the We-B research centre–Working for e-Business. In 2000 she assumed the role of world president of the Information Resources Management Association (IRMA). She has previously held senior academic posts in Hong Kong and the UK. Her research interests relate to information systems strategy and benefits evaluation in virtual organizations with a particular emphasis on social, political and cultural challenges in an e-business environment. She is recognized as an international researcher, with over 150 refereed publications in journals and international conferences. She is on the editorial board of six prestigious IS journals and participates in a number of joint research projects with international collaboration and funding.

Terry Anthony Byrd is associate professor of MIS in the Department of Management at the College of Business, Auburn University. He holds a BS in electrical engineering from the University of Massachusetts at Amherst and a PhD in management information systems from the University of South Carolina. His research has appeared in *MIS Quarterly, Journal of Management Information Systems, Decision Sciences, OMEGA, Interfaces* and other leading journals. His current research interests include the strategic management of information technology, information technology architecture and infrastructure, electronic commerce, and information technology implementation.

Phil Carter is director of the Auckland University of Technology's Computer Systems Usability Laboratory. He is also program leader for the bachelor of business and master's of business in information technology. He holds a doctorate in Information Systems from Massey University. Prior to study in IT, Phil lived for several years in Taiwan, witnessing its transition from martial law to greater freedom and transparency of government. He is currently awakening to the living tradition of his Maori ancestors and seeking to embody the philosophy of valuing the community, caretaking the land, and formulating and expressing knowledge in creative and artistic forms, such as the non-scripted theater of action methods and psychodrama.

Scott Chapman attended Brigham Young University, where he received a bachelor of arts (BA) degree in Korean literature and language and a Juris Doctor (J.D.) degree. He is currently a candidate for a master's of business administration (MBA) at the University of Nevada, Las Vegas. Mr. Chapman has clerked for the Honorable Judge Ray M. Harding, Jr. in the Fourth Judicial District of Utah, has clerked for the Law Offices of Kim, Shin and Yu in Seoul, South Korea, was a certified mediator for court-sanctioned alternative dispute resolution measures in Utah and was a member of the Willem C. Vis International Moot Arbitration Team in Vienna, Austria. Currently, Mr. Chapman is admitted and practices law in Las Vegas, Nevada, in the US District Court, District of Nevada, and in the United States Court of Appeals for the Ninth Circuit. Mr. Chapman is a member of the American Bar Association, the State Bar of Nevada, the Clark County Bar Association and the J. Reuben Clark Law Society.

N. Ben Fairweather, PhD has been a research fellow in the Centre for Computing and Social Responsibility at De Montfort University, Leicester, UK, since 1996. Prior to this he completed a PhD in environmental philosophy at the University of Wales, Cardiff. He is associate editor of the *Elsevier Journal–Telematics and Informatics: An Interdisciplinary Journal on the Social Impacts of New Technology.*

Joseph T. Gilbert is an associate professor of management at the University of Nevada, Las Vegas. He teaches in the areas of business strategy, organizational theory and business ethics. He holds bachelor's and master's degrees in philosophy and a doctorate in business administration. He has published several articles and book chapters in the area of business ethics. Dr. Gilbert currently team-teaches (with an attorney) an MBA-level course in law, regulation, and ethics.

Sandra C. Henderson is a doctoral candidate of MIS in the Department of Management at Auburn University. She holds a master's of accountancy with a concentration in accounting information systems from Florida State University and a BS in Accounting from Albany State University. Her research has appeared in *Information & Management* and several proceedings. Her research interests include information privacy, electronic commerce, and systems development.

William Hutchinson is the associate head of management information systems at Edith Cowan University in Western Australia. He has had over 20 years experience in information systems in the government sector and the oil and finance industries. Dr. Hutchinson has published numerous papers on system design and information warfare.

Karen D. Loch is the director of the Institute of International Business and an associate professor at Georgia State University. Her current research interests span international IT transfer and social and ethical concerns of information systems. She has published in journals such as *MIS Quarterly, Information Systems Journal, Communications of the ACM, Journal of Global Information Management, Academy of Management Executive, Journal of Business Ethics, and DATA BASE,* and a book on IT education. She serves as global editor for the *Journal of Global Information Management,* as associate editor for the *Journal of Global Information Technology Management,* and as a review board member for *Information Resources Management Journal.* She reviews regularly for other leading IS journals.

Mark G. Lycett, PhD is a lecturer at Brunel University, UK. His research interest lies in systems development. In particular, he is interested in the interaction between new development approaches/technologies and strategies,